The Sober Diaries

*How one woman stopped drinking
and started living*

Clare Pooley

CORONET

First published in Great Britain in 2017 by Hodder & Stoughton
An Hachette UK company

1

ISBN 9781473661875
eBook ISBN 9781473661882
Tradeback ISBN 9781473661899

Typeset in Celeste by Palimpsest Book Production Limited,
Falkirk, Stirlingshire

Printed and bound by Clays Ltd, St Ives plc

Hodder & Stoughton policy is to use papers that are natural, renewable and recyclable products and made from wood grown in sustainable forests. The logging and manufacturing processes are expected to conform to the environmental regulations of the country of origin.

Hodder & Stoughton Ltd
Carmelite House
50 Victoria Embankment
London EC4Y 0DZ

www.hodder.co.uk

For Juliet

My flame-haired friend who burned
so brightly and died too young

THE MONTH WHEN I FINALLY REALISE
THAT THE VINO HAS TO GO

DAY 0 0 0

SOMETHING HAS TO CHANGE

On a scale of one to ten, today is languishing at around a minus five.

It's a Sunday, so I have a hangover, obviously. But this is the Sunday after my birthday party, so today's hangover is a particularly special one. A humdinger. A prize-winner.

My brain seems to have shrunk to the size of a marble, and it's banging off the sides of my head like a game of pinball. I'm sweating alcohol and drowning in successive waves of nausea. I keep clutching at the worktop in my kitchen like a desperate sailor clinging on to a life-raft. This is not a good idea, because I keep catching sight of my grey, puffy face reflected in the polished granite. Yikes.

Even on a good day (which this is obviously *not*) the noise level in my kitchen would be unbearable. Maddie (aged six) is playing Minecraft and yelling something about having 'spawned' in a nest of creepers. Kit (aged eight) is watching, on YouTube, *somebody else* play Minecraft (and I'm fairly sure they just used a totally inappropriate word), and Evie (aged eleven) is practising her scales on her clarinet.

Whenever Evie plays a minor scale the dog howls as if his life is ending (he's sensitive). I desperately want to tell Evie to *put the damned instrument down,* but what kind of a mother yells at her child for voluntarily doing her music practice?

Just as I'm thinking that things can't possibly get any worse (always a bad idea), the doorbell rings. I'm still in my nightie and, believe me, it's not the sort of garment you want anyone to see you in, not even Jehovah's Witnesses or the man who reads the gas meter.

I do the only sensible thing and duck down below the kitchen units, out of sight of the window. Now not only can my unwanted visitor see three seemingly unattended children in my kitchen, but they can also hear them yelling 'MUMMY! WHAT ARE YOU DOING ON THE FLOOR?!?'

I'm aware, as I sit it out and wait for whoever is on my doorstep to give up, hoping that they won't call social services, that the rational response at this point in time is to vow to not touch another drop of alcohol for several days, if not weeks. I need to sweat it out and rehydrate. But I also know that the only thing in the world that is going to make me feel any better is *another drink.*

I glance at the kitchen clock from my crouching position. *Is it broken?* It's barely moved since I last looked at it. Just after 11 a.m. Not drinking before midday is one of The Rules. If you drink in the morning you're an alcoholic, right? But after twelve, particularly at the weekend, is perfectly okay. Everyone knows that.

I open the cupboard and reach past the packets of Rice Krispies and Weetabix (no chocolate cereals in my house, because I am a Good Mother, most of the time) to investigate the bottles of drink. There's an open bottle of red wine with about two inches left in the bottom. It is very unlike me to leave a bottle unfinished. I must have fallen asleep (passed out) before I managed to drain it. Yay! It's A Sign. That wine is there for a reason. It's saying *'Drink me!'* like an adult-rated version of *Alice in Wonderland.*

4

I can't possibly pour the wine into a glass. My children are pretty used to Mummy having a glass of wine permanently welded to her hand, but even they might baulk at the sight of one at 11 a.m. So, I take out a mug from the cupboard and pour the dregs of the bottle into it.

Only minutes after I've knocked back the wine the throbbing in my head subsides to a gentler hum. And that's when I look down at the mug in my hand and see what's printed on it:

THE WORLD'S BEST MUM.

I hate myself.

Something has to change.

To be honest, I've known for several years that it was all starting to go wrong. I can't remember the last time I went a whole day without a glass of wine. On a regular weekday I'll have a large glass while helping the kids with their homework. Then a second glass while preparing the evening meal. Then I'll hide that (more empty than full) bottle in the back of the cupboard so that I can open a brand-new one when John – the long-suffering husband – comes home, and we'll share it over dinner. (When I say *share*, what I actually mean is that we'll both have some, but I'll make damn sure that I get more than he does.)

So, if I make myself add that all up (which I try very hard not to do, obviously), it's more than a bottle of wine *every day*.

Then there's the weekend. Hurrah for the weekend, when lunchtime drinking is perfectly acceptable – obligatory even. And there's usually a social event. So, on a Saturday or a Sunday (probably both) I can easily polish off two bottles.

Oh My God. I'm drinking nine or ten bottles of wine a week. Now, I am pretty adept at closing my eyes, sticking my fingers in my ears and going 'la la la la' whenever anyone mentions the government guidelines but, even so, I know that this is well in excess of the recommended levels. Around *100 units.* I confessed to fourteen the last time I was quizzed by a medical professional. Surely they know we all lie?

It has to stop.

I take a brutal look at myself. I'm forty-six years old, but I'm quite sure I look older. I'm *raddled.* I'm the sort of woman that my mother would describe (and she does) as having 'let herself go'. I'm two stone overweight, and most of that is on my belly. If I stand up straight and look down I *can't see my feet*! I've started to hate taking buses as people often offer me their seats. A friend of Maddie's asked me, in front of a bunch of other mums, about 'the baby in my tummy'. I told him, through gritted teeth, that it was actually cake. He looked horrified. Perhaps he thinks I'm going to give birth to a vast blueberry muffin.

Sleep is another major issue. I *get* to sleep easily enough. Rather too easily, actually. I can't remember the last time I made it through to the end of a movie before passing out on the sofa. But then I wake up at about 3 a.m., tossing and turning, sweating booze and hating myself. I usually manage to drop off to sleep again at about 6 a.m., just before the alarm goes off.

Then there's the wine witch. That's the pet name I've given to the voice that seems to have taken up permanent residence in my brain, which turns even the most solid of resolutions into dust, whispering things like 'Look! There's only a small amount left in the bottle. You might as well finish it, or it'll go off!' Or 'She's poured a WAY larger glass for herself than she's poured for you. Tip another slug in while no one's watching.' The wine witch is a great fan of the concept of 'me time'. 'It might be only 5 p.m., but you've had a hard day. You've spent all day being bossed around by people under the age of twelve and now it's grown-up time. *You've earned it.'* And the killer: 'Everyone else is doing it too . . .'

I'm constantly broke, but, funnily enough, I've never thought to blame this on the wine. I've economised on pretty much everything else – going out, clothes, 'grooming' – but I'll still shell out a small fortune on wine every week, because if you're drinking Chablis you're a connoisseur, not a lush, right?

What kind of an example am I setting my children? I don't want them to grow up thinking that all adults need buckets of alcohol in order to cope with the ups and downs of everyday life. Just last week, when I was picking Maddie up from school, her teacher pulled me aside and said 'I have to tell you something funny that happened today! I was hearing Maddie read, and the book was called *A Cup of Tea.* I said "Does Mummy like to drink tea?" and she replied "Oh no. Mummy likes to drink wine!" Ha! Ha! Ha!'

'Ha! Ha! Ha!' I'd echoed, a forced smile on my face, but inside I died a little.

It feels like my whole life has been sucked into a bottle of Sauvignon Blanc. I used to be so fearless, so ambitious and optimistic. I travelled through the Far East for months on my own at nineteen, and was on the board of a major advertising agency by the time I was thirty. Yet now I feel anxious all the time. And the booze, my trusty old pal, that used to take the edge off and make me feel invincible, I suspect is only making things worse.

The obvious solution is to *cut down,* to drink moderately and sensibly. But I've been trying to do that for *years.* I've done Dry January. (Well, most of it, anyway. I started a bit late and stopped a bit early.) I've done Sober September. Each time I manage a short stretch without alcohol, I swear that I have now 'recalibrated', that I've seen the light and completely changed my relationship with booze. From now on we will have a perfectly healthy and functional relationship. But, like an abusive partner, the booze comes back fighting, and within a few weeks I am back to where I started, only more so.

I've tried only drinking at weekends (but the weekends start on Thursday, and end on Tuesday). I've done only drinking when I go out (then found I was going out an awful lot). I've given only drinking beer (which doesn't count as proper alcohol) a go, and alternating alcoholic drinks with water.

None of it works. Despite seeing myself as a strong, determined person, I'm totally unable to stick to any of my resolutions for longer than a week or two.

I have to stop completely. Maybe not for ever (I can't possibly think about for ever), but at least for the foreseeable future. So, this glass I'm clutching is my last. Tomorrow is Day One.

Is it possible to live without alcohol in a world where you're more likely to be offered a glass of wine at a playdate than a cup of tea? Where Facebook is filled with references to 'wine o'clock'? Where every social event is fuelled by gallons of booze? *Is there life after wine?*

I guess I'm going to find out . . .

DAY 001

HOW ON EARTH DID I GET HERE?

I blame Bridget Jones. Not just Bridget – the *Sex and the City* girls and their cosmopolitans have an awful lot to answer for too, as have the *Absolutely Fabulous* Patsy and Edina, constantly cracking open the Bollinger. (I obviously don't want to blame *myself* for the fact that I seem to have become a sad, middle-aged lush and am having to contemplate a life *without booze*.)

I didn't see Bridget Jones as caricature, I saw her as a *role model*. I loved her neuroses, her imperfections and her granny knickers. I loved her humour and the way she cut through all the 'emotional fuckwittery', and I loved the way she ate like a normal woman, smoked like a chimney and drank like a fish.

I loved Bridget because I pretty much *was* Bridget. So much so, that when I was thirty and the BBC were looking for people to feature in a documentary about the 'real-life Bridget Joneses', they called me. I reluctantly agreed to take part in a small segment of the film – a singletons' dinner party. I turned up, along with seven other singles, at the appointed Chelsea restaurant, and was told that the film crew would be a while setting up, 'so do, please, help yourself to free drinks at the bar.' No one's ever had to offer me free drinks twice. An hour later, nervous and tanked up with booze on empty stomachs, we were all flying. Or at least, I was.

In a Herculean effort to stand up for the rights of women to be single and happy, I waved my wine glass around and proclaimed 'Look. I've got a great job, a really cool car, and I own my own flat. Why on earth would I need a man to make myself complete?' Job done. Or so I thought.

I wasn't expecting anyone to actually *see* the documentary. My friends were all far too busy working and partying to be indoors watching TV on a Thursday night. (And this was before the days of Sky+ and catch-up TV. You had to set a timer on your VHS machine, which was far too much hassle.) So, imagine my horror, when ALL WEEK, on prime-time TV, the BBC ran a trailer featuring only one person: me. There I am, slightly tipsy, saying 'Look. I've got a great job, a really cool car, and I own my own flat.' Then the serious, male voiceover cuts in: 'So why can't these women find the one thing they *really want*: *A MAN?*'

Everyone saw it. Everyone saw me slapping female emancipation in the face and being pronounced un-whole.

But it didn't stop me loving Bridget. After all, she gave us all an *excuse* to drink too much. She made downing gallons of Chardonnay with one's friends cool. She made drinking home alone, while singing badly to power ballads, de rigueur.

Back then, in the 1990s, we saw drinking as our *duty* as good feminists. It was the era of the ladette, of keeping up with the boys and beating them at their own game. The drinks companies noticed this and rolled out the female-friendly wine bars – all soft lighting, sophisticated menus on chalkboards and wine served in 250ml glasses (one third of a bottle). And drinking was part of the work culture as well as the play culture. In fact, in my creative industry, we had a bar IN THE OFFICE where most of the important networking took place, and I had a huge expenses budget, which I was expected to use wining and dining my team and my clients.

I assumed that I would stop drinking with quite such abandon after I got married and started having kids, but I was of the generation that had been told we could *have it all* – and I was trying to juggle a big top job and small babies without a wife at home to stop the ship from sinking. I would end up trying to change an exploded nappy while dealing with a call from my finance director. I'd miss class assemblies so that I could be yelled at by demanding clients and petulant creative directors. I'd run home from a day keeping hundreds of balls in the air and immediately have to switch into calm, happy mother mode to read *The Gruffalo* to my babies. Only copious amounts of booze enabled me to make the switch from one persona to the other and provided a release from the inevitable stress and the knowledge that – for the first time in my life – I was failing at everything.

I realised that I was driving myself crazy. Whenever I was at work, my heart was with my children. Whenever I was with my children, my head was filled with work. Plus, I was paying a vast proportion of my salary to a nanny so that she could do the job that I desperately wanted to do myself. Time was flying by in a whirlwind of dropped deadlines and missed developmental milestones. I couldn't bear the idea of not being part of my children's childhoods.

So, when my third child was born, I finally quit the rat race in order to be a Perfect Mum. My house was going to be a happy haven of freshly baked cupcakes, craft tables and carefully planned playdates. How the gods must have laughed, because, while being able to stop work to bring up your gorgeous babies is obviously an honour and a privilege, anyone who's done it knows it's not a walk in the park. Or rather, it's *endless* walks in the park – with wet wipes, breast pads and emergency rice cakes, pushing swings until your arms go numb along with your mind.

After a year or two, I started feeling like I'd lost my identity, lost myself. I was no longer 'Clare the advertising babe', or the Group Head, or Board Director. I was only ever defined in relation to other people – John's wife, or Evie's mummy. It was as if without them I didn't exist. I even lost my name, as everyone now referred to me by my married name, and my maiden name (which I'd used at work) was consigned to distant memory.

I was also starting to worry that I wasn't setting a good feminist example for the children. I remember going to a Mother's Day event at Maddie's nursery when she was just three. All the proud mums sat in a semicircle on those teeny-weeny chairs, made for teeny-weeny bum cheeks, while the children took turns telling us all what they wanted to be when they grew up.

'I want to be a fireman!' said one, as we all went 'Aahhhh'. Then there was a would-be doctor, a teacher, an airline pilot. I waited in suspense to see what my little darling would come up with. Finally, it was her turn.

'I want to be a mummy and talk on the phone and go to the gym,' she said. I smiled at her encouragingly, and clapped enthusiastically, while thinking *NOOOOO! You're going to discover the cure for cancer, broker peace in the Middle East or invent the next hadron collider.* Still, at least the other mums thought I was fit. Ironic, since I hadn't actually been to the gym for months.

Wine was my oasis of sanity, a release from the stress of toddler tantrums and the boredom of nappy changing and Monkey Music. A glass of wine could put the zing into a late-afternoon playdate with a girlfriend, and the Zen into post-children's bedtime. At the end of a long, frazzled day I could pour a generous helping of Chablis, dance around the kitchen and think *Yeah, baby, she's still got it.*

I used wine to wind down, to rev up, to celebrate, to commiserate, to socialise and for 'me time'. But then the day came when I realised that I couldn't do any of those things – relax, party, de-stress – *without the wine.* Like Helen Titchener in *The Archers* (OMG, my cultural references are all so horribly middle-class, I am a cliché), all my self-confidence had been slowly stripped away to the point where I believed that without wine *I was nothing.* Without the booze I was timid, boring and anxious, and yet I knew that it was the drink that had – slowly, insidiously, over a number of years – put me there.

So, here I am, at the end of a Day One that has felt as long as a week. Battered, bruised and still hungover – but fighting.

DAY 003

EXHAUSTION

I've gone three days without booze on numerous occasions. I've given up for weeks, even months at a time. But this is different, because I know it's not temporary. The light at the end of the tunnel has been well and truly snuffed out.

I remember breaking up with my first big love when I was in my early twenties. I spent days sobbing, believing that I'd never be happy again. I spent hours listening to 'our' songs, trying desperately to rewrite the future in my head without him in it. He was constantly on my mind as I replayed, in slow motion, every moment we'd spent together, poring over old photographs and letters (yes, they were 'a thing' back then). *Was it really so bad?* I asked myself, and any girlfriend patient enough to listen. *Surely I was happier in that relationship, however imperfect, than I am now?* Life without him seemed drearily monochrome where it had been gloriously technicolour.

And now, a quarter of a century later, I feel much the same. I can't stop thinking about booze, my errant ex-lover. It's on my mind all the time. I read anything I can get my hands on about alcohol. Amazon keep turning up with another package of books about stopping drinking, which I add to the growing stash under my bed. I am, I fear, turning into a madwoman.

I've been cooking in the morning and leaving food in the fridge for John to heat up when he gets home, because cooking, for me, is totally entwined with drinking. Many an evening I've spent with a wooden spoon in one hand and glass of wine in the other, talking to an imaginary camera crew as I juggled with herbs and channelled my inner Keith Floyd, the drunken TV chef.

As well as being mentally exhausted by my booze obsession, I'm physically shattered. I feel like I'm wading through Play-Doh. It's much like the early stages of pregnancy, but without all the excitement of *Woo hoo! We've created a whole new life! How clever are we?*

I forgot my PIN yesterday – a number I've been typing into cashpoint machines and supermarket pin pads for *decades*. The only thing that manages to cut through the fog in my brain is the crashing headache that's been coming and going for the last two days. But, despite the exhaustion, I can't get to sleep. I'm used to being gradually eased into the Land of Nod by the anesthetising effects of a few glasses of wine, but for the last two nights I've been awake for hours, brain whirring, staring at the ceiling, while John slumbers, snorting away like a happy warthog, beside me.

And now it's six o'clock, the most difficult time of the day. I've cooked the children's supper, we've done homework, they've had their baths and they're happily sitting in front of the television. All the time the booze is calling me, like a persistent stalker, saying *give me just one more chance. We can make it better this time. We won't repeat all the old mistakes. You KNOW you love me. You're miserable without me, just look at you!*

But I know, deep down, that it's all lies. It's never going to be different; in fact it's only going to get worse, and if I don't walk away now there's a danger that I never will.

I run myself a hot bath and light some aromatherapy candles someone gave me for Christmas many years back. That helps, for ten minutes or so. I go on a cleaning frenzy, just to keep my hands occupied. I'm usually a bit of a domestic slut, but after three days of not drinking my house is *gleaming*. I check my watch: it's seven o'clock, but I feel like I've done as much of today as I can manage, so I round up the children and announce that we're all going to bed. Yes, Mummy too.

The four of us pile into my bed, followed by Otto, the very enthusiastic terrier. Otto does not know he's a dog. He is, as far as he is concerned, another sibling, and his 'brother and sisters' are very happy to play along with this misconception. Otto inserts himself in between me and Kit, sighs happily and farts noxiously, causing howls of anguish from the children.

Before I had children, I'd imagined a little troop of mini-mes (with maybe just a passing resemblance to their father). As it turned out, none of them look like me at all, or like John, or even like each other. Right from day one they've been totally different, completely unique and I know I'm going to spend my whole life just getting to know them.

Evie is my eldest. Eleven is a magical age, when you're past the childish tantrums but haven't yet hit the teenage years. I wonder how long it'll be before she decides that climbing into bed with her mother and her siblings (and the dog) isn't cool. Evie amazes me. She has huge amounts of self-confidence and completely believes that she can do anything she sets her mind to, whether it's coming top of the class in maths, making the netball team or baking an extraordinarily complicated chocolate cake – and usually she's right.

Then there's Kit, three years younger, my little left-handed boy who thinks in a completely different way to me, has a wonderful turn of phrase and sense of humour and teaches me something new every day. If I'm occupying a space in the kitchen that Kit is after for some game he's playing he doesn't just ask me to move, he takes me by the hand, leads me to a different place and says, solemnly, 'Congratulations. You have been successfully relocated.'

Although Maddie is now six, she'll always be my baby. Maddie has us all wrapped around her little finger. She has oodles of charm, and ever since she was tiny, total strangers have rushed over to exclaim about her cuteness. At this point Evie and Kit tend to roll their eyes and say, somewhat sarcastically, 'Yes, she's just like a real person, only smaller.'

If Evie wants something she'll spend days over a fancy PowerPoint presentation, quoting statistics and research and arguing her case with all the skill of a top barrister, whereas if Maddie wants something she just starts to cry. On demand. Big, fat tears streaming down her face and dripping off the end of her nose until all of us fall to our knees begging her to let us know how we can make her happy again.

All three children are obsessed with working out who is my *favourite child.* I keep telling them that I have no favourite, and that choosing a favourite would be like trying to decide between a strawberry pavlova, a chocolate roulade and an English trifle. Each are equally delicious but in very different ways. This response is greeted with howls of derision and leads, inevitably, to an argument about who is the pavlova and who is the trifle.

The four of us (and the dog) lie, limbs all entwined, taking turns reading from a Famous Five book and a Harry Potter. I find myself wondering, idly, whether the butterbeer they sell in Hogsmeade is alcoholic or if it's more like the lashings of ginger beer drunk by the Famous Five to wash down their tins of sardines.

I look over to my left, to the empty space where my ever-present glass of wine would once have been. It may have sat, quietly, unobtrusively, to the side, but I realise that the actual space it occupied was right in the middle, sticking its elbows out and shoving everyone else aside. Because of that glass of wine, and its many friends, I skipped over endless pages of the children's picture books, and wrapped up years of precious bedtime routines as early as possible. I gave up work so that I could spend more memorable moments with my children, then spent the next few years constantly trying to run away from them.

When, I wonder, did I stop using alcohol for celebration and start using it for liberation? Liberation from the mundanity of everyday life and from the realisation that it had not turned out as I'd hoped.

But no more, I declare, silently. It's time to do parenthood properly, adulthood properly, *life* properly. I'm going to be the sort of mother who gets her children to eat kale crisps, carries antiseptic spray in her handbag and remembers to do her pelvic-floor exercises.

After an hour of reading, and before John even gets home from the office, I turn out the light, hoping that John won't mind moving three comatose children into their own beds when he gets home.

Maddie leans over and whispers right up against my face, 'Namaste'. Her fingers are entwined in my hair, as if to ensure that I don't leave her once she's fallen asleep. Her breath is warm and smells of strawberries and chocolate, revealing her claim to have brushed her teeth as a big fib.

'Namaste,' I reply.

'Do you know what that means, Mummy?' she asks.

'No,' I confess.

'It means *I see God in you.*'

And I see God in them. And that's what will get me through.

| DAY | 0 | 0 | 7 |

IS ANYONE OUT THERE?

I'm not sure I can do this on my own. I wish there was someone I could talk to, but I'm far too ashamed. I've told John, casually and in passing, that I've quit drinking, but I don't think he's taking it seriously at all. To be fair, he's heard it all before, and I'm sure he expects me to be back on usual form by the weekend.

I've made some pretty bad decisions over the years, but marrying John was not one of them. I loved him the minute I met him, nearly twenty years ago, in Scotland, on New Year's Eve. He was wearing a kilt, above a really nice pair of knees, and I've always had a weakness for men in skirts. He made me laugh – a lot – and he was one of the kindest people I'd ever met. We became best friends, but, back then, I was still in thrall to the bad, arrogant boys. The ones who'd make you feel grateful for their time and attention, however begrudging. So, it was four years before John and I kissed. I felt my foundations morph from sand to rock, and wondered why on earth I'd taken so long.

Since then, John has loved me patiently through years of increasing overindulgence and bad behaviour.

To be fair, he's not perfect either. He has a terrible habit of leaving wet towels on floors, and dirty plates on top of the dishwasher rather than in it. There is more tummy to love than there was fourteen years ago, and a little less hair. He's Scottish, and plays to the stereotype of being somewhat 'careful' with money. He has been known to put gaffer tape over the central heating controls to stop me turning them on in November. But I wouldn't have him any other way.

Whenever I've been in trouble, John has done his best to

help, not always entirely successfully. I remember once, a few weeks after Evie was born, when he came back from work to find me sobbing uncontrollably as I had mastitis – boobs like rocks and a terrible fever – compounded by two weeks of not sleeping for more than two or three hours at a stretch.

'What can I do to help?' he'd asked, helplessly, as I wept and Evie howled.

I'd spoken to the community midwife, a nineteen-year-old trainee who had no idea what it felt like to have a set of gums clamped to your cracked, bleeding nipples for hours on end, and she'd told me that putting cold cabbage leaves inside my maternity bra might provide some relief. This sounded totally improbable, but at that point I was willing to try anything.

'Please can you go to the shop and buy a cabbage?' I'd sobbed.

He came back, an hour later, with a (leafless) *cauliflower*, explaining that all the local shops were out of cabbage.

'What am I supposed to do with *that*?' I'd yelled at him.

'Er, eat it?' he'd replied, not unreasonably.

I threw the cauliflower at his head (and drank a pint of wine instead), which seemed, at the time, to help both me and Evie.

So, the point is, I know that if I talked to John and told him just how bad things had got he'd do his very best to understand, and to help. But I can't. Maybe because I don't really want to confess, even to myself.

I've not emptied the booze cupboard or the wine rack, nor have I asked John to stop drinking. I figure that if I can get used to ignoring booze in my own home, I'm much more likely to succeed when I go out. But John is a considerate soul, so he is trying not to drink in front of me. He is also a moderate drinker – damn his eyes. He can drink one glass of wine and then . . . stop. How does he do that? And what is the *point*? One glass of wine has never, ever been enough for me.

It seems crazy that when I quit smoking, fifteen years ago, I was able to tell the world – proudly. All the non-smokers cheered, welcomed me with open arms and promised whatever help I needed. My friends still puffing away looked at me enviously and admired my strength and resolve. But now I'm ditching another addictive drug and I feel I can't tell anyone.

I'm doing an amazing thing – for me, and for my family – and yet I'm scared that everyone will think I must have been a bad mother, an irresponsible lush. And, perhaps even more frightening, I'm worried that, now I've quit, they'll think I'm *boring,* and I'll never be invited out again.

But, right now, I really need some friends. I need someone to hold my hand and tell me I can do this. I need someone to tell me what to expect. I need someone to tell me that it's all going to be okay in the end.

Isn't that what Alcoholics Anonymous is for?

Which brings me to the other question that's been bugging me: *Am I an alcoholic?*

This is not a new query. For at least the last two years, usually after a spectacular weekend-long bender, I've been googling *am I an alcoholic?* I then get offered a variety of quizzes (which is great, I love quizzes). I can always answer YES to several of the questions. (*Have you tried to stop drinking for a week or so, but failed after a few days*? Well yes, endlessly. *Do you drink alone?* Of course, doesn't everyone? Anyhow, I'm not alone. The kids are here. And the dog. *Have you ever felt remorse after drinking?* Is the Pope Catholic?)

But, reassuringly, there are always several questions that I can answer NO to. (*Do you drink when you first wake up? Have family and friends told you to stop drinking? Do you have black-outs?*) After I've answered all the questions I click the button for the magic answer, and it says *You may have a problem with alcohol.* No shit, Sherlock. I kind of knew that, that's why I did your stupid questionnaire in the first place! What I want to know is *am I an alcoholic?*

The truth is that, whether or not I am an 'alcoholic', I know I am addicted to alcohol, in the same way that, back in the day, I was horribly addicted to nicotine. Alcohol is an extremely addictive substance, and if you drink enough of it over a long enough period of time (which, let's face it, I did) then you're bound to get hooked. And once you're hooked, as with any drug, there's no going back. You quit or, eventually, you die. But doing it alone is *hard,* and I'm sure that AA could help . . .

The problem with AA is that it's the polar opposite of Soho House – it's a club that welcomes everyone, but absolutely no one chooses to be a member. Because alcoholics have a terrible image. You immediately imagine tramps quaffing methylated spirits in gutters, smelling of wee, and mothers lying face down in pools of vomit while their children forage for scraps. People assume that alcoholics are weak-willed and selfish, and even if the alcoholic manages to quit, we see them as doomed. Sentenced to survive for ever without the world's favourite drug, taking one day at a time and reliving past misdemeanours in dusty basements while drinking sweet tea from plastic cups. Alcohol is the only drug in the world where, when you stop taking it, *you* are presumed to have a problem, a disease, while those still indulging are viewed as 'normal'.

Yet many of the best people I know are 'overly enthusiastic drinkers', or ex-drinkers. We're the people who don't do anything by halves, who grab life by the short and curlies and throw ourselves in at the deep end. Okay, so we might have a teensy little problem with *moderation,* but we are immoderate in all things – in love, in friendship, in work and in motherhood.

In his Temperance Address in 1842, Abraham Lincoln said of 'habitual drunkards': 'There seems ever to have been a proneness in the brilliant, and warm-blooded to fall into this vice. The demon of intemperance ever seems to have delighted in sucking the blood of genius and of generosity.' *Brilliant, warm-blooded, generous geniuses.* I'll take that, even from a man with dubious facial hair.

So, I'm sure I'd meet some incredible people through AA (especially in the nearby Chelsea meeting, which is, apparently, stuffed full of B-list celebrities), I'm sure they'd welcome me and I'm sure they'd help me. But I just can't make myself do it.

I'm scared that all the tales of terrible 'rock bottoms' will only serve to make me feel that my bottle-of-wine-a-day habit is perfectly acceptable. I'm not kidding myself. I'm certain that if I carried on drinking all of that would be in the post. I know that addiction is progressive, and that one day I could lose my family, my home, everything, but *I'm not there yet*, and I have no intention of getting there.

I'm terrified of bumping into someone from the PTA while I'm going in, or coming out. I hate the idea of surrendering to a Higher Power, and I loathe the thought of all the rules. (I'm not at all good at rules. That's why I'm in this proper pickle.)

I just can't imagine standing in a church hall, in front of a bunch of strangers, and saying 'My name's Clare, and I'm an alcoholic.' Even if I can make myself say the A-word, I don't want to define myself by a negative. I want to stand up and say, proudly, 'My name's Clare and I'm a non-drinker.' I want to deal with it, put it behind me and get on with the rest of my life.

So I type 'How do I stop drinking?' into Google, and I find the most extraordinary thing. There are women, all over the globe, just like me; women who've quit drinking and are writing about it. Writing about how their love affairs with booze ended, about their hopes and fears and their day-to-day struggles. Telling the world all the things they can't tell their closest friends.

I can't stop reading. I curl up in bed with my laptop, gorging on the private lives of ex-drinkers. Now I know that I am not alone.

I leave a few comments on my favourite blogs, feeling like the new girl at school tentatively offering the cool girls a Marlboro Light and hoping to be accepted into the gang. Then I think *Why not go one step further? Why not set up your own blog, make yourself properly accountable, tell the whole World Wide Web what you're doing? Then there's really no turning back.*

So I do. Me – the technophobe who has to call her husband at work to ask how to download an email attachment. I find a programme called Blogger, which makes it all fairly easy, and set up a simple, not very pretty, text-only blog. Then I write my first post, confessing to all of it, telling anyone out there just what a mess I've made of my life. I type away, feeling like a dumpy, middle-aged version of Carrie in *Sex and the City*, although I'm pretty sure that Carrie didn't type with one hand while removing dried-up Rice Krispies from the kitchen worktop with the other.

Incredibly, when I check my blog stats half an hour later, my post has been viewed three times! I get terribly overexcited until I realise that it's just me, reading and rereading my own blog.

I've double- and triple-checked everything to make sure I'm completely anonymous. I've called myself SoberMummy, because I'm hoping that every time I type out my pseudonym on the keyboard it'll reinforce the fact that *Mummy is now sober*. Also, it means I get to sign off each post with my initials: SM. Just one '&' away from *Fifty Shades of Grey*. Racy.

I've called the blog Mummy was a Secret Drinker, because I feel like there is a whole dark side to my life that no one (not even John) is aware of. All those mums at the school gate, who see me always organised, hosting coffee mornings, raising money for charity and volunteering for class rep, have no idea. They've never seen me drunk or out of control. I rarely drop a ball. I'm probably pretty irritating, come to think of it. Which makes me think, *If no one knows my secret, then how many other mums just like me are out there? Who else is standing at the school gate, stealing the kids' Haribos to smother the smell of stale booze?*

SOBER MORNINGS

Sunday morning, and what a difference a fortnight makes.

I remember, when I was a child, thinking that if I dug a hole deep enough I'd end up in Australia, where everything would be kind of the same, except we'd all be standing on our heads. Well, giving up alcohol has been a bit like that – everything feels upside down and back to front.

In the *drinking days,* I lived for Friday and Saturday nights; I died on Sunday mornings. But now, I dread evenings, which are only made bearable by eating mountains of cake, but Sunday mornings are my reward.

For years, my nights have been dark and full of terrors. I've been plagued by insomnia, waking up at 3 a.m. most nights, letting my overactive mind turn small issues into insurmountable problems with all the skill of a prize-winning novelist. I've tried lavender pillows, homeopathic drugs, prescription drugs, hot milk, aromatherapy baths, meditation and exercise, but I never thought to blame the booze.

But at last, now I've mastered the skill of dropping off sober, which took a little practice, I am sleeping for a solid *nine hours* of deep, uninterrupted sleep. No more psychedelic dreams, no more getting up to wee again and again, no more trips to the fridge for cold water to combat the raging thirst, no more turning molehills into mountains.

This morning I drag myself out of sleep, like a butterfly clambering out of a chrysalis (note that this is the *only* way in which I resemble a butterfly), and initially I'm all muggy-headed and heavy-limbed, but fifteen minutes later and I'm bouncing around like the Duracell bunny on speed.

While the rest of the family are still sleeping and the house is quiet, I do some research, and it turns out that the link between alcohol and insomnia is a well-proven one. To feel refreshed you should, ideally, have six or seven cycles of REM sleep. After drinking you typically have only one or two, which is why you feel exhausted the next day. You're also likely to wake up several times to wee, because alcohol is a diuretic, and the weeing and sweating dehydrates you and makes you thirsty. Plus, alcohol can make you snore, or even cause sleep apnoea. All of which adds up to just a few hours of poor-quality, fitful sleep.

Not only does lack of sleep make you tired and unable to function properly, but it's terribly bad for our health. It exacerbates depression and weight issues, it's bad news for your skin, puts strain on your heart and it increases your risk of colon and breast cancer.

God, I love sleep. It's the next best thing to chocolate. It's even making me think that being sober might actually be *a really good thing*. Plus, a study by Amie Gordon and other researchers at UC Berkeley found that couples who regularly get a full night's sleep are more likely to have happy, successful relationships.

The other thing that's transformed my mornings is the lack of a hangover. I've had some chronic ones in the past. On one memorable hungover Saturday, I managed to reverse my car over a raised mini roundabout that I couldn't see in the rear-view mirror. To my horror, the car stopped moving and I realised that I was balanced *on top of the roundabout* with all four wheels suspended in mid-air. I had to clamber out of my car (still dressed *in my pyjamas)*, to beg help from four security guards.

'Don't worry, madam,' said one of them, kindly, 'people do that all the time.'

'Do they really?' I asked, relieved.

'No,' he replied, as they all cracked up. They actually had to cling on to each other for support, they were laughing so much.

I realise now that one of the differences between problem drinkers and 'normal drinkers' (curse the lot of them) is their attitude to hangovers. I was always astounded by those people who would turn down a glass of wine at Sunday lunch because they'd drunk too much the night before and couldn't face it. Surely they realised that the only effective cure for a hangover was to *drink more*?

I was an enthusiastic proponent of 'hair of the dog'. The expression comes from a time when it was believed that the way to cure rabies was to put the hair of the dog that bit you (presuming that you could catch it) on the rabid dog bite.

Unlike this cure for rabies, 'hair of the dog' as a hangover cure does have a sound basis in science. Alcoholic drinks contain methanol, which is a poison and makes you feel terrible, and doctors treat methanol poisoning with ethanol – or, as it's better known, alcohol.

Another reason why alcohol cures a hangover is that many of the symptoms you experience – the irritability, headache, shakiness – are caused by the early stages of alcohol withdrawal. It's actually your body craving *more*. So, when you give it more – they stop. Simples.

I share all of this with my blog readers. *Are there any?* In a way, it doesn't really matter if no one ever reads my posts, because it's like free therapy. I type away, sharing my fears, my hopes and all the day-to-day struggles that come with quitting booze, and afterwards I feel lighter, clearer and more resolute. I press 'publish' and my words fly out on to the internet, taking many of my woes with them.

Then, I spot something new: underneath my latest blog post it says *1 comment*. It's from someone called 'Whimsical': *Big bravo to you. Thanks for sharing your story x*

I feel like I've just been given a huge great bear hug by the World Wide Web. I can see my grin reflected in my computer screen. There is someone out there!

Feeling buoyed up, I round up the troops for a trip to the local indoor play centre.

A soft-play area with a chronic hangover is a special kind of hell. The combination of the noise of a few hundred shrieking children, that indescribable odour – a mixture of fried food, sweat, disinfectant and dirty nappy – and an alcohol-induced dehydration, queasiness and headache is truly dreadful. In the old days, I would hunker down in as quiet a spot as I could find, clutching a cup of coffee and counting the seconds until it was all over.

But today is different. Today, all rested, sober and perky, I can see it all through the children's eyes. Hundreds of overexcited small people charging around having fun. A myriad of different colours, sounds and textures. It's a veritable wonderland.

Until a breathless Evie and Kit come to find me.

'Mummy, Maddie's got stuck at the top. She climbed up there fine, but she's too scared to come down. We tried to help her, but she wants you.'

Oh, great. I have to navigate four massive storeys of inflatable obstacles. Tunnels. Ladders. Slides. Rope bridges. All designed for an average-sized eight-year-old, not a middle-aged mum with a pronounced wine belly.

Hangover or no hangover, there's only so much soft play any reasonable adult can take.

DAY |0|2|1|

THE WINE BELLY

I haven't quit drinking in order to lose weight but, I have to confess, the idea of dropping a few pounds is a major incentive. I weigh twelve stone, which – at five foot seven – is at least two stone overweight, and I have a horrible wine belly.

Over the years I've tried endless diets: the F Plan (endless fibre), the Beverly Hills diet (lots of fruit), Scarsdale Medical diet (detailed meal plans), Hay diet (complicated rules about protein and carbs), cabbage soup diet (just what it sounds like), the Cambridge diet (milkshakes), Atkins (no carbs), Dukan diet (more no carbs), low GI diet (only certain sorts of carbs) and the 5:2 diet (two days fasting a week). Just writing that list makes me feel hungry.

All of them would work for a while. I'd lose up to around ten pounds in a month. But they were impossible to stick to long term, and as soon as I started eating normally again, the weight would pile back on, as if to punish me for my foolish optimism.

I did the exercise thing too. Jane Fonda's workout. Rosemary Conley's hip and thigh workout. Stepping. Spinning. Running. Large rubber band things. Blow-up balls. Callanetics. Weights. Body Pump. Body Attack and that funny machine that you stand on while it vibrates. Just writing that list makes me feel exhausted. I did get fitter, but not much thinner, and nothing seemed to shift the belly.

I'm not *monstrous* (yet). I'm a UK size fourteen. (I'm in denial about this and try, whenever possible, to squeeze myself into a twelve. If God had meant us to be skinny She wouldn't have invented stretch fabrics.) But as I sit here in my trusty jeans, a little roll of flab – like a child's rubber ring in the swimming pool – is hanging over my belt. Lovely. If I lie down in the bath and grab my belly fat with both hands (which I have done, when I was feeling masochistic), it is – ironically – about the size of a bottle of vino.

The problem with being relatively slim except for the vast wine belly is that it makes you look five months pregnant. And there is nothing worse than some poor woman asking you when it's due. Plus, if you're at a party, knocking back the vino while looking up the duff, you get some very hostile looks from the Pregnancy Police.

While I'm obsessively googling everything related to alcohol, I do some research on wine bellies. It turns out that not only is it not the best look aesthetically, it's also really bad for your health.

It is, apparently, way better to be obese all over than to be relatively skinny with a beer/wine belly. A recent study by researchers from the Mayo Clinic in Minnesota (published in the *Annals of Internal Medicine*) showed that normal-weight adults who carried fat around their middles had *twice the risk of early death* than those who were overweight or obese but with normal fat distribution.

The reason belly fat is so dangerous is that it doesn't just sit under the skin and wobble (like the bingo wings or thunder thighs, both of which I'm on more than nodding terms with); it wraps itself around your vital organs and massively increases your risk of stroke, heart disease, cancer and type 2 diabetes.

I decide to take all my measurements, as a baseline, so that when I find myself transformed into a goddess I can look back at them and chortle in horror. The only tape measure I have is one of those metal ones for DIY, so I end up tying myself in knots, literally, with pieces of string that I then measure against the metal tape.

According to the NHS, a woman's waist should ideally measure less than 32 inches. Between 32 and 35 is classified as 'high', and over 35 inches is 'very high'. They also suggest that you measure your waist to hip ratio (inches around the waist, divided by inches around the hips). For women, this ratio should be less than 0.85.

Now, despite the fact that my BMI is only just above the 'normal' range, my waist measurement at *36 inches,* and my waist to hip ratio at 0.87, put me well into the danger zone. I run the risk of being killed by my muffin top.

I'm quite sure that the booze is to blame. Alcohol has 7 calories per gram, making it the second most calorie-rich micronutrient after fat. A bottle of wine usually contains *at least* 600 calories. That means that if you drink a bottle of wine a day you are consuming *two extra days' worth* of calories a week.

There are two other reasons why alcohol leads to piling on the pounds, which I'm certainly very familiar with. One is that drinking makes you lose your inhibitions, so, at the end of the meal you're likely to think 'Death by Chocolate? It'd be rude not to! Tiny, dainty chocolates with coffee? Why the hell not? *Just one more wafer-thin mint.'* The second is the dreaded hangover. Because your body is dehydrated and it needs energy to recover from the previous night's marathon, you crave fat- and carbohydrate-rich foods, which is why a fry-up, a greasy bacon sarnie or a blueberry muffin (one of your five a day!) always hits the spot in a way that fresh fruit and no-added-sugar granola is never going to.

It's also true that red wine contains something called 'resveratrol', which can help you burn fat, BUT (and it's a big but, or – in my case – a big butt), only if you drink no more than one small glass a day. Excuse me for a minute while I grab my belly fat and roll on the floor laughing.

I post all my measurements on the blog, which feels a bit like walking naked into a room full of strangers, along with a summary of my research. Then, for good measure, I decide to stand on the bathroom scales for the first time since I quit, three weeks ago. I'm feeling kind of smug *in advance.* This is the moment when I get to see some positive results from all this damned *denial.* This is payback time, baby.

So I strip off, go to the loo, even cut my nails to get rid of any possible excess weight, and stand on the scales.

Bugger, balls and damnation! I've GAINED three pounds! I stand on one foot. Same result. (I clutch the handbasin and immediately lose half a stone, but even I acknowledge that this is cheating.) Where is the logic and the fairness in that? I catch sight of myself in the bathroom mirror. Naked, deranged and STILL FAT! Why? Why? Why?

If I'm completely honest with myself, I think I know the answer, and it's *cake.* After a decade of smoking to wind down and reduce stress, followed by another decade of heavy drinking, my automatic response to any negative emotion (or positive emotion, come to think of it) is to stick something in my mouth. And, when you're having a pretty miserable time, nothing hits the spot quite like cake.

My other new habit is *hot chocolate*, which, I've discovered, has magical powers. When I'm wrestling with the wily wine witch of an evening I make a cup of hot, sweet, comforting chocolate, wrap both hands around it and I'm transported back to my childhood, to a simpler time before the old crone wrapped her arms around my neck and jabbed her talons into my spine.

But, having identified the culprits, I'm not at all sure that I can do without them. Or want to. Right now, I feel like chocolate is a necessary food group. Frankly, I've given up every other vice I've ever had and I'm not letting go of this one, at least not yet.

On the plus side, while my bathroom scales may be the harbingers of doom, I swear that my face has got less puffy, not so *jowly*. And while the belly is still *huge*, the 'jeans that don't lie' seem to fit much more easily. Added to which, Evie said this morning, 'Mummy, I think your butt has got less saggy.'

Talk about damning with faint praise – and I was just starting to glow with satisfaction when she continued 'Your boobs are still droopy, though.'

I bit back the urge to yell that this was almost entirely the fault of her and her siblings, especially Maddie, who refused a bottle for nearly a year. (She doesn't take after her mummy, does she?)

DAY	0	2	6

OH GOD, IT'S FRIDAY

I used to love Fridays, where the weekend starts at lunchtime and anything is possible.

Friday has always been a special day of the week – a significant day. When I was little it was all about no homework. In our house, Friday evening was my mother's night off cooking. As my dad was unable to even boil an egg, this meant it was *takeaway night.* Fish and chips, or chop suey, in front of *It's a Knockout, The Two Ronnies* or *The Generation Game* (We'd shout raucously over the conveyor-belt challenge: 'Deep-fat fryer! SodaStream! Don't forget the cuddly toy!')

When I was a teenager, one of my best friends, Lou, was Jewish, and she would invite me to Friday-night supper (Shabbat). I loved it. I seriously considered converting to Judaism (but giving up bacon sarnies was a deal-breaker). All those candles, rituals, generations of family around the table gently teasing each other over Bubba's chicken soup with dumplings.

As I got older, and started working, Friday became even more special. The end of the working week. We'd often start celebrating at lunchtime, with a team trip out to a local Pizza Express. We'd return half-heartedly to our desks, shuffle some things around and postpone as much as possible to Monday morning, then we were *out on the town.* Letting our hair down. Going wild. We'd earned it!

I had a boyfriend back then who rode a bicycle with a big butcher's basket on the front. He would collect me from the office bar on Friday evening and I would climb into the basket (still clutching my drink) with my legs sticking out the side, and he'd ride us into Soho or the West End, where we'd blag our way into the latest, hottest, members-only club.

Then I became a full-time mum, but I still had a special place in my heart for Fridays. Friday was the day when I'd often have a lunch arranged with friends (and a glass or two of wine). If not, then it was a perfectly valid excuse to open a bottle as soon as school was out, either with a friend over a 'playdate' or – if necessary – on my own. (In this, it appears, I was not alone.) Laura Donnelly from the *Daily Telegraph* cites a recent report backed by Alcohol Concern which found a huge increase in 'stressed mums turning to wine after the school run'. Laura quotes Alison Wise, director of Drink Wise, saying 'There is a real problem with drinking that starts after school. It used to be a cup of tea, now it's a glass of wine at 3.30pm instead.'

Many a Friday afternoon was spent letting the children run wild around someone's playroom, ignoring the occasional shouts of 'Mummy, Archie *bit me*!' or similar, while a handful of mums set the world to rights over a glass or two of Sauvignon Blanc. I remember one gloriously sunny week in a local park, feeling happily tipsy when one of my friends nudged me and said 'Clare, isn't that Kit at the top of that tree?' And, sure enough, there he was, about twenty foot up in the air and unable to get down. And I hadn't even noticed.

None of the children ever came to any harm, but perhaps that was more a matter of luck than of judgement. I realise now that I spent the last few years running with scissors, and it's pure chance that I never fell and stabbed myself, or anyone else.

So, I loved those lazy, hazy (sometimes crazy) Friday afternoons; but a few years ago, Fridays started scaring me. Whatever method I was currently employing to 'moderate' (no drinking on weekdays, only drinking beer, no drinking alone, etcetera), the gloves were always off on a Friday. And it was getting out of control. Despite all the promises I'd made myself, the wine witch would start yabbering on at me from lunchtime onwards: *Come on! It's Friday! You deserve it! You're a grown-up, you need to have some fun. You've been so good.* Inevitably, I'd start drinking by 4 p.m. latest, so by the time the husband got back from work I was most of a bottle of wine down already, and by 9 p.m. I'd be grumpy, argumentative or asleep.

Now I categorically hate Fridays. I wake up to the radio alarm and, for a few precious moments, I forget. I think *Yay, Friday!* Then I remember that I have absolutely nothing to look forward to except an evening wrestling with my inner demons.

So today I think I'll try something new: *alcohol-free beer.* There's a fair amount of discussion about 'fake alcohol' in the Sobersphere. Some say it's a godsend, others that it's the work of the devil and bound to catapult you off the wagon faster than you can say 'teetotal'. I figure that, since beer was never my drug of choice, alcohol-free beer is unlikely to be a trigger for me. Fake wine, however, I'll steer clear of for the time being (apart from anything else, the general consensus seems to be that it all tastes terrible).

So, on the way to pick the kids up from school I drop in at Sainsbury's. In the beer aisle, I discover Beck's Blue. It looks pretty much like the real thing. I pick up a six-pack and take it up to the till.

Now, here's a confession: I used to buy wine on rotation from several different shops because I was worried that the cashiers would clock how much I was buying and *judge me*, particularly at this Sainsbury's near the school, as I use it quite a lot. I used to get really irritated by the fact that the same cashier seemed to be on duty whenever I went in. I would say to the children, loudly, as I hauled my bottles of vino up to the till, 'Mustn't forget Daddy's wine!' or 'Godfather Duncan's coming for supper!' with an eye-roll. Needless to say, the children thought I'd gone slightly mad. They weren't wrong.

I approach the cashier with trepidation, before I remember that I have absolutely nothing to be ashamed of (for a change). I put my alcohol-free beers on the counter and find myself, yet again, talking too loudly as I say 'Why is there an age restriction on these when they are *alcohol-free*? Isn't that funny? It's not as if there's *any alcohol* in them! Ha ha!' Still acting like a mad lady. I would love to know whether cashiers ever give a toss about who's buying what and wonder which of the mums they serve are secret lushes. I suspect that the only person ever judging me was myself.

I collect the kids from school and one of the mums calls over to me, 'Hey, Clare! Haven't seen you for ages! Why don't we go out for a few drinks?'

'I've quit the booze for a while,' I reply, 'on a bit of a detox . . .'

She looks crestfallen and shoots off, calling over her shoulder, 'Let me know when you're back on the sauce!'

'I can still go out, you know!' I yell after her, 'I can drink water! Mocktails!' But she's gone. And I'm officially a pariah. I suddenly come over all weepy, so go and stick my head into the lost-property cupboard, with which (thanks to Kit) I'm intimately acquainted. Luckily, the odour of abandoned, sweaty rugby socks brings me round quite quickly.

We get home and the kids pile out of the car. They're all staring at the ground outside our house. The water board recently dug a huge hole in the pavement and filled it in with wet concrete in which some local wag decided to draw a 5-foot penis. Oh, great. Luckily, they are not a talented artist.

'What's that, Mummy?' asks Maddie.

'It's a rocket, darling,' I reply.

'That's so funny, it looks a bit like a—' I silence Kit with a hard stare and usher everyone quickly into the house.

'Mummy!' says Maddie, reaching into her school bag and bouncing up and down on the balls of her feet in excitement. 'I've got a surprise for you! Guess who I got to bring home?'

Oh, God, it's the class bear. That's all I need.

I quickly rearrange my face into an ecstatic smile.

'Well done darling!' I say, in an enthusiastic tone that's fooling no one. 'We're so excited to have you here, Billy.'

Evie and Kit have both bought the class bear home in the past. Ostensibly it's a way for the class teacher to reward pupils for working particularly hard and to practise their writing, as they have to fill in a little diary (ideally with photos) detailing what the class bear got up to over the weekend. In reality, the mothers use it as a way to show off to each other about what perfect lives they lead.

Evie dives into Maddie's bag to find Billy's diary. She and Kit start flicking through and sniggering.

'Look! Billy went to see the Elgin Marbles at the British Museum last weekend. He's been to a concert at the Royal Albert Hall. He's done a Mandarin class with someone called Jasper. There's even a picture of him at the top of the Eiffel Tower! And look what he did at half-term! He went scuba-diving in the Maldives!'

Six eyes turn to look at me. Eight, if you include Billy's shiny brown buttons.

'What are *we* going to do with Billy, Mummy?'

I make it as far as 4.45 p.m. (*plus ça change*) before cracking open a 'beer', while trying to figure out a suitably impressive weekend itinerary for Billy. Perhaps I should ask Evie to show me how to use Photoshop, then we can crop Billy into all sorts of educational landmarks.

Spookily, my alcohol-free beer looks just the same as the real thing (apart from not quite as much head), tastes just the same and even makes me feel light-headed. *Drunk. Woo hoo!* I double-check the bottle. It *is* alcohol-free. Either they're playing a sick joke or my head is so finely tuned to expect to feel tipsy that it's slipped into that mode automatically.

It helps, it really does. It makes me feel a bit more 'adult', a bit more celebratory. Then I eat a slice of carrot cake bigger than my head. (It's a vegetable, so doesn't count. Even the icing was *lemon* based.) That helps even more. But I'm still fed up. I'm fed up with being 'boring'. I'm fed up with the constant dialogue in my head about alcohol.

I do a deal with myself. I will keep this up for another seventy-four days, until day 100. That's a nice round number. Then, if it still isn't getting any better, I'm throwing in the towel.

THE MONTH WHEN I DO A LOT OF WEEPING

| DAY | 0 | 3 | 3 |

NOT THE GIRL HE MARRIED

Thirteen years ago, my husband married a party girl. A *bon viveuse*. Until recently (thirty-three days ago, to be precise) our lives revolved around entertaining friends over boozy Sunday lunches, getting happily plastered at parties and cooking elaborate dinners accompanied by expensive wine. 'Date nights' generally involved meals out at the latest restaurant with aperitifs, wine and digestifs, followed by a nightcap. But now he's married to a teetotaller. I signed up to this – he didn't. He wanted me to cut down (drastically). He didn't ask (or want) me to stop completely.

Before I quit, in my low moments, usually around 3 a.m., I'd have visions of the husband leaving the puffy, boozy, raddled wife and running off with a younger, slimmer, more vibrant version. Now when I'm feeling morose I have the same vision, but in this one they are happily sharing a bottle of wine in a romantic bistro, while I sit at home alone with a glass of water in my hand.

There's a lot of help and discussion for families of problem drinkers, but not much help – as far as I know – for husbands of non-drinkers. For better, for worse, for richer, for poorer, for drunker and more sober . . .

I haven't yet confessed my fears to John (although I've poured them out on my blog, obviously) as he's too kind to ever admit to any pangs of regret, so I worry that whatever he says I won't believe him, but this evening I just can't help myself.

'Darling,' I say, 'can I ask you a question?' He looks like a rabbit caught in the headlights. John is a stiff-upper-lip Scot – he doesn't do 'talking about stuff'. He went to boarding school at the age of seven. His mind is whirring, running through his mental filing cabinet of 'appropriate answers for tricky conversations' in advance.

'Does it bother you that I've stopped drinking? Do you miss having a drinking partner?'

John looks relieved. At least I hadn't asked him 'Does my bum look big in this?' He always struggles with the correct response to that one.

'God no, it's a wholly good thing,' he replies. I press him for more. I want to know details. The benefits are, apparently, as follows:

1. I no longer fall asleep while watching TV, so we can genuinely share a box set.
2. I'm less grumpy.
3. I don't keep him awake tossing and turning at night-time.
4. He doesn't have to drink really fast to make sure he gets his share of a bottle of wine.

I grill him for any negatives. He thinks hard, then replies, 'I don't get as much access to the TV remote control.' Then he hides behind his newspaper, like a tortoise sticking his head back in his shell. Conversation over. Men. Simple creatures. Don't mess with their sleep, their TV-watching or their comfort blankets and they're happy.

The truth is, I suspect, that the idea of losing a drinking partner is only terrifying to we addicts, not to the 'normal' drinkers.

But if I tried to take away his remote control permanently? *That* would be a deal-breaker . . .

DAY	0	4	0

I AM KHALEESI

Day 40, and, in my quest to beat the evening wine cravings, I'm reading up on visualisation techniques.

Visualisation has been around for centuries and has roots in meditation, prayer and hypnotherapy. Many top sportspeople use visualisation. Arnold Schwarzenegger famously took the visualisation techniques he used in bodybuilding and applied them to acting and politics.

I find a website called easyvisualizationtechniques.com which quotes Arnie saying: 'I visualised myself being and having what it was I wanted. Before I had my first Mr Universe title, I walked around the tournament like I owned it. I had won it so many times in my mind that there was no doubt I would win it. Then I moved on to the movies, the same thing. I visualised myself being a famous actor and earning big money. I just knew it would happen.'

The complete improbability of a scarily pumped-up Austrian with an unintelligible accent becoming Governor of California makes me think that maybe there's something in this visualisation malarkey.

There are, I discover, three ways to use visualisation on the road to getting and staying sober. The first is in relaxation and stress relief. The idea is that around wine o'clock, instead of thinking about Pinot Grigio, you find a quiet spot and imagine yourself in your 'happy place'. You use all your senses – smell, feeling, sounds, colours, taste. Cravings, apparently, only last ten minutes (although it feels like an awful lot longer), so this can help you ride the storm.

I try it. I lie in the bath, close my eyes and imagine that I'm back on an island in Thailand on my gap year with Buck, the gorgeous Texan with whom I had a memorable holiday romance. Buck had a tattoo in Thai on the sole of his foot. He said it translated as 'the Buck stops here'. In reality, it probably read 'stupid, gullible tourist'. I can hear palm leaves swaying in the breeze, feel the sand between my toes and taste the cool Singha beer on my lips. Uh-oh. It appears that all my darned 'happy spots' revolve around booze.

Eventually I settle on imagining my thighs gripping the back of a horse, galloping along a Cornish headland with my arms wrapped around the rippling, glistening six-pack of Ross Poldark, fresh from his morning's scything in the fields. It is, thank goodness, virtually impossible, even in my fevered imagination, to drink a glass of vino while on the back of a galloping stallion.

The second way to use visualisation is the Arnie way: to imagine your future success. Here you picture yourself where you want to be in a year's time. I try it. I imagine a sober, skinny, beautifully dressed and groomed me, at the book launch of my soon-to-be-bestselling novel, surrounded by friends, family and my proud, happy, well-behaved and well-adjusted kids.

Future visualisations are believed to help with focus, confidence, motivation and self-esteem. Knowing what you are working towards and *really believing it can happen* is the first step, so they say, to changing your life. There are even those who claim that visualising a positive future can actually *make it happen.* This is referred to as the 'law of attraction'. It sounds like poppycock, but there are many studies showing that people who think positively have more positive outcomes, and vice versa, so perhaps there is something in it.

Scientists have proven the power of perception and of the

subconscious, over and over again. For example, think about the use of placebos in medicine. I love the fact that if I say to my children 'Mummy will kiss it better' *and* I kiss the 'ouch', it really *does get better.* Because they believe it will be so. (Admittedly, if they manage to chop off the end of a finger, this will not work and off to A&E we shall go.)

But my favourite way of using visualisation is what I think of as the 'kick-ass method'. Allen Carr (author of *The Easy Way to Stop Drinking*) suggests visualising your cravings, or your 'inner addict', as a writhing snake or a monster. Every time you deny the snake a drink it dies a little. You have to keep going until it's well and truly despatched. One small sip and it leaps back into life.

In a similar vein, I like to imagine the 'wine witch'. It's easier to beat your inner addict when you picture it as a vile, manipulative crone and not just your own subconscious. I take this one step further and imagine myself in 'kick-ass' persona, battling with, and beating, the enemy with great style and panache.

I remember using a trick like this when I was promoted to the board of my ad agency. When I went, nervously, into board meetings as the youngest, and one of the only female, directors, I would picture myself as Madonna circa 1987 wearing one of those cone-tipped bras and leather hot pants. I also imagined that my nipples could fire laser guns on demand. Needless to say, I swaggered into those meetings with far more confidence than I'd have had without Madge.

Apologies to Madonna, to whom I will always be grateful, but I have updated her. I am now Khaleesi from *Game of Thrones.* Khaleesi – aka Daenerys Targaryen, Mother of Dragons – strong, wise and beautiful. You would never, ever see Khaleesi reach for the Chablis when in a spot of trouble. Oh no! She would let loose her army of Unsullied. Khaleesi would never have a problem overcoming a little addiction. This woman can walk through flames and come out unscathed!

So now, when the wine witch comes tapping on my shoulder, I picture Khaleesi and set free my three dragons, who burn the evil bitch to a cinder without hesitation or wavering. (It's important to ignore the end of Season 4 when Khaleesi's dragons turn bad and start frying small children.) Take that, ugly crone, and don't try messing with me.

DAY 0 4 4

WHEN THE WINE WITCH WINS

Since I quit drinking I've been sleeping so deeply that I've not remembered any dreams, until last night when I dreamed, vividly, of Juliet.

I met Juliet when I was twenty-six, and a friend of mine introduced her to me as his new girlfriend. Juliet and I immediately fell in (platonic) love.

Juliet had wild, untameable red hair and freckles, and she crackled and fizzed with an energy that was tangible. Spending time with her was like eating a huge mouthful of popping candy. She was fiendishly clever and fiercely loyal and, like me, she smoked like a chimney and drank like a fish. When I was with Juliet I felt *more*. More attractive, more witty, more alive.

I should have known then that a flame that burned so brightly would inevitably die young.

Juliet and I would go to smart restaurants and talk until the waiters started putting chairs on the tables around us. We'd finish the first bottle quickly and Juliet would wave it at a waiter, crying 'Excuse me, my man, could we please have one exactly the same as this, but *full*?' and she would tip back in her chair and guffaw with laughter.

We would spend long nights at her flat or mine, dancing like no one was watching to the anthems of our youth: Duran Duran, Siouxsie and the Banshees, Toyah Willcox. We read poetry out loud (pretentious, I know, but we were *young*). We promised each other that we'd grow old together, becoming eccentric geriatrics dressed in purple velvet and ancient mink with the heads still attached, terrorising youths with our walking sticks and drinking Martinis with abandon.

Juliet was ferociously fearless (when drunk, when sober, she was riddled with insecurities), and persuasive. She would always manage to convince someone that she was 'perfectly able to drive'. She was, she'd say, a *brilliant* driver and, in fact, even better after a few drinks.

One day, after we'd all been to a wild weekend country house party, she decided she was perfectly able to drive home rather than stay the Sunday night like the rest of us. We, much to our shame, let her. She crashed her car on the M1.

Mercifully, no one was hurt, but it shook her up big time. She realised she wasn't invincible. She ditched the high-powered consultancy job she hated and moved out of London, away from temptations, to live more soberly and follow her dream of writing. She wrote the way she lived – with great gusto, originality and humour. Her emails were side-splittingly funny. John read some of them out at her memorial.

I'm ashamed to say that, wrapped up in the self-obsession of youth, I didn't speak to Juliet as much as I should have done after she left town. In the year that she was away I never once went to visit.

One night Juliet had a friend over. He wasn't yet a boyfriend – I think they were just 'testing the water'. They got drunk. She wanted to buy some cigarettes, but – having holed herself up in the countryside – the nearest shop that would be open was several miles away. She spun the usual line about being an even better driver when drunk.

Juliet's car careered off an empty country road and ended up upside down in a ditch. The not-yet, and now never-to-be, boyfriend was trapped for hours, dressed in his pyjamas, next to her corpse. She wasn't even thirty years old.

Many years later, John and I were driving in Africa with Evie and Kit (who were then a toddler and a baby) in the back. The visibility was terrible – lashing rain and fog. I fell asleep. In my dream, I saw Juliet, as clear as day. She shouted 'WAKE UP!' I woke to see that the road was splitting into a dual carriageway. John hadn't noticed and was heading straight towards two lanes of oncoming traffic. I yelled. He swerved. I honestly believe that Juliet saved our lives. I wish I'd been able to save hers. (John thinks I should stop telling this story as 'it's all a bit woo woo' and makes me 'sound like a hippy'. I think he has no soul.)

That's the thing about the wine witch. She cuts brilliant lives short, and ensures that others are only half lived. She makes children grow up thinking it is normal for adults to drink all evening, every evening. She fixes it so mothers are woken up in the middle of the night by a stranger telling them their only child was found dead in a ditch, next to someone she barely knew.

I remind myself that I'm not just doing this for me. I'm doing it for my husband and my children, and I'm doing it for my feckless, fearless, flame-haired friend – Juliet, who I will never forget.

DAY |0|4|7|

THE DINNER PARTY

It's Saturday afternoon and, after days of spring showers, the sun is shining, so John and I take Evie, Kit, Maddie and the dog to Holland Park.

I watch the children playing hide-and-seek in the adventure playground while John sits on a bench, reading the weekend *Financial Times.* I wonder whether I should tell him that he needs to start putting sun lotion *on top of his head,* but decide not to ruin the moment.

Suddenly, out of nowhere, I'm hit by a wave of elation, a bolt of pure *joie de vivre* and *love* like I haven't felt since the legendary Judge Jules played the decks at the Cross back in 1995.

I've read about this feeling with eager anticipation. It's called the 'pink cloud' of early sobriety. For a few minutes, I float along on my pink cloud feeling that anything is possible and nothing can go wrong, then *poof,* and it's gone. Evie, Kit and Maddie resume usual hostilities. Evie's teasing Kit about something, so, unwilling to take on his bigger sister, he kicks (the totally innocent) Maddie when he thinks no one is watching. Maddie bursts into tears, half of John's newspaper blows away in the wind and the dog runs off with a bread roll stolen from someone's picnic basket.

I stare longingly at the rapidly retreating pink cloud. Is that it? Will it ever come back?

And now it's 6 p.m. – wine o'clock – again, and the cravings have returned with a vengeance, exacerbated by the fact that I need to get ready to go out to a *dinner party.* I root around in the wardrobe of despair for something half decent to wear, brief the babysitter and then drive myself and John to Laura's house.

Driving. Now there's a bonus. No more night buses, no more tube trains filled with rowdy revellers, no more expensive taxis.

I decide that I'm not going to make a big deal about not drinking; that way I don't have to deal with all the questions it'll inevitably raise. Maybe no one will even notice. Even if they do, they probably won't think it worth mentioning. They'll just assume that I'm driving, or detoxing, or something.

We park the car and walk into the large, stuccoed Kensington house that has been the backdrop to many of my drunken antics over the last fifteen years.

'John! Clare!' shouts our host as we walk into the basement kitchen, which is already filled with people. 'What will you have to drink?'

'Errr, don't suppose you have a Diet Coke?' I reply.

Everybody stops talking and about eight pairs of eyes swivel around to stare at me. Well, that went well.

'I'm driving,' I add, lamely.

'Why on earth didn't you take a taxi?' Laura asks me. 'Anyway, you can still have a glass or two!'

'Thanks, but I won't. I'm . . . detoxing.'

She shrugs and hands me a Diet Coke, which I clutch with both hands like a toddler clinging to a comfort blanket.

I start chatting to Laura's son, who's the same age as Evie and has been bribed to take coats and hand out crisps. He asks whether he can borrow my phone to show me something on Instagram. I pass it over.

'You shouldn't keep so many windows open, you know,' he says, 'it makes everything run slower and uses up loads of data.' With a display of manual dexterity way beyond the capability of any adult, he starts closing down screens. To my horror, my iPhone screen is suddenly filled by my blog. He stops and squints at it.

'Mummy was a Secret Drinker?' he reads, slowly and loudly. In my mind his voice, clear and unbroken as a choirboy's, is echoing off the walls and ceiling of the crowded kitchen.

I'm horrified! While I'm happy to share all sorts of details of my life with strangers all over the world, the idea of anyone I actually *know* reading about my sordid secrets, anxieties, and even my waist and bum measurements, makes me feel sick.

I grab my phone back, hoping that no one heard him and blushing as red as the beetroot salad sitting on the kitchen table.

'It's just a blog I was reading. Totally *crazy* lady. Won't bother subscribing to that one, ha ha,' I gabble.

There are about ten of us for dinner, all standing around chatting, and I feel disconnected. Like an observer rather than a player. David Attenborough seems to have taken residence in my head, and he's narrating the scene like a nature documentary: *And here we see a representative group of adult drinkers in their natural habitat – the 'kitchen supper'. Note how they try to impress each other with their complicated rituals and fancy plumage . . .*

As I look around the room I notice that everyone seems incredibly *sober*. Until forty-seven days ago, by this point in the evening I would not have been. I would have been seriously merry. Doesn't everyone have a few glasses of wine at lunchtime on a Saturday? And a 'sharpener' or two while getting ready to go out? It appears not. Who knew?

We sit down for dinner and, despite feeling edgy and uncomfortable, I realise that I'm actually much better company sober. I manage to talk, in equal measures, to the men on my left and my right. In the old days, I would have stuck with the more interesting one, leaving the poor chap on the other side floundering. I also would have got stuck on 'transmit', seeing other people talking as just a convenient pause for me to be able to work out which tired old anecdote to wheel out next. This evening I'm properly *listening.* I'm genuinely *interested* in what other people have to say.

But I'm finding the effort of not reaching for a glass of wine *exhausting.* I'm sure I'm grinding my teeth and, once I've finished eating, which I seem to do well before anyone else, I have no idea what to do with my hands. I fight the urge to sit on them.

I escape to the bathroom, lock the door and sit on the loo, listening to the muffled sounds of slightly sozzled merriment from the kitchen. I get my iPhone out of my bag and log on to my blog. I find this comment from one of my favourite readers, Kags. She says: *I'm sure that I speak for many of us followers when I say that, as much as we spur you on staying sober, your blog is what keeps us all on the straight and narrow too. Knowing there is this little band of strong and independent non-drinkers out there all feeling the same keeps me sane and sober.*

I can't let them down. I take a deep breath and re-enter the fray.

Strangely, it seems that most people do not get drunk at a dinner party. I'm mortified. I've spent the last few years happily getting merrily wasted myself (never embarrassingly so; never staggering, vomiting or (very) abusive, but probably fairly slurry by the end), just assuming everyone else was doing the same. But of our ten, at least two others drink no more than two or three glasses of wine all evening and, even several hours into the party, no one is obviously plastered.

As soon as it's late enough to leave politely we do. Enough is enough. Time to drive home. For years, I've had a fear of police cars, just in case I'm still over the limit from the night before, or have miscalculated my units, but tonight I am *longing* to be pulled over. I really want a uniformed officer to ask me exactly how much I've had to drink this evening so that I can say 'Not a drop, officer. Would you like me to breathe into your breathalyser?' You have to get your kicks somewhere.

Despite the lack of random police roadblocks, this evening was, I think, a success. I managed not to drink without breaking down or killing anyone. I had a good time. I was – I hope – a good guest. I'll wake up tomorrow without a hangover. But I still feel really sad. I still fear that as people realise I'm no longer 'joining in' I will get left out. I worry that as I dry out all the invitations will dry up. I know that this is shallow of me, but being sociable has always been part of my *raison d'être*. And, since I spend most of my day with people under the age of twelve, evenings are often my only chance to talk to grown-ups.

Why am I doing this? Is it really necessary? Was I really that bad?

WEEPING

I'm multitasking: doing the ironing while mainlining Jaffa Cakes and catching up on *Poldark* on the telly. It's amazing how clean and orderly your house gets when you get sober. Cleaning and ironing really help take your mind off the *not drinking* thing. It's like a less indulgent version of mindfulness – it keeps you focused on the moment and your hands occupied. Plus, there's a lovely synergy between cleansing everything around you and cleansing yourself. A fresh start. A clean sheet of paper. Right now, I'm finding newly laundered bedlinen almost as exciting as a chilled bottle of Sancerre used to be. How sad is that?

Anyhow, back to the point. Here I am, watching telly and ironing the husband's shirts when, apropos of nothing, totally out of the blue, I start sobbing. Profusely. Snottily. And I'm not even sad. Nor is Poldark – he's just discovered copper in his mine and they're all celebrating.

As if in sympathy, there's a crash of thunder outside and it starts pouring down with rain. Big, wet drops cascading over my inadequate gutters and running down my blotchy face.

Now, I'm British. I don't do weeping. Stiff upper lip and all that. The only time I remember being this emotional for no apparent reason was shortly after Evie was born. I was a mass of hormones, still in shock from being suddenly propelled into motherhood, and it took me two days to get over the scene in *Finding Nemo* where Nemo's mum, along with hundreds of his unhatched siblings, was eaten by a shark.

I feel a bit like an onion that's gradually had its layers peeled away, leaving me all raw and vulnerable. I'm *overwhelmed* by emotion. It's not bad crying – it's actually rather cathartic – it's just I feel like a pillock.

I've read a lot about how we drink in order to avoid emotions; we're stressed, we drink, we're scared, we drink, we're happy, we drink. As a result, we fail to grow up. The fabulous Caroline Knapp, author of *Drinking: A Love Story*, writes 'I'd never really grasped the idea that growth was something you could *choose*, that adulthood might be less a chronological state than an emotional one, which you decide, through painful acts, to both enter and maintain. Like a lot of people I know (alcoholics and not), I'd spent most of my life waiting for maturity to hit me from the outside, as though I'd just wake up one morning and be done, like a roast in the oven.' And that's so me: an oven-ready chicken wondering when I'm going to get cooked. I still feel nineteen years old at heart.

Apparently, when we stop drinking we don't mature immediately. It's as if we have to be 'pared down' before we can build ourselves up again, before we can choose to deal with our lives and emotions properly, soberly, and become a real-life grown-up. A perfectly done roast.

So here I am, all raw and weeping over my newly pressed laundry.

I do more research online, trying to find a way out of my black hole before I start driving myself mad. It turns out that feeling like I am, at this point in time, is perfectly normal. I am irritatingly predictable. There are, it seems, several stages of 'recovery'. The 'honeymoon period' is characterised by feelings of confidence and optimism about your life and a sense of well-being and being in control.

Sadly, the phase that follows 'honeymoon' is called 'the wall', and generally runs from around day 46 to 120. The 'wall' phase is all about boredom, depression and questioning. Oh, God – that doesn't sound much fun. How high is this wall? Is it a low, crumbly, Cotswold drystone wall, or is it like the mile-high wall of ice in *Game of Thrones*? How do I get over it and, crucially, what is on the other side?

I ask this final question to my blog readers and one experienced hand, a fellow blogger called Ainsobriety, replies with one word: *Freedom*.

I need a plan to help me scale the wall. I've come across the expression 'self-care' in many of the articles and books that I've read. Now, I'm pretty sure that self-care is supposed to be all about healthy nutrition and exercise – beginning to repair the ravages caused by years of boozing. But today, because of the weeping thing, I am *broadening* the definition of self-care to include a little 'self-indulgence'. Hell, I think I deserve a bit of that by now.

I sit down and, for the first time ever, calculate how much I used to spend on wine. I didn't drink cheap plonk. In my head, if the wine cost over £10 a bottle it made you a connoisseur as opposed to a common-or-garden lush. So I spent, on average, about £12.50 per bottle. And I drank (this is a conservative estimate) about ten bottles a week. That's £125 per week. More than £500 per month! That is a MASSIVE proportion of my total housekeeping budget.

I must have been aware of how much I was spending (I have a degree in economics for God's sake), but because it was filed in the 'total necessity' part of my brain, along with loo rolls and detergent, I never stopped to question it. There I was, week in, week out, in the supermarket looking for the buy-one-get-one-free offers and swapping expensive brands for own labels when it came to my groceries, and yet I was spending more than £500 per month, £6,000 per year, on booze.

That's the terribly, awfully, embarrassingly bad news. Here's the good news: I have now saved myself *£500 a month*. Yay! Go girl. Let's shop!

So, I go out on to the streets washed clean in the rain, and breathe in the fresh tang in the air, as nature has, temporarily, won the battle for supremacy against the London pollution. I walk to the flower stall and buy some gorgeously fragrant flowers for my house (one bottle of wine). I book myself a pedicure in time for the spring (two bottles of wine) and I get my eyebrows threaded (which makes me cry even more, but at least I have an excuse) (one bottle of wine).

Over the last few years I have not bothered very much with 'grooming'. All that waxing, tweezing, tanning, blow-drying nonsense was way down the pecking order compared with buying, and drinking, wine. Plus, I was so grumpy, bloated and lacking in self-respect that whenever I did do any of that stuff it felt like putting lipstick on a pig. But now I'm feeling just a little bit sexier. I have more time. I have more cash. So, I'm saying 'Farewell, ugly duckling', and 'Hello swan!'

THE MONTH WHEN I OVERDO THE SOCIALISING

DAY 0 6 2

DODGING THE BULLET

We are incredibly good at only seeing what we want to see and hearing what we want to hear. When I was a properly committed smoker, I was confronted by large government health warnings in bold, capital letters whenever I picked up a packet of cigarettes. I'd seen all the pictures of tar-soaked, blackened lungs. I knew the statistics – that half of all smokers will eventually die from their habit. But did I think any of that applied to me? Hell, no.

Yet now, whenever I walk past a group of young women standing outside a bar, smoking, I want to grab them by the shoulders and shout 'Why are you doing that? What exactly do you think you're *gaining*? Do you think it looks *sexy*? Don't you know you're *killing yourself*?' It's only once you extricate yourself from the clutches of an addictive drug that you can rip the sheep's clothing off the wolf and see it for what it really is.

As a society, we are adept at ignoring the dangers of alcohol. We assume, not unreasonably, that a drug taken legally, openly, boastfully, by the vast majority of the adult population must be pretty harmless. We see the government guidelines as exactly that – just guidelines, to be ignored whenever they're inconvenient. We skip over any newspaper articles about liver damage and addiction and leap on those detailing even the most insignificant benefits of a small daily glass of red wine.

I would happily uncork a bottle, telling myself that wine counted as one of my five a day (it's made of *grapes)* and congratulating myself on living a Mediterranean lifestyle. I'd imagine myself at a ripe old age, sipping my vino in the sunshine like those ancient, wizened and desiccated ladies dressed in head-to-toe black, living on obscure Greek islands, revered by their hordes of grandchildren and great-grandchildren, until the age of 110 when they pass away, peacefully, during an afternoon siesta.

It's only now, after two months sober, that I can clearly see the damage that alcohol does.

In 2010, Professor Nutt, a former government chief drugs advisor, published a study in the *Lancet* looking at the relative harms of twenty different drugs based on harm to the users themselves, and to society as a whole.

We spend a fortune educating children on the dangers of heroin and worrying about the problems of illegal drug addiction, when, according to the Nutt Report, *by far* the most harmful drug of all (when you consider the combined impact on the individual and society) is the one we don't even see as a drug – *alcohol.*

Even when you discount the impact of alcohol on communities and the wider economy and just look at the danger to the individual user – in terms of addiction, mental and physical damage – alcohol is still one of the most harmful drugs. It is more dangerous than any of the drugs tested except heroin, crack cocaine and methamphetamine. More deadly than tobacco, than cannabis, than cocaine, ecstasy or ketamine. If alcohol came on the market now, it would never be legalised.

You would never find a group of mums at the school gate joking about how they were dying to get home to rack up a line of cocaine, and yet use of a much more harmful drug is not only acceptable, it's expected, to the extent that *not* taking it makes you weird.

The reason alcohol is so harmful is partly because it is extremely addictive. We have convinced ourselves that only a small, unfortunate group of people who are born with the disease of alcoholism will ever get addicted to booze. Yet the Nutt Report concluded that alcohol was more addictive than any drug apart from heroin, cocaine, nicotine and barbiturates. Public Health England estimates that 1.6 million people in the UK are dependent on alcohol – 10 per cent of the total number of drinkers.

As well as being dangerously addictive, alcohol has a terrible impact on our physical and mental health.

I knew, of course, that drinking too much could lead to irreversible cirrhosis of the liver, but I thought this was a disease suffered only by sad old men – the types you find sleeping on park benches surrounded by empty cans of strong cider.

This is categorically not the case. Liver specialists in hospitals all over the country are reporting huge increases in the numbers of women in their thirties and forties being admitted with liver disease, and they tend to be those in higher-end executive jobs who see booze as an intrinsic part of their lifestyle, not as a drug that's slowly killing them.

This problem is exacerbated by the fact that one area where women will never be equal to men is the way in which their bodies cope with alcohol.

I've spent years drinking with men, matching them glass for glass. Often those men were drinking beer, while I was drinking strong wine. I forgot that, while I may be their equal (and, I like to think, more than) mentally, I will never be their equal physically.

Women generally weigh less than men and have a lower

level of a key metabolising enzyme that helps us break down alcohol. Added to which, the hormone oestrogen intensifies the effect of alcohol. As a result, women become dependent on alcohol much faster than men. And alcoholism is, apparently, twice as deadly for women as it is for men. On average alcohol-dependent women will die *twenty years* earlier than those not addicted to alcohol.

But alcohol doesn't just affect our livers. Women who consume four or more alcoholic drinks a day quadruple their risk of dying from heart disease, and are five times more likely to have a stroke.

Excessive alcohol consumption is also linked to cancer, particularly breast cancer. According to breastcancer.org, research consistently shows that alcohol increases a woman's risk of hormone receptor-positive breast cancer, to the extent that women who drink just three alcoholic drinks a week have a fifteen per cent higher risk of breast cancer than teetotallers.

Professor Dame Sally Davies, the Chief Medical Officer, was reported, somewhat controversially, by the BBC as saying that there is *no safe level* of alcohol consumption and that she considers the risk of breast cancer every time she contemplates a glass of wine.

Alcohol affects our mental health as well as our physical health, and is strongly linked to depression. Experts also say that chronic heavy drinking causes cognitive decline over time – leading to impaired memory and decision-making, anxiety and emotional issues. This alcohol-related damage is often undi-agnosed and confused with dementia, or seen as just an inevitable part of ageing.

As wine o'clock comes around again and I'm flexing and unflexing my fingers and glancing wistfully towards the fridge, I think *Is that nightly glass (or three) of wine worth twenty years of my life? Is it worth burdening myself and my family with a breast cancer diagnosis?* And, with a sigh of resignation, I make myself a hot chocolate.

DAY 0 7 0

SOBER HAIR

Day 70, and it strikes me, looking fleetingly in the mirror (past the age of forty it doesn't do to linger at mirrors) this morning that *something has changed.*

And it's my hair.

There are many benefits I expected to accrue when I quit drinking – like weight loss, better sleep, more energy and so on, but bouncy, springy, look-at-me hair was not one of them. My hair has gone all exuberant, confident to the point of pushy. *American.* It's so big that it deserves its own postcode.

I google 'sober hair'. It appears I'm not imagining it. Hair, like your skin, suffers from dehydration when you drink, and goes all dry, brittle and split-endy. Plus, alcohol depletes your iron levels, which makes your hair *fall out.* My older friends tell me that the menopause is disastrous for hair, so I see this as my hair's last hurrah. Enjoy, you lovely little follicles. It's your chance to shine.

This hair thing is very good timing, because tonight I have an *ordeal.* My old Cambridge college is holding a drinks do at the House of Lords.

I still remember when I got the letter containing the results of my Cambridge application and interview. I was with my friend Philippa. I poured us both a vodka and orange for courage, despite the fact that it was only 11 a.m. (that didn't augur well). I unfolded the letter with shaking hands and quickly scanned down until I found the words 'We are pleased to be able to offer you . . .' It was the proudest day of my life.

So tonight I'll look around the room at all of us, supposedly some of the brightest and most promising of our generation. Many of my cohort are now government ministers, top lawyers, brain surgeons, newsreaders, best-selling novelists and rich-as-Croesus financiers.

And what am I? An ex-boozy housewife. All that promise left pickling at the bottom of a bottle of Chablis. Not for the first time, I wonder why I didn't carry on the career (which I was very good at) and leave a highly paid nanny (with far more experience and expertise in childcare than I) to bring up my three children. I quickly remind myself how much I adore the little blighters, how fast they grow up and what a privilege it is being able to stay home with them for a few years.

I've not done a drinks party yet. What are they *for* if not to drink? The clue, surely, is in the name. And I know from pregnant days that they are useless at providing non-alcoholic drinks at these things. Warm orange juice or elderflower cordial. Drinks for children and grannies. No virgin mojitos for the sophisticated alcohol-free lady, oh no.

So, I have decided to treat my new, perky hair to a professional blow-dry. Cost: two bottles of wine equivalent – exactly what I would have drunk tonight in the old days. I might be standing, quivering, in the doorway, but my hair will be way ahead of me, propping up the bar and flirting with the waiter.

The Big Hair and I arrive at the House of Lords. Typically, it's pissing down with rain, so I wrestle with a giant umbrella, desperately trying to protect the expensively coiffed locks.

I was wrong about the selection of soft drinks on offer. There's no elderflower cordial – only warm, sticky, processed orange juice. Not even mineral water, let alone virgin mojitos.

Not only do I not want to drink orange juice, but my bright-orange tumbler shouts NON-DRINKER loudly in the sea of classy wine glasses. I can't see one other glass of orange juice being drunk. As a result, people are constantly remarking on my strange choice of beverage. I explain that I'm temporarily off the booze so I can be 'beach body ready' for the summer. What a joke! I haven't been 'beach body ready' for *twenty years*! In any case, we always go to Cornwall in the summer, so I end up encased in a full body wetsuit, not a teensy-weensy bikini. 'Beach body ready' in Cornwall actually involves laying down as much subcutaneous fat as possible as insulation. Amazingly though, no one bats an eyelid at my ridiculous excuse, they just accept it and move on.

I feel like one of the ghosts at a feast in Harry Potter: I'm there, everyone can see me and even talk to me, but I'm not able to participate properly since I'm actually in a different, but parallel, dimension. Everyone else is fully rounded and solid, while I am just an ethereal hologram.

Eventually, I find some old college mates and am chatting happily. Then two ladies approach me (who I don't recognise) and shriek 'Clare Pooley! We saw your name on the list and *had* to come and find you. You probably won't remember us – we were two years below you – but you made a huge impression on both of us!'

Oh dear. I smile, weakly.

The first one says 'You were my college mother.' (Oops, should have remembered her!) 'I asked you what one piece of advice you would give me and you told me something that I have never, ever forgotten. In fact, it has become my life motto.'

Did I? Gosh, how extraordinary. I have depths so hidden that even I wasn't aware of them! I bask in an unusual glow of self-satisfaction. I am obviously very wise.

'What did I say?' I ask, intrigued.

'You said that you can never wear too many sequins!' she replies.

Ah. Profound.

The second lady joins in. 'I remember you too!' Oh God. I have a feeling that this is not going to end well. 'You were famous for running down the corridor naked except for a strategically placed yucca plant, claiming to be Eve in the Garden of Eden.' I offer up a silent prayer of thanks that Facebook had not been invented then, thereby saving Evie, Kit and Maddie from evidence of their mother's past misdemeanours.

I feel a wave of nostalgia for my younger, unforgettable (even if for the wrong reasons), exuberant self, and sip on my yicky, sticky orange juice.

Once the drinks start winding up, Saskia and I head out for dinner.

I knew Saskia long before we both turned up as undergraduates at Newnham College. We both lived in Brussels as teenagers. We used to offer to take our family dogs (we had a boundlessly energetic Labrador, she had a rather ditsy retriever) for a walk so that we could meet surreptitiously in the woods for an illicit cigarette. Years later, Saskia's dog died of cancer. I blamed myself.

I love catching up on the five years since we last met up. (Five years! How did that happen?) And it's fine not drinking. But – I have to confess – I miss that feeling of your shoulders relaxing, tension reducing and the wave of bonhomie and positivity that comes with a few glasses of wine. I feel too *rigid,* too *overly aware* and analytical of everything I'm doing and saying.

I force myself to remember the last time I attended the same event – five years ago. I probably had at least one glass of wine before I left home. I then drank about three glasses at the drinks party – large ones on an empty stomach. By the time I got to dinner (there was a group of five of us) I was feeling lethargic.

I remember worrying that I was slurring slightly, plus being convinced that I was horribly boring as I was too drunk and exhausted to think up any witty repartee, or to properly follow the conversation. Needless to say, I woke up with a horrible head the following day and had to do the school run.

So tonight isn't perfect. It's not easy. I miss my former self. But the self I miss was the one of twenty-five years ago, not the more recent one. And I suspect that I am now, sober, more like the twenty-year-old me than I was five years ago.

DAY |0|8|0|

ANXIETY AND GARDENING

I've been rereading Jason Vale's book *Kick the Drink . . . Easily!* When I first read this book it was a revelation. I began to realise that life without alcohol might just be, not only bearable, but actually enjoyable. As I turned the pages I was nodding away. It all *made sense.* Well, nearly all of it.

There was one bit of Jason's logic that just didn't ring quite true. Jason writes that alcohol has *zero benefits.* Now I had many 'triggers' that made me reach for the bottle – feeling miserable, feeling happy, feeling stressed, feeling anxious, feeling pretty much anything at all, come to think of it, and alcohol *really did seem to help.*

But Jason says that your negative emotions are, at least in part, *caused* by the drink. Heavy drinkers are, he writes, constantly experiencing withdrawal symptoms when they are not drinking, and these exacerbate the feelings of stress, anxiety and depression. If you quit, he argues, you will feel as good as you used to after a few drinks *all the time.*

Nice logic, I thought, but you're pushing it a bit. Alcohol may be evil in many ways, but it does have some positive effects. But now, after eighty days, I am starting to get what he means. Here's why:

I found, in the last few years, that I was becoming increasingly anxious. About stupid little things. I'd have mini panic attacks about nothing. If I had some (slightly) bad or annoying news via phone or email I would get a knot of anxiety in my stomach. It would wriggle away there like a tapeworm. And the best way to kill it, or at least to numb it for a while, was to drown it in Sauvignon Blanc.

This bothered me. I'd run huge global ad campaigns with multimillion-pound budgets. I'd managed a group of around sixty employees. And here I was getting totally stressed out about a patch of damp in a bedroom, a tax return or a less than perfect school report.

I thought maybe I was just out of practice, getting old or perimenopausal. I didn't blame the drink. In fact, I thought the drink was the solution, not the problem.

But I realised last week that I hadn't felt that noxious knot in the stomach for a while. I'd had a number of issues crop up – don't we all – and I'd just dealt with them.

When you drown your problems with booze they don't go

away, they just get forgotten for a bit, fester and get worse, like mouldy bits of cheese that the children have dropped down the gaps between the car seats. (Or is that just my car?) Then your inability to deal with them effectively destroys your confidence even more. It's like you're Superman and someone's stuffed kryptonite down your pants.

When you deal with your problems sober, straight away, your confidence grows. You find the kryptonite hiding in plain sight, chuck it away and feel your power returning. Going to my college reunion the other night reminded me of how brave and fearless I used to be. Nothing fazed me.

And it's coming back. Oh yeah, baby.

Anxiety is, however, impossible to avoid all the time and it's a major trigger – the thing most likely to have me salivating over John's bottle of wine sitting chilling in the fridge. So I've been researching various 'healthy' ways of dealing with it. Here's a great one: *gardening.*

It's believed that gardening helps because it provides a sense of 'control', which is the psychological nemesis of stress and anxiety. Plus, the act of gardening is a form of mindfulness – it makes us focus on the 'now' and takes our minds off problems in the past, or fear of the future.

According to the mental-health charity MIND, researchers have proven that gardening boosts self-esteem and improves mental and physical health. That's why they've funded 130 eco-therapy projects across England.

Even *looking* at gardens helps produce a sense of calm and can help patients recover faster from surgery. The notorious New York jail Rikers Island uses horticultural therapy to calm prisoners and prepare them for release.

I realise that it's all very well *reading* about horticulture, but in order to feel the benefits I really ought to *do it.*

This is a daunting prospect.

The thing about being a high-functioning ~~alcoholic~~ dependent drinker is that you have to learn to *prioritise*. There are not enough sober hours in the day to keep absolutely everything working perfectly, so you learn to pick your battles.

In my life, priority number one was keeping the children (and husband) happy. Properly fed, clothed, achieving. Homework done, music practice done, playdates arranged and executed, home-made costumes created for various 'dress-up days', cakes baked for bake sales, and so on. That, in itself, is a full-time job.

Next in line is the house. We have an old, relatively big (for London) house that we can't afford to maintain properly. So not only do I have to make sure that it's clean and tidy, but I'm constantly running around with pots of filler, damp-proof paint and so forth, trying to stop it looking as if it's about to fall down (which it is).

After the house and its other inhabitants comes me. And, as I've mentioned, personal grooming had started to slip a little, as had the self-care. Who has time for appointments with the gym, the dental hygienist and the well-woman clinic when there's serious 'socialising' (aka drinking) to do at the weekend, as well as all the house-kids-and-husband stuff? Not me.

And right at the bottom of the list? The garden. It's all too easy to shut the doors and just pretend it isn't really there. Especially in the winter. Between the months of October and March the only member of the household who spends any time in the garden is the dog. With inevitable consequences.

Once an engineer from Sky arrived unexpectedly early for an appointment to fix a satellite dish. It had been raining for several days and I hadn't been into the garden to 'clear the lawn'. The man from Sky refused to erect his ladder on our lawn due to 'health and safety' and hotfooted it back to Sky HQ. (This makes him sound like an angel. He wasn't. He was just a regular chap with a, not unreasonable, fear of dog poo.) God I felt like a slut.

But now I have aeons more time and I'm on a mission, to improve my outside space and my mental health. So, over eight hours of back-breaking work, I *totally transform* my garden. I manicure the lawn, weed the borders and take all the old, broken, plastic garden toys to the dump. I plant lots of little bedding plants and I train honeysuckle and clematis over the old Wendy house. I make a little herb garden and I order an outdoor sofa online (cost: a massive thirty bottles of wine equivalent, but worth it).

And it's worked! Not only is my garden looking lush (the only lush in the house now), but the *act of gardening* has given me a real high. My new plants will, hopefully, thrive and grow, providing a living 'sober counter'. And we won't have any more problems with our satellite TV.

Now I'm shattered, the kids are in bed and I've crashed on the sofa with Jason Vale (the book, not the man). John is laughing uproariously at something on the computer. He spots me staring at him, stops abruptly and looks up guiltily.

He's reading my blog.

Now, I've suspected for a while that he sneaks a peek from time to time, but here's proof. Caught in the act. And he didn't appear to be laughing *with* me. He was laughing *at* me.

'What's so funny?' I ask, cocking The Eyebrow of Fear.

'Where is this large house in Chelsea that you write about?' he chortles.

I explain that I'm trying to remain *anonymous,* so can't confess to living in Fulham. And since I was going to have to invent a location I might as well upgrade postal districts. I've always wanted to live in Chelsea.

'We don't have a "lawn", it's more "a patch of grass" and well done you for mowing it, but it's hardly "manicured". And what's this "herb garden" you've described? Surely not the three pots of weeds sitting outside the kitchen door? Where is this nirvana? Can I go and live there? Even better, can we sell it and retire?'

Ha ha.

I point out to John that it's in his interests that I view things through rose-coloured spectacles because, despite thirteen years of marriage and the ravages of time, I still think he's the most gorgeous guy around.

I'm slightly mortified that he's found my online diary but, in a strange way, I'm also rather relieved that after years of hiding my escalating vino consumption, now I really don't have any secrets from him. (Apart from the new outfit in my wardrobe, waiting to be described as *What? This old thing?*)

DAY |0|8|4|

REBEL WITHOUT A CAUSE

I hate the word 'sober'. I looked up the dictionary definition. It means *serious, sensible and solemn*. Other, equally ghastly, synonyms are: *grave, sombre, severe, restrained, conservative, strict, puritanical, unemotional* and *dispassionate*. None of that is me. It just doesn't fit with the view I have of myself.

You see, I've always seen myself as a bit of a rebel. I've never liked rules, or rather I liked them being there so they could be broken. Drinking and smoking fitted neatly into the image I had of myself.

I was at Roedean School just outside Brighton, which was, back then, an extremely traditional, very strict, girls' boarding school. Don't feel sorry for me – I loved it. So many opportunities to *be naughty,* so many rules to break. In my final year, my bedroom led on to a flat roof. I used to climb over my desk, through the window and huddle, late at night in the gale-force winds (we were on a cliff), smoking with my best friend, Selina. I was, literally, the gateway to rebellion.

(Gorgeous Selina, over 6 foot tall in her bare feet and with white-blonde hair, then caused total mayhem by escaping from school with a sexy American, ten years older than her, who she married on a beach in Mexico. But I digress.)

One of my favourite mini-rebellions was the 'cockroach incident'. I saw some photos in *Tatler* of the Roedean boarding houses after a recent makeover. They look like luxury boutique hotels. This was not the case back in my day, when my house (the imaginatively named House Four) was *riddled* with cockroaches. They'd make themselves scarce during the day, but at night-time they'd come crawling out of the walls and floors, searching for dropped crumbs of tuck. Being relatively fearless, I volunteered to complain to our ferocious housemistress, who was rendered even more terrifying by the fact that a recent stroke had caused her face to droop on one side.

I knocked on the door of her study while my friends loitered outside, backing me up from a safe distance.

'Madam,' I said, for that's how we had to address our teachers. 'Please can something be done about the cockroaches. Annabel woke up last night and found one crawling up her arm. They're everywhere.'

'Don't be ridiculous!' thundered my housemistress, spraying saliva from her asymmetric mouth. 'There ARE no cockroaches! And even if there WERE cockroaches, which there are NOT, it would be entirely YOUR fault for keeping tuck in your bedrooms. GET OUT OF MY SIGHT.'

This made me very cross. One thing I was not was a liar.

So I organised the giant cockroach hunt. Over the course of the next week we got up in the middle of each night and, armed with Athena poster tubes, chased those prehistoric-looking insects around the linoleum-floored bathrooms and bedrooms until we had a whole Quality Street tin filled with live, squirming, aggrieved roaches. The next day I took the tin down to the HM's study.

'Madam, please can we discuss the cockroach situation again?' I asked, politely.

'How many times do I have to tell you THERE ARE NO COCKROACHES?'

At which point I placed the tin on her large, leather-topped desk, took the lid off and walked out of the room.

Her screams could be heard in the dining rooms, about half a mile of corridor away. Rentokil were called. I had to ring the early-morning bells for a week.

I saved the best rebellion until my final term, once my A levels were safely in the bag. It was a tradition at Roedean that the leaving year played a prank. These were usually rather innocuous. My friends and I were about to change that.

We booked, to arrive during our final assembly when the whole school would be seated on the hall floor and all the teachers on the raised platform, a stripogram. We asked him to dress as a policeman, to walk up to the headmistress, to strip right down to his tiny pants and then to present the headmistress, Mrs Longley, with a red rose.

The day arrived. So did the stripogram. With a reporter from the *Sun* newspaper. That was not part of the plan. The stripper did his thing. You could hear a pin drop in the hall as 500 jaws hit the floor. Mrs Longley looked as if she might be about to have a heart attack. She was rooted to the spot. Not so the rather large, but surprisingly agile, deputy head, who bounded down the aisle like a charging rhinoceros, ripped the camera out of the reporter's hands and removed the film from the camera and the reporter from the premises.

Our end of term ball was cancelled.

Most of my best friends from that time, and the next twenty years, were the people I met huddled in groups, in cold gardens or on windy fire escapes, smoking, or the last ones remaining at a party in the early hours playing drinking games.

I chose advertising as a career because it seemed like the antithesis of a 'sensible' job. Regular, enthusiastic drinking was obligatory. You could smoke *everywhere*. (I remember one of my team asking if we could ban smoking in status meetings as she had asthma. I thought this would be an outrageous infringement of civil liberties so, instead, I told her that she didn't have to come. It strikes me now that I was not a very responsible boss.) You were expected to be a bit wild. I wore suits (sometimes), but the collars were trimmed with fake fur.

The early 1990s were party days. I worked hard and played hard. I burned the candle at both ends, and in the middle. We spent weekends camping in fields at impromptu festivals, and at clubs like the Cross, the Fridge and the Ministry of Sound. I was intimately acquainted with dawn over the city, and some-times slept on the sofa in my office (which was, conveniently, right next to Annabel's nightclub) since there seemed no point in going home.

Then, nearly fifteen years ago, I quit smoking. It took me a while to adjust the image I had of myself to exclude the ubiq-uitous cigarette – the badge of the rebel (as I saw it), the smoky haze of mystery and promise, my personal soft-focus lens. But I still had my drink . . .

And, until I quit, when I was feeling boxed in, squashed and squashy, a boring, podgy, middle-aged housewife, alone at home with the chores – I'd pour myself a glass of chilled Sancerre and have my own little party for one. And now it's gone. My last remaining vice. My final rebellion. And I am a sober, slightly skinnier, middle-aged housewife.

What next? I know all about cross-addictions. The last thing I want (or need) is an internet porn habit, bulimia or an online bingo addiction. So here's how I try to see it . . .

If 80 per cent of the adult UK population drink, then who's the rebel? Who's zigging while the others are zagging? Who's at the frontier, pushing the boundaries? I am. So stick that in your bong and smoke it.

Plus, I have my little blog, my own private rebellion, my subversive secret. Sometimes when one of the other mothers asks what I'm up to I say 'Oh, I've started writing a blog.'

'Really? Does anyone read it?' they ask incredulously.

'Oh yes, thousands of people, all over the world. From India and China to Ukraine, Antigua and Oman – all over the place.'

'What's it about?' they ask, agog.

'Oh, this and that. Nothing kinky or illegal,' I reply enigmatically, and walk off. Still a rebel.

The problem is, in an effort to prove to myself that I am not boring, and that you can still be a cool rebel without the booze, I appear to have overdone it. Rookie error.

I've invited two families round for a barbecue lunch in order to show off my newly pimped-up garden. In typical Bank Holiday weekend fashion, as soon as we fire up the barbecue it begins to rain. We move inside and start eating at around 2.30 p.m.

By 3.30 p.m. we've all eaten way more than we should have. Unlike the old days (when, by this stage, I'd have given up any pretensions of 'proper hosting'), I remember to offer everyone coffee and chocolates. I clear all the plates, load the dishwasher, and they all just sit there *drinking*.

Don't get me wrong. It's great fun. The conversation is hilarious, and at several points I laugh until I cry. But I feel *itchy*. I desperately want to be able to turn down the dimmer switch, slump in my chair and just go with the flow. I'm way too upright and *aware* to be able to spend *four hours* at a table without eating or drinking.

I find myself analysing everything I'm saying as I'm saying it. *Was that funny? Why am I telling this anecdote? Is this gossip really appropriate?* In the old days, I just *said stuff* without thinking. It probably shocked people, or upset them from time to time, but it was easy. It was natural.

Funnily enough, I now remember being this analytical about conversation way back in my teens and early twenties. Probably the last time I did lunch and dinner parties relatively sober. Apart from when I was pregnant, and that was easy. You could just sit back in your chair, quietly and serenely stroking your precious bump, channelling your inner madonna (the original one, not the pop star), then leave early without any qualms.

By 5 p.m. I want to stand on my chair and shout 'RIGHT! You've eaten my food. You've drunk my booze. Now just EFF OFF out of my house.' But I love them all, and they're having fun, and I can't.

At 7.30 p.m. they all head home. I have a crashing headache and realise that I've been *literally* gritting my teeth for several hours. I'm proud of myself, but utterly exhausted. All I want to do is to hole up in my safe little house with my safe little family and watch *Mad Men* with a cup of hot chocolate.

I've realised that quitting booze is a bit like learning to walk again after an accident. You need to take *baby steps*. And this weekend, I've been trying to run a bloody marathon, with only the minimum of training.

PAWS

It's half-term, so the kids, dog and I have decamped to my parents' house.

Many of my readers talk about troubled childhoods – divorce, bullying or abuse. They often refer to feeling like they have a 'hole in the soul'. My experience was nothing like that.

I have amazing parents. When I rerun the movie of childhood memories in my head, it's a happy melange of Monopoly, butterscotch flavoured Angel Delight, guinea pigs, pogo sticks and that endless hot summer of 1976. The slightly less than ideal turn my life has taken can, in no way, shape or form, be laid at the door of my parents. Although, I have a slight suspicion that a genetic predisposition to addiction runs through my father's family.

When I was little, I thought my father was a soldier, often away in battle. When my mother discovered that this is what I'd told my teacher and my friends she quizzed me about it. It turned out that I'd got the wrong end of the stick when he'd said he was going to Iceland to fight the Cod War. He was actually a civil servant in the Ministry of Agriculture, Fisheries and Food, being sent to negotiate fishing rights.

Dad is one of the cleverest men I have ever met. He won a scholarship to Cambridge (to Clare College, my namesake) and then scored off the charts in the civil-service exams. He's also incredibly principled. He was extremely successful, and much admired, but I have an inkling that if he'd been prepared, ever, to lie or dissemble he would have ended up in the top job – but he never would.

Dad is also brilliantly witty. When he worked for the European Commission, he was famous for his hilarious April Fool's memos. One year he circulated a spoof request for Common Agricultural Policy funding from an imaginary co-operative of geriatric Scottish ladies who were hand-knitting testicle warmers to improve the sperm count of Highland rams. He had to own up before too much council time was spent debating the merits of the application.

My mother met Dad when she worked with him in Whitehall, although, as was expected in those days, she quit work when I was born. When my little brother started primary school she started a teacher-training degree, but then my dad was posted to Brussels and, yet again, she gave up her career.

I can see how successful my mother would have been by the way she approached everything she touched. When my brother wanted to be a Cub Scout, she volunteered to help and quickly became Akela. Within a year or two she was running the Cub Scout movement for the whole of the Benelux region. When the BBC threatened to take Radio 4 off long wave (meaning that Mum wouldn't be able to listen to *The Archers* or *Woman's Hour* any longer) she mobilised the expat community, printed T-shirts, bumper stickers and banners and organised a march on Parliament. The Beeb, wisely, crumbled in the face of my mother.

But, despite being at the haven of my parents' house, these last few days I've felt despondent and tetchy. And I'm *tired*. Physically tired and emotionally drained.

I sleep like a log, a good seven hours, but wake up feeling

exhausted. Then, by mid-afternoon, I'm falling asleep in a chair. By the evening I've run out of the energy to do anything except collapse in front of the telly.

So, I google something along the lines of 'fatigue after quitting alcohol'. I get all the usual stuff about withdrawal symptoms in the few days after stopping. I know that. I remember the total exhaustion of the first week. But this is Day 88. (Two fat ladies. I empathise, girls.)

Then I find all this stuff about Post-Acute Withdrawal Symptoms, also known by its, inappropriately cuddly, nickname: PAWS.

Oh, bugger.

Apparently, PAWS is the second stage of withdrawal from alcohol (or any form of drug) and occurs after the initial intense physical withdrawal stage. As the brain chemistry gradually returns to a new equilibrium it tends to fluctuate, causing emotional, physiological and physical symptoms.

These episodes appear to be cyclical – some people swear they are lunar, occurring every twenty-eight days or so, or literally at the full moon. Good God, I'm a werewolf! The 'pink cloud' phase followed by 'the wall' is the first episode of PAWS, but these symptoms can reoccur for *up to two years*!

The good news is that each episode gets shorter and less intense, disappearing within a few days. And if you're aware of them and ready for them you can cope. Apparently, being unprepared for an attack of PAWS is a major reason for relapse. You think everything's improving, then BAM! It feels like you're back to the beginning. You lose faith that it's ever going to get better and reach for the bottle.

Symptoms of PAWS include: mood swings, anxiety, irritability, tiredness, low enthusiasm, variable concentration and sleep disturbance (including bad dreams in which you drink heavily).

I also read that a number of people experience terrible memory lapses during episodes of PAWS. This is actually a relief to discover, as it may explain why two days ago when I was asked in a shop for my postcode I *couldn't remember it.* I've had that postcode for nearly a decade. I had a panic that I was getting early onset Alzheimer's. Imagine – two decades fuzzy through drink, a few months lucid, then off with the fairies again!

So, what do I do about PAWS? Here's what it says on addictionsandrecovery.org: *You can't hurry recovery. But you can get through it one day at a time. If you resent post-acute withdrawal, or try to bulldoze your way through it, you will become exhausted. And when you're exhausted you will think of using* (drugs or alcohol) *to escape.*

So basically, I just have to go with the flow. Ride it out, like PMS.

As always, I share my new knowledge on Mummy was a Secret Drinker. It's now getting hundreds of page views a day as people all around the world stumble (possibly literally, given the subject matter) across me. I get lots of comments from people who, like me, are relieved to find out that they're not losing their minds.

LushNoMore (I do love her pseudonym) says:

Your post today could not have been more perfectly timed. I am bawling my eyes out here for what I thought was no reason apart from tiredness. Hooray – I'm normal! I don't feel very normal though. I feel like a big freak. I don't get these mood swings. Psycho swings sums it up better.

The blog is proving to be great therapy. Until I've written my blog post for the day I feel all antsy. The words go around and around in my head until I can corral them into a straight line and make them sit still on a virtual piece of paper. Then I blast them into the internet and feel . . . peace. But, even better than that, it makes me feel less alone, and it seems I'm also helping people. Having spent the drinking years being incredibly selfish, it feels good to be doing something worthwhile.

DAY 0 9 1

THE WINE WITCH

For me, the single most telling sign that you are no longer in control of alcohol, but it is in control of you, is when you instinctively understand the concept of the 'wine witch'. I only met her about three years ago. Until then, if you'd mentioned her name I would have had no idea what you were talking about. Some people refer to her as the 'inner addict' or the 'monkey on my back'. Men often talk about a 'devil' or a 'wolf'. But, for many of us women in the sober online world, 'wine witch' describes her perfectly.

At some point (for some, as soon as they start drinking in their teens, but for many of us not until our forties) she starts whispering in our ear, and from that moment on she becomes an increasingly intrusive presence.

The wine witch starts rather innocuously. She begins by saying 'Are you sure that's going to be enough? Why not buy another bottle just in case you run out?' Then she gets a bit more competitive. Like 'Didn't he pour himself a much bigger glass than he poured you?' She moves on to deviousness: 'Have a glass or two before you go out, then you won't need to drink so much when you're there.' And ends up just plain weird: 'You need to find somewhere else to put all those empty bottles or the neighbours will see your recycling bags and *judge you.*'

The only way to shut up the wine witch is to drown her out – to give her as much alcohol as she wants. As soon as you try to cut down, to moderate your intake for any reason, she gets increasingly loud and insistent. 'ONE GLASS? THAT'S NOT ENOUGH! BARELY TOUCHED THE SIDES! WHAT ARE YOU? A WOMAN OR A MOUSE?' That's when you see what you're really up against.

Long-haul flights are a good case in point, because flying is one of those times that requires copious amounts of booze – to celebrate going away, or to commiserate when coming home. Plus, however much you sort of get the whole science of lift and drag, and differential airspeed over the curved wings, it still seems counterintuitive that such a massive hunk of metal is going to stay in the sky. And there's always that fear that your baggage is on an entirely different aeroplane, or that forty-five minutes isn't long enough for you to make your connecting flight. A drink helps unravel that knot of anxiety.

Now, I loved flying on business trips. You were plied with free drinks, from the moment you got on the plane – 'Complimentary champagne, madam?' – to the moment you dropped off to sleep on your fully reclined flat bed – 'Digestif? Nightcap?' But economy flights with the family were an altogether different proposition.

I became *convinced* that British Airways had changed their alcohol policy, that they'd become more parsimonious with the vino. Because whereas I used to be perfectly happy on long-haul flights, they now made me super-stressed. Surely they used to give you more than one drink pre-dinner and wine with dinner? Now I suspect that the only thing that changed was me.

By the time we'd been through the interminable security and check-in queues and boarded the plane, I'd be desperate for a drink. I'd have to wait until we were in the air and the drinks trolley finally came out. I'd be riveted to the slow progress of the trolley down the aisle. *For God's sake get a move on!* Then, after dinner, and having downed the two smallish drinks I'd been given, I'd wrestle endlessly with the dilemma of whether I could call the stewardess over to ask for another teeny-tiny glass of wine without being *judged.*

At moments like these the wine witch would go loopy. 'CALL THE DAMN STEWARDESS! WHO CARES WHAT SHE THINKS!'

So, when I first came across the term 'wine witch', on the fabulous Soberistas website, it was like a light bulb switching on. Not only had someone named my nemesis, but I was obviously not the only one who'd met her.

I like to think that every day you go not drinking, you drain more of the wine witch's energy. Mine is now pretty much in a coma. She's still there, but she's weak, and she's not talking any more. The great thing about having the measure of your enemy is that knowledge is power, and with that power you can beat her.

As I drive home after collecting the children from school I congratulate myself on how well I'm doing, on how brave and selfless I am, and on how I'm turning into a great mother. I should know by now that pride inevitably precedes a fall.

I can hear a volley of electronic 'pings' coming from my handbag. I groan. It must be one of the class WhatsApp groups chattering about nut-free snacks or lost items of clothing. As soon as we get home I check my phone.

Bad news, ladies. Jocasta has nits. Thought you should know so you can check your babies.

Archie too. I've found a super earth-friendly, hypoallergenic treatment. PM me for details.

School nurse told me they're everywhere. Upper and lower school. Am combing my lot now.

I immediately feel itchy. I'm convinced I can feel armies of headlice marching over my scalp. I look over at the children, just as Kit lifts his arm and starts scratching his head furiously. I hand out the nit combs and we sit in a circle combing each other's hair like a group of grooming gorillas.

'Got one!' shouts Evie, who's combing Kit.

'I've found two on Maddie!' replies Kit, not to be outdone.

'Look at your roots, Mummy!' shrieks Maddie. 'You need to go to the hairdresser for some more—'

'Never say dye!' I growl at her.

Before long it becomes clear that the whole family are riddled.

'Daddy's not going to be happy if he's got nits,' says Maddie, always the master of understatement.

'Well at least they'll be easy to find,' says Kit, with a grin. 'There's nowhere for them to hide!' There is no joy greater for an eight-year-old than pointing out the indignities of ageing.

Sod the namby-pamby organic, chemical-free shampoos. We're bringing out the big guns. I napalm everyone's heads with some noxious-smelling liquid from a bottle featuring a rather terrifying skull and crossbones. We then spend what feels like hours combing, washing and drying hair, by the end of which I'm shattered. Luckily, it's bedtime and I figure that, for once, we can skip the reading.

'Mummy,' says Kit, 'don't forget I need to hand my Roman project in tomorrow.'

Aaarrrggghhh! The Year 4 Roman project. Enough to drive any mother to drink. I should have remembered. I saw several smug parents yesterday handing in the Roman project twenty-four hours early. One boy delivered his dressed in gladiator costume and clutching an intricate scale model of the Colosseum. Another appeared to have written his up in beautiful calligraphy on hand-made paper wrapped into scrolls and tied with purple ribbons. There's no way they did those projects by themselves.

We spend the next two hours trying to shape Kit's Roman project into something acceptable and, by the time I've got everyone into bed and corrected some of Kit's more heinous spellings (using my left hand in order to mimic his scruffy writing), I've had enough.

I collapse into a chair. I thought I'd got the wine witch under control, but she's now back with a vengeance. I'm drumming my fingers, which are aching to wrap themselves around a wine glass, on the arm of my chair. To try to keep my mind and fingers occupied I grab my phone and log on to Facebook.

Stupid mistake. My newsfeed is filled with pictures of people drinking at parties, dinner tables complete with large bottles of wine in the foreground and the inevitable memes joking about mums and their wine.

Because it's 5 o'clock somewhere!
Keep your friends close. Keep your wine closer.
Be kind. Be helpful. Bring wine.

Someone's even posted a link to a designer handbag that doubles up as a *wine dispenser*. It looks like a regular bag, and can still carry your phone, purse and make-up, but it holds two litres of wine in the lining, accessible via a discreet and handy tap. How I would have loved that in the olden days.

What is the point of me going through all of this when *absolutely everyone* is drinking, all of the time? It's a perfectly acceptable way of winding down at the end of the day. It's fashionable. It's *continental.*

Why am I making life so *hard* for myself? No one can be expected to recover from an evening of killing lice and writing up Romans with *a cup of tea.* Right now, even a non-alcoholic beer feels about as useless as those silly little arms on a Tyrannosaurus rex.

It is at times like this that I curse my decision not to ban booze from the house. I've been so determined to keep everything as normal as possible, to have an open bottle of wine available for John, or for guests. AA advise strongly against this. They say that if you hang out in a barber's shop, eventually you'll get a haircut. I told myself that I was stronger than that, and there's no point in running away from alcohol when the whole world is swimming in the stuff.

But now, knowing that there's half a bottle of my favourite white wine chilling in the fridge is driving me insane. I walk back and forwards to the fridge, so many times that I'm surprised I haven't furrowed a groove in the floorboards, while a battle rages on in my head. Eventually, I open the fridge door and pour out a large glass.

THE MONTH WHEN I CELEBRATE 100 DAYS AND
IT STARTS GETTING EASIER

DAY	0	9	3

DECLUTTERING

I didn't drink that glass of wine.

I sat down at the kitchen table and stared at it. I sniffed it. I picked the glass up and swirled the chilled, honey-coloured wine around. Then the door opened and John walked in. He looked at me, he looked at the glass in my hand, he looked shocked. I jumped a mile, spilling much of the glass I was holding over my hand and the kitchen table. I felt like I'd been caught naked with the man come to read the gas meter.

'You're not drinking that, are you?' he asked. 'You've done so well, don't ruin it now.'

And I reminded myself how far I'd come. I read back over this diary – starting at Day 0, which I would never want to repeat – and I reminded myself that I'd promised I'd make it to 100 days before admitting defeat. So, I emptied that glass down the sink, told John that he probably had nits and went to bed.

And now I'm so glad I kept going, because today I feel completely different. To misquote Kate Moss, no wine tastes as good as sober feels. I'm surfing that happy pink cloud and, what's more, it's exactly *three months* since I quit. One quarter of a year. Who'd have thought it?

I wouldn't have made it here without my friends in the sober blogging world. All those kindred spirits who've made me laugh, made me cry and amazed me with their strength and generosity.

I feel that if I'd had that glass of wine I'd have let them all down, and if I'd caved in I might have caused many of my virtual friends to topple over like dominoes. The internet has saved me.

But there are many moments when it isn't enough. There are times when you just want a *hug*. Something tangible. A friend with a *face* and not just a made up name.

If I'd had the nerve to go to AA, then today I'd be taking a cake along to the church hall to celebrate with a crowd of real people who knew the physical me, not just my virtual avatar. They'd be clapping and patting me on the back, sharing my cake and giving me a three-month coin. So today I feel a little blue about hiding behind my screen with my sad little made-up name.

To cheer myself up I decide to spend the day *decluttering*.

The thing about high-functioning ~~alcoholics~~ heavy drinkers, is that it's all about external appearance. If everything *looks* as if it's in control, then we can kid ourselves that it really is. We're like swans – apparently gliding effortlessly over the water, but in reality paddling like crazy through all the fish poo.

So many of us have homes that look, on the surface, in pretty good order, but if you peek into the cupboards, under the bed or in the cellar they are filled with clutter and dust balls. When you're drinking a lot you simply don't have time to deal with loads of *stuff,* to work out where it goes or what to do with it. So you shove it in a drawer and pour another glass of vino.

And, here's the spooky thing: we do exactly the same thing with our minds. Oh dear, here's a pesky emotion that I don't really like and don't know what to do with. Hide it in a recess and pour another drink.

When we get sober we start clearing out all those rejected and neglected emotions that haven't gone away but have sat there getting mouldy and making us all sluggish and dysfunctional. So I suppose it's no surprise that I've started feeling the need to do the same thing with my environment. I've had a go at the garden already, now it's time to tackle the house.

Before starting on 'project show home', I decide to do some research by reading up on feng shui, which is all about the link between our surroundings and our spiritual selves. I have to confess that I'd always filed feng shui in the 'Life's too short for all that up-itself nonsense' drawer, but now it's starting to make sense.

An article on thespruce.com claims that

Clutter is low, stagnant and confusing energy that constantly drains energy from you. Depending on the feng shui area of your home and where your clutter is located, it can also negatively influence, or even completely block, the flow of energy and events in many areas of your life.

According to feng shui, we are like plants, and we cannot grow without space and light.

Blimey, no wonder my life's in such a mess.

Funnily enough, the two areas of my house that I've started decluttering first are my kitchen and the entrance to my house. Having done some (quick) research, I've discovered that the kitchen is the area that is related to your health, *especially your liver.* How spooky is that?!? And the entrance to your house is known as the 'mouth of chi' and where your house gets its 'energy and nourishment'. If your 'mouth of chi' is all blocked you're screwed (executive summary).

According to my research, the best way to declutter is to take one small area at a time and spend no more than thirty minutes on each session. In those thirty minutes you separate all your clutter into three piles: 'keep', 'bin' and 'don't know'. You only keep stuff that you love, or is useful and you have a place for. If you don't love it, or have no use for it and nowhere to put it you ditch it, ruthlessly. You put the 'don't know' box away for a few months, then go through it again doing 'keep', 'bin', 'don't know' until it's eventually empty.

I find myself singing that terrible song from *Frozen*, 'Let it Go', as I merrily throw things into a box for the charity shop like a woman possessed.

By the end of the day, when John and the kids get home, I'm physically and emotionally exhausted, but I'm also on a (totally legal and non-toxic) high. Not only have I created much more *space*, but I'm also creating order out of chaos. I put up a hook for the dog leads by the front door, and pegs for all the children's school bags, while muttering *a place for everything, and everything in its place.* And all those bowls filled with bits of *stuff* have been emptied out and categorised. I've even created my own version of a Japanese koi carp pool in my new 'herb garden' with an old fish tank and the children's tadpoles. I had to pause for a while as I got positively weepy over a pair of bright-orange Versace jeans (in a size ten) from my clubbing days.

I fight the urge to declutter the husband, who is currently sprawled, messily, over the sofa watching back-to-back episodes of a programme about teenaged mermaids with Maddie.

'Why are you watching this?' I ask as I pass him, clutching a bin bag. Three blonde teens prance across the screen in barely-there bikinis. His eyes are on stalks.

'There's something in it for everyone,' he replies, not taking his eyes off the action.

I have a long way to go, with both the physical and the emotional clutter (I haven't been anywhere near the cellar – known in our house as 'the Pit of Despair'), but I can see chinks of light starting to break through. Or perhaps that's just more tiles falling off our roof.

I put the kettle on for a congratulatory cup of tea and go to collect the mail from the letter box. In it is a letter addressed with handwriting that, despite the fact I haven't seen it for a decade or more, I immediately recognise.

It's from Philippa, a friend I've known for thirty years and who now lives in America. She is the only person I actually know (apart from John) who reads my blog. I gave her the link right at the beginning because she's been there. Not only has she been sober for nine years, but she did a postgraduate degree in addiction studies. Who better to confess my sins to?

I sit down with my cup of tea and open the letter. Inside is a congratulations card and Philippa's own AA three-month sobriety coin. It's a solid, tangible thing from a real person who has not only thought about me, but given me something very precious of her own. I start crying. Good, big, fat, happy tears.

Thank you, Philippa. It means more than you can possibly imagine.

DAY |1|0|0|

REFLECTING

I've made it to the big one, oh oh! Woo hoo! Go me!

Whereas AA celebrate three months, the sober blogging world tend to celebrate 100 days. This is, they say, *a milestone*, as it is after 100 days, or thereabouts, that things start to get better.

I was intending to celebrate by myself (and with my virtual crew), but it turns out that there are advantages to the husband sneaking the odd peek at the blog. When I was still half asleep this morning he presented me with a 100th birthday card! (Bet they don't sell many of those.)

Not only that, but he's also bought me a gorgeous necklace – a silver elephant on a chain. I could invent something about 'elephants never forgetting', or make a joke about the size of my arse, but the truth is he just knows I love elephants.

He is a Good Man. A Keeper.

So, since it's a *special day*, I've been reading back over this diary from the beginning and doing a bit of reflection.

There I was, all bright-eyed, bushy-tailed, enthusiastic and naive, like the new girl starting at secondary school. You think that you've made it – you've done the work, passed the exams and *you're in*! – then you realise that you know nothing. You look around and notice that no one else is wearing their socks pulled up or their skirts at regulation length. You don't know your way around. You don't know the rules. You're totally out of your depth.

Now I've done the 'Am I an alcoholic?' exam, and I've done the 'Surely I can just have the one?' modules (also known as

'Is this really it? For ever?'). I've done lower fourth and upper fourth and I'm into lower fifth! But I realise that I have a way to go before I'm a cool know-it-all, confident sixth-former. I've only just started on 'Introspection' and 'Who the hell am I, anyway?' and I have no idea what comes after that. I've not even been given the syllabus.

I think about what I would have told my lower-fourth self to expect 100 days ago so I can post it on my blog for all the new girls following on behind. Here's what I come up with:

You will sleep more, and better, than you've done in years, but will be more tired than you can imagine. You'll discover that hot chocolate has magical healing powers, and that there really is a point to alcohol-free beer. You might feel ten years older and wiser, but you'll look five years younger. You'll discover a passion for cleaning, tidying, weeding, sorting and clearing out – both literally and metaphorically – and will read, obsessively, everything you can find about alcohol, alcoholism, alcoholics and anything else beginning with 'alc'. You'll find that that knot of anxiety you lived with for years was *caused by* the drink, not solved by it. Your best friend was actually your worst enemy. You will become an obsessive navel gazer (not to be confused with a naval gazer – someone who stares at seamen), constantly wrestling with questions like 'Who am I? Who was I? How did I get here? Where am I going?' And while you're learning all of this, you'll meet some incredible fellow travellers. People who will make you laugh, cry and think. Hugely strong, brave and inspirational people sharing your journey.

But, you know what? There would have been no point in (the older, wiser) me telling (the younger, more naive) me any of this, because one of the main things I've learned is that *there are no shortcuts.* There's a quote, often attributed to Winston Churchill (he didn't actually say it, but it does sound like something he would have said), 'if you're going through hell, keep going.' And you do just have to keep putting one foot in front of the other, one day at a time until, eventually, you get through the battlefield. And now, after 100 days of just keeping on going, I'm there!

I log on to the Soberistas website and read some blogs written by newbies on Day 1, or Day 7, or 14, and I almost (but not quite) feel jealous of the fact that they're standing there at the beginning of a journey that will change their lives. The first 100 days are hard, but also more intense and rewarding than I could ever have imagined.

I float on my pink fluffy cloud (disguised as a battered Toyota people carrier) to High Street Kensington for lunch with my girlfriend, Sam.

Sam is a gorgeous blonde who looks like a classic Kensington yummy mummy. But you patronise her at your peril, for she has a PhD in primatology from Cambridge, a subscription to the *New Scientist* (which she actually *reads*) and raises vast sums of money for elephant conservation. Which is why I'm not surprised when she immediately spots my silver one.

'I LOVE the necklace!' she says. And, for some reason, I find myself telling her what it's for, telling her that I've quit drinking, possibly for ever. I wait for her to look horrified and to start shouting *WHAT ARE YOU THINKING? You are so BORING! I never want to see you again!* But she doesn't.

'God, I'm so relieved. I was trying to work out how to break it to you that I really don't feel like a boozy lunch today. I have stuff to do.' Awesome. So, feeling like I'm on a roll, I tell her about my secret blog and, not only is she not shocked, but she's *impressed*. She gives me a massive hug and tells me how proud she is of me. I make her solemnly promise not to tell anyone and not to try to track down my blog. I may have had a momentary flicker of courage, but enough already.

When I get home I log on to Mummy was a Secret Drinker and find more than twenty messages from women (and one man!) all over the world congratulating me.

Apparently I rock. Perhaps I do!

It's only now that I remember I'd given myself a get-out clause at 100 days. I'd vowed that if it wasn't getting easier by now I'd quit quitting. But, at this moment, that seems like the most foolish idea in the world. There's no way I'd want to start again, right back at the beginning. So, here's to the next 100 days. I'm ready.

I'm celebrating (secretly) this evening at a pub quiz night. I'm looking forward to being as intellectually sharp (or not) at the end of the evening as at the beginning. That'll be a first. I am a little miffed, however, that my proposed team name 'The Big Fact Hunt' has been vetoed. Some people have no sense of humour.

DAY 103

DRINKING ALONE

Someone's left a comment on my blog that's been niggling away at me. They said *anyone who drinks alone has a problem IMHO*. It got me thinking: when did drinking alone stop being a stigma? Or maybe it still is a stigma, but just one I, and most people I know, discounted as old-fashioned and irrelevant.

The 'line that shall not be crossed' as far as I was concerned, was drinking before midday, and being deceitful about drinking. (Things like hiding bottles, and lying to the husband and friends. Lying to the GP doesn't count, obviously.)

If I had seen *drinking alone* as a danger sign, I would have crossed that metaphorical line *twenty years ago*. At that point I wouldn't have had to quit altogether, I would have just reined it all in, and carried on as a happy, moderate, normie with no inkling whatsoever of the wine witch.

Whenever I did one of those online questionnaires entitled: 'Are you an alcoholic?' (and I did loads of them, mainly when drunk) and I got to the question 'Do you drink alone?' I'd mentally discard it. Drink alone? Of *course* I do. Doesn't everyone?

My drinking career started off socially, but, by the time I got to Cambridge, there were 'social' drinking events pretty much every evening. Then, when I left university, I rented a house with three university friends who were trainee doctors. No one knows how to let off steam better than a medic. Our house was 'social drinking central' most evenings. Everyone pretended not to notice the sink overflowing with mouldy plates and put their cigarettes out in the dregs of their coffee mugs.

After a year or two I moved into the relative serenity of a small flat on the noisy Wandsworth Bridge Road with a friend from college – Katie. We lived together, happily, until she met Mark, and two became three.

I liked Mark. He was, like all the best people, slightly barmy. He ran a fireworks company and erected a giant rocket launcher on our flat roof (which you could access by clambering out of the sitting-room window). If he and Katie were home in the evening and wanted a little peace and quiet, he would launch a massive rocket over Fulham, a shot across the bows, which I would see from whichever bar I was at and know to keep pounding the streets for a little longer.

Mark's third great love (after Katie and pyrotechnics) was practical jokes. He started rigging up bangers around the flat to catch me when I got home. I'd open the door at 2 a.m., slightly the worse for wear, and BANG! The door would explode. Eventually I got wise to the exploding door trick, and would be ready for it. Then, one evening, I got through all the doors without any problem, and went into the bathroom. I lifted up the lid of the loo and nearly had a heart attack as a huge bang ricocheted around the flat.

Predictably, I got tired of living in a war zone, constantly checking for landmines and exploding lavatories, and of playing gooseberry to love's young dream. So, at the age of twenty-six, I bought my own flat.

I found a large one-bedroom in Fulham for the price of £80,000 (I got a ninety-five per cent bank loan and a five per cent loan from my parents). That wouldn't buy you enough space in London to park a moped on these days. I had so few possessions that I was able to move with the help of a friend's VW hatchback, and a friendly black cab driver.

That first evening in my new flat, on the first floor of a terraced Victorian cottage in the Sands End area, built for workers of the Imperial Gas Light and Coke Company, I sat in my only chair (a brightly coloured Habitat deckchair) in my new sitting room. The only other furnishings were two ornate candlesticks from the Conran Shop, my stereo system, a yucca plant named Alan and a packing case that doubled as a coffee table. I had never been so happy.

So, did I toast my achievement with a glass of Perrier? Hell, no! Obviously, I opened a bottle of champagne (Laurent Perrier, ironically) and drank half of it (that was plenty in those days) *on my own.*

Given that I now lived alone, it stood to reason that I would drink alone. I never questioned it. In fact, being able to go to my own fridge, after a hard day of kicking ass in the cut-throat world of advertising, and pour myself a large, chilled glass of Chardonnay (as it was in those days) felt terribly grown up.

It was sophisticated. Emancipated. Not sad! Oh no! Bridget Jones drank alone. Carrie Bradshaw drank alone. It's what young, independent, single women did.

As I grew up, got married and had children, pouring oneself a large glass (or three) of vino once the children were in bed (and then earlier and earlier) was all part of being a busy, stressed-out mum. Every day you'd hear someone say something along the lines of 'God I need a glass of wine', or making jokes about 'Mummy juice'. And we sure as hell wouldn't wait for company before getting stuck in (and blitzed out).

But, I now see that the problem with drinking alone is that that's when the vino morphs from being 'social lubrication' to 'self-medication'.

When you drink socially, you drink for the buzz, the relaxation, the shared change of mood. When you drink alone, you drink because you're stressed. Bored. Angry. Lonely. Soon you find that you're drinking to numb any emotion at all. You're staying up late with your glass of wine having morose conversations with Siri. And that is NOT HEALTHY (obviously).

Plus, if you only drink socially, you're more likely to drink about the same as your peers. Drink alone and you set your own measures. A glass becomes a third of a bottle. You 'pre-load' with several drinks *before* you join your friends. You assume that everyone does the same, then suddenly realise that you're an outlier.

So, I believe that one of the best things we can do for our children, and all today's young people, is to bring back the stigma of drinking alone. If the government poured some cash into an ad campaign portraying solo drinking as sad, desperate and *a problem*, they would save a huge amount of money down the line in treating the immediate and knock-on effects of problem drinking.

Which got me thinking: *If I was asked to advise teenagers on responsible drinking, what would I say?*

At this point I have to pause a little and chortle at the thought. Wouldn't that be a bit like asking Elvis to talk about healthy eating, or Casanova to discuss responsible sex?

These are the rules I would give them, and that I wish someone had given me:

1. Don't drink before 6 p.m.
2. Stop drinking as soon as you feel, even a tiny bit, out of control
3. Don't drink more than three times per week and
4. Never, ever drink alone
5. As soon as you find yourself unable to stick to 1–4, and/ or find yourself being dishonest about your drinking, to yourself or others, GET HELP.

God, how I loved drinking alone . . . (and that says it all, really).

On the way to bed, I stop off in Kit's room. He's spread out like a beached starfish, all tangled up in his duvet. His hair is all rumpled, and, because he's recently become obsessed by the great Victorians, he's grown his sideburns ridiculously long. I consider cutting them off while he's sleeping, but resist and just carefully straighten out his covers and then reach under his pillow to remove the tiny little, surplus to requirements, tooth he'd placed there earlier. I replace it with a pound coin.

The tooth fairy has a bad reputation in our house. She's known as being somewhat unreliable. On several occasions,

I've had to explain that she's got stuck in traffic, didn't know we were on holiday or hadn't got the news of the lost tooth in time, when the truth is that she'd drunk a bottle of wine, fallen asleep in front of a Swedish crime drama (try reading all those subtitles when half drunk) and forgotten.

But now the tooth fairy, like Mummy, is a reformed character.

MODERATION

It is definitely getting easier. I can go for hours, even days at a time without thinking about drinking at all. Being sober has started to be the *new normal*. It's no longer a huge effort. I think back to the drinking days and they're not as vivid. That drunk girl in the movie of my memory just doesn't feel like me.

But while I can't remember the bad times so well, I sure as hell remember the good ones. The first, much anticipated, drink of the evening – the one that makes your shoulders relax and your mind unwind. The first rosé of the summer, shared with a girlfriend in the sunshine while the children run under the garden sprinkler. The first glass of champagne on Christmas Day, while peeling sprouts and listening to the chatter about what Santa delivered this year. The welcome cocktail as you arrive, finally, at a holiday destination. And then I hear the whisper . . .

. . . you've overreacted! Silly old you. Sure, you needed to cut down, hell doesn't everyone? But quit totally? For ever? What were you thinking? It's not as if you were REALLY bad – a proper

ALCOHOLIC. *You were just a bit overenthusiastic! You never blacked out, vomited into gutters or had sex with strangers.*

I put my hands over my ears and reply, through gritted teeth, *But why would I* want *to start drinking again, even if I could do it in moderation? I'm getting used to being sober. I feel healthier. I sleep better. I'm skinnier. I'm nicer. I'm a better mum, a better wife . . .*

Then it gets insulting: *But it's* vanilla. *You're* boring. Live a little! *You've never coloured inside the lines before. It's just* not you.

I remember my blog: *What about my online friends? They rely on me. I'd be letting them down.*

It laughs. *Don't flatter yourself! You're not the only sober blogger. You're a mere drop in the ocean of the World Wide Web. And your 'real-life' friends would love to have you back drinking again. They've missed the real you.* You've *missed the real you.* Then, even more quietly: *Bet the husband does too . . .*

Now you've done 106 days of not drinking you'll have recalibrated. You're older and wiser. You've got the T-shirt and the three-month coin. You'll never go back there again. Of course you can drink moderately, like a normal person. Why not just give it a go? If you don't like it, you can always stop again.

Moderation. The elephant in the room. The giant enchilada. The hairy chestnut.

The M-word is hugely emotive in the sober blogosphere. It causes endless angst and virtual handbags at dawn. People fall out over it and storm off websites in virtual huffs, trailing angry emojis behind them. The reason this subject is so highly charged is that, for most of us, 'moderation' is the holy grail, the ultimate fairy-tale ending. You see, we may not want to go back to the dark days of drinking a bottle of wine every night and waking up every morning filled with self-loathing, *but* we'd love just a few *special ones*, just once in a while.

Every time a 'properly thirsty' (how many euphemisms can I come up with to avoid using the word 'alcoholic'?) drinker announces that, after a good long period on the wagon, they're going back to drinking 'moderately' we feel this surge of hope. We think *If he/she can do it, then surely I can too?* And that's why it makes everyone so upset.

Celebrities do this all the time. They do the rounds of the comfy sofas on daytime talk shows, talking about 'my rehab hell', but then, a year or two later, they announce that they're back to having an occasional cocktail once in a while, no prob-lemo. A few months later there are photos of them all drunk and disorderly, wrapped around a much younger stranger on a dancefloor and flashing their pants as they fall out of taxis. But, in the meantime, we are all shown the oasis in the desert, the song of the siren, the alluring shimmer of false hope.

I know, because I've been there endlessly in the past, that having one glass of wine after a long stretch sober will not lead to a three-day bender and me ending up knickerless in a gutter. Oh no. It's far more insidious than that.

I don't actually enjoy that first glass all that much – it tastes sort of vinegary, not the way I remember. I think 'See! I don't even like it that much any more! Ha ha. Put the cork back in the bottle and leave it there for ever. Or, at least until it's a *really* special occasion.'

Two weeks later. It's a *mildly* special occasion. I think 'I can have a glass of wine. I did so well last time. It's been two weeks already. Hurrah, I'm cured!' Then I'd drink three glasses of wine. And within two more weeks I'd be drinking every weekend, then every time we went out, then every day except Monday and Tuesday, then every day after 7 p.m. . . . yada,

yada, yada. Back to square one, just more bruised, beaten up and exhausted.

The truth is, I am not one of nature's moderators. I'm an all-or-nothing person. Moderating *anything* is not my forte. Plus, if I want proof of how *not normal,* how obsessive my relationship with booze is, then all I have to do is to read back over around 100 blog posts on the topic. Anne, my sober blogger friend, wrote recently *A normal drinker does not feel the need to write a sober blog.* That's me. Bang to rights.

Bill Wilson, the co-founder of AA, said that the test of whether or not you are an alcoholic isn't whether you can go for a few days or a few weeks without drinking (which I can, and have done several times), it's whether you can have *just one drink and then stop.* He says (in AA's *Big Book*), *try to drink and stop abruptly. Try it more than once. It won't take you long to decide.* And that I couldn't do, not without stapling my hands to the table and driving myself mad.

AA are very black and white about moderation. They say 'once an addict, always an addict' and one glass just leads to more, and more, and more.

There are neurological and physiological reasons for this. When the brain is 'excessively and repeatedly' exposed to alcohol (that'll be me then!) its natural systems of craving and reward are screwed up. When we drink, our brain's reward system is artificially activated, and it produces dopamine. Dopamine is the brain's 'feel-good' chemical, a natural high. Over time, the brain susses out that it's producing far too much of the stuff, so it compensates by kicking into reverse gear and *actively decreases* our base levels of dopamine.

That's why, gradually, drinkers feel more and more depressed, and start to believe that only alcohol will make us feel better. We're not actually wrong. Drinking enables us to produce dopamine again. What we fail to understand, however, is that it was drinking that caused the problem in the first place. Effectively, we reach a tipping point where alcohol stops being the solution and starts being the problem.

The good news is that as soon as we stop drinking our brain gets back into balance, and starts producing the happy hormone again all on its own. In fact, in the beginning it can *overcompensate.* A bit like a rubber band pinging back into position, it initially overshoots. This is why ex-drinkers experience the 'pink cloud' stage, followed by a series of ups and downs as our brains struggle to find equilibrium again.

The bad news is that by now our brains have been hard-wired to believe that *alcohol equals pleasure.* Years of our dopamine levels being controlled by alcohol have, in effect, created the 'wine witch' in our heads. And the only way to shut up the wine witch is *to not drink.*

AA use an analogy to explain why alcohol addicts can't drink 'normally' again – that of cucumbers and pickles. They say that you can stop a cucumber turning into a pickle, but once it *is* a pickle it can never be a cucumber again. And, let's face it, my cucumber days are long behind me. I've been well and truly pickled.

I know all of this, and just writing it down really helps, but sometimes it feels that as it gets easier it also gets harder. Two steps forward, one step back.

FREE BOTOX

Only two and a half weeks until the end of the school year and it's all gone crazy. With three children at London primary schools, the schedule for the next nineteen days includes two sports days, two prize-giving ceremonies, three class socials, bake sales, the summer fete and the inevitable dress-up days. Last year all of this would have been accompanied by, approximately, nineteen bottles of vino.

It has been decided (by a language teacher who has, no doubt, never been on the other end of one of these requests) that tomorrow Maddie's year should all go to school dressed as something *French*.

Since I am now (I keep telling myself) a really efficient and responsible mother, I have resisted the urge to perform my usual trick of ordering something off Amazon, made from a material so cheap that it'll fall apart after being worn once and is likely to burst into flames at the mere sight of a light bulb.

Now, the night before 'French day,' I'm regretting this. I scan through my mental Rolodex of stuff in the house that might do.

'I have an idea!' I announce. 'Maddie can go as a baker.' I grasp at a word I haven't used since O level French, back in the dark ages. 'A *boulanger*. She can wear one of Mummy's aprons and we'll give her a basket of patisserie to carry!'

Three children look at me, witheringly.

'You made me go as a *boulanger*,' said Evie, 'and Kit too. It was rubbish. And I got into trouble because one of the croissants had *almonds* on it.' She says the word 'almonds' as if they were arsenic, which, according to the school nut-free policy, they are.

The school are even more paranoid about nuts right now, ever since one of Kit's best friends nearly killed the form teacher. He gave him a lovingly home-baked (with peanut butter) cookie. Then, in front of the entire class, the incredibly popular and, it transpires, nut-allergic Mr Evans went into anaphylactic shock and was carted off in an ambulance. I congratulate myself on the fact that, despite not being the best parent in the universe, I have yet to hospitalise a teacher.

'I want to go as the Eiffel Tower,' announces Maddie.

'Brilliant idea!' declare her siblings, in a rare display of solidarity. 'We'll help you.'

Oh, joy.

We stop off at the art shop to buy card, paint, glue and tape. By the time we have all the necessary supplies I've spent enough to get to Paris and back.

We make Maddie a little pointy hat and cut out two large triangles of card, which we hang over her shoulders using an old pair of my tights. Kit and Evie then paint a remarkably realistic rendition of the Eiffel Tower on to her front and back.

By the time we've finished, everyone is covered in paint, so I frantically bathe the troops and get them into bed so I can get ready to go to Sally's party.

I've known Sally for twenty-five years. I met her when she started going out with an ex-boyfriend of mine, and we eventually worked out that we liked each other more than we liked him.

Sally is one of those incredible people who keeps in touch with pretty much everyone she's ever met. She told me recently that she'd updated her address book to remove out-of-date contacts, and had deleted 500 entries. I don't think I've ever known 500 people. So, going to a party of Sally's is like turning up at a recording of *This is Your Life*. People you haven't seen for decades crop up around every corner; like the boy I used to lust after in microeconomics lectures, the girl who broke my heart by running off with my boyfriend in my second year and the girl I shared an office with as a graduate trainee.

By the time John and I arrive at the party it's heaving. I drink, in quick succession, two virgin mojitos, which look and taste just like the real thing and, irritatingly, cost just as much. How is that fair?

At least four or five people comment on how great I look. I keep being asked if I've been on holiday (if only), and the women are looking at me quizzically, checking for signs of Botox or other 'work'.

I am, according to several people, looking five years younger. Yay! One old friend (he is, admittedly, rather drunk) even says 'ten years younger' but then ruins it by adding 'you were looking *rather raddled*'.

I nip to the bathroom and study myself up close in the mirror, and it's true. My face is less puffy – I have a jawline for the first time in years. I have far fewer lines, and my skin is all plump and rosy. Plus, I have white, shiny eyes. I'm still not Renee Zellweger, but then, even Renee Zellweger isn't Renee Zellweger these days.

So, there you have it, sober is the new Botox. But it's cheaper, and you can still raise your eyebrows. What's not to like?

By 11 p.m. the room has emptied out a fair bit, so I leave the husband going strong and *drive home*.

As I'm drifting off to sleep I realise that I know exactly where my handbag is.

This may not sound like a big deal, but this handbag has been a huge source of angst for several years. It's a beautiful, black quilted Chanel bag that John gave me for my fortieth birthday. I am determined to keep it safe for ever, and to pass it on to one of my daughters (who spend a rather unnerving amount of time discussing who gets what when I die).

The Chanel bag only comes out for parties and special events so, in the old days, by the time it got home its owner was usually drunk. I would take my clothes off (but not my make-up, which would end up smeared all over my pillow) and collapse into bed, then wake up a couple of hours later in a panic, trying to work out what I'd done with my bag. Had I brought it home from the party? Did I leave it in the taxi? Eventually, I'd have to get up and scan the bedroom with the torch on my iPhone (presuming I could *find* my phone), then go downstairs and search the kitchen until I found the bag. By then there'd be no chance of getting back to sleep until dawn.

But this evening I'm snuggled up, face thoroughly cleansed and moisturised and bag all present and correct back in its happy place in my wardrobe. Result.

SPORTS DAY

This morning I discover that there's one thing even better than waking up without a hangover, and that's waking up next to someone *with* a hangover. Obviously, I wouldn't wish any ill on the long-suffering husband, but he's a *fabulous reminder* this morning of what I'm missing. Our bedroom smells like a brewery, and his breath could pickle an onion at twenty paces. He's bloodshot, puffy and grumpy.

Looking at the husband makes me think, in a rather mean, smug way, of an AA saying: *Drinking today is just borrowing tomorrow's happiness.* In my early drinking days I would be trading massive fun on a night out for a minor headache the following day, but in the latter years it was a case of minor enjoyment the night before in exchange for a massive downer the following day (or days).

There is a physiological reason for this trade-off too. Drinking alcohol releases that dopamine in the brain, which gives us a high, but over the following days we have a corresponding dopamine 'crash', which makes us feel miserable.

This then gets me thinking that maybe I have, in effect, borrowed all my future booze ration and drunk it already. Perhaps you have a set amount in your lifetime that your brain can cope with and, given that I've drunk about four times what I should have for the last twenty years, I've used it all up. Nothing left in the wine bank. Funnily enough, that thought makes me feel a bit better. At least it seems *fair,* much like Kit wolfing down all his Halloween booty in twenty-four hours while his sisters eke theirs out over several weeks. He doesn't complain (much) about it because he knows it was *his choice.*

I try to feel sympathetic towards John, who must be having the day from hell. And I feel great! Which is just as well because today is Kit's sports day . . .

I think back to one of Evie's sports days about four years ago. We'd been out late the night before. I woke up with a chronic hangover. I packed the picnic for the traditional parents–kids lunch that follows the event, and included a bottle of white wine (which I'd decided was the only way to cure the headache).

Somehow I managed to get through all the endless egg and spoons, beanbags on heads, etc., while corralling a toddler, small baby and dog. I invented some acceptable excuse for, yet again, ducking out of the hugely competitive mothers' race, where former CEOs, fashion models and tiger mothers elbow each other aside for a chance to be seen as heroines in the eyes of their children.

(The first year I did Sports Day, I made the mistake of stepping up to the starting line, thinking it would be a good laugh. I knew I'd misjudged when I realised that I was wearing strappy sandals and everyone else was changing into running shoes *with spikes.*)

Then we all gathered for the picnic and I realised quite quickly that no one else had packed any alcohol.

Undeterred, I brandished my bottle of wine and was faced with a dilemma: I desperately wanted other people to join me so I didn't look like a ghastly old soak (which I was, obviously), BUT I didn't want so many to join in that I was only left with a small glass myself. I was pushing with one hand and hoarding with the other, finding it all horribly stressful.

Plus, the refusals made me feel terribly guilty. They'd say things like 'No thanks, I drank far too much last night!' (me too). 'Thanks, but I'm driving' (me too), 'I've got too much to do this afternoon' (and me) and 'Really shouldn't, I'm out this evening' (yup, so am I).

But today, hangover-free, I drop the Eiffel Tower off at school. The look of excitement and pride on her face as she struts in, ponytail swinging jauntily, putting all the children dressed in Breton striped tops and necklaces of onions to shame, makes the whole last-minute arts and crafts debacle worthwhile. Then I head off for sports day, which goes swimmingly, except for the terrier peeing on one of the kitbags and running off with a child's sandwich, at which point I tut loudly and say 'Whose dog is that?'

TODDLER TANTRUMS

Up until now, I've been surfing the zeitgeist. Every day the number of people finding my blog increased. Every week there seemed to be another article in the press about the dangers of drinking too much. It felt like I was at the forefront of a huge wave of change.

And then the sun came out.

People are no longer googling *Am I an alcoholic?* and stumbling across me. They're googling *How to make the perfect glass of Pimm's* and *Best cocktails for a barbecue.*

Journalists are having way too much fun at drinks parties on the terrace of the House of Commons to be bothered with writing about the evils of alcohol. Everyone is off to weddings, festivals and Wimbledon, all fuelled by a vast great lake of booze.

I feel like the sole storm cloud threatening a fabulous picnic. I'm King Canute trying in vain to hold back the wave, shouting above the noise of the roaring tide, 'Think about your liver! What about your dopamine receptors? Don't forget the wine belly!'

Statistically, one third of the UK population confess to drinking more in the summer (and those are just the ones who admit it and are sober enough to do the maths). It adds up to *an extra* 333 million pints of beer and 67 million more litres of wine. After the Christmas season, the summer is our booziest.

How I loved summer afternoon drinking. All those Pimm's parties in the quads at Cambridge in May week (which, bizarrely, was in June). A glass (or three) of cold rosé in the garden. Boozy barbecues, drunken picnics and poolside cocktails.

But now, for the first time *ever*, I am looking forward to January. Cold, dark, bleak January when *everybody* decides to cut down, if not totally give up, on the booze. In January, I will be *normal*. In January, the tide turns again, and I'll be up there surfing the wave, standing on my pro-board doing cunning stunts (careful how you say that one), while all the newbies are floundering around in the shallows.

In the meantime, I have found a new way of thinking about, and dealing with, wine cravings: seeing them as toddler tantrums.

There are, as any seasoned mother knows, several ways of dealing with toddlers who are lying on the floor flailing their limbs around and screaming.

The first is to *give in*. You give the toddler what they want and they shut up (for a while). But this only teaches them to kick off even more frequently, and with more volume. That's what I did for decades with the booze. Feel like a drink; have one.

After a while you realise that this method is only making things worse, and you discover a new technique: *distraction*. The toddler has a tantrum. You bring out a favourite toy and start making up a story. End of tantrum (for a while).

This is a great technique when you first quit drinking too. You feel like a drink; go for a walk, have a bath with bubbles and candles, eat cake, write a blog, read a book, do the gardening, clean the house – whatever works.

That's what I've been doing for the last three months. Then, I realised that, like managing the errant toddler, there is a whole new – and more effective – solution: *dealing with the root cause.*

After months, or years, of trial and error, you start to realise that, inevitably, toddler tantrums are not about what they think they are about. For example, the toddler has a tantrum because they want to watch another episode of *Peppa Pig*. It's totally out of proportion. They yell until they're red in the face. Then blue. They go rigid. They've actually forgotten what the issue was in the first place, but can't get out of the funk.

Here's the truth: *it's not about* Peppa Pig.

They are, almost certainly, hungry. Or tired. Or bored. Or overstimulated. What they need is a rice cake and a nap. Not more television, or distraction with another game (they'll still be hungry and tired, and there'll be another tantrum later – but worse).

The same is true of cravings. You can give in to them (very bad idea). You can distract yourself (it works but, in the end, it only delays the problem). But really what you need to do is to see the craving as a *warning signal.* It's like the light flashing on the car dashboard.

That warning signal isn't actually saying *I need a drink.* My body does not need a drink. After three months off the booze, I am not in the slightest alcohol dependent. I have just got used to dealing with *any* warning signal by drowning it in alcohol. What I need to do is to find out *what the warning signal is really telling me.* What is the tantrum *actually about?*

In my case, the flashing light is usually anxiety related. There's no point ignoring it and going off for a long bath, because the root cause of the anxiety won't go away. I have to breathe deeply, work out what the problem is and how to fix it, then put a plan in place. Like a grown-up! *Then* I can go and have the long bath with the problem sorted.

And seeing the cravings as my *friend*, alerting me to a problem, means that I can deal with all those niggly issues straight away, and then my life will be all calm waters and smooth sailing. (Yeah, right.)

But if this is true, and cravings really are my internal toddler tantrums, then that means there is a . . . *Ninja level: avoiding the tantrum.*

By the time I got to child number three I was a ninja mother (relatively speaking). Maddie hardly ever had tantrums because I could see well in advance if she was getting hungry or tired. I had routines. I always had healthy snacks. I had prevention strategies and contingency plans.

I didn't let the fear of tantrums interfere with what I wanted to do, and nor can I avoid all situations that will trigger an alcohol craving, but I can plan in advance and make my life easier. I've learned, for instance, to take my own alcohol-free beers with me if I'm staying with friends for a weekend; I write endless lists and get stuff done before it becomes urgent and more stressful. If I have a tough evening coming up I try to catch forty minutes' sleep during the day so my batteries are recharged.

I guess that, over time, I'll develop more and more of these strategies until eventually I'll be a proper grown-up. No more tantrums. No more cravings. (Or hardly any. Let's face it, even grown-ups have tantrums from time to time.)

Today is a great distraction. My mother, Evie and I do a girls' trip to the Alexander McQueen exhibition at the Victoria and Albert Museum.

I've always been a bit sceptical of those who claim that high fashion is art, but I was wrong. I'm blown away. The exhibition is brilliantly curated. Each room has a different theme – Highland Rape, Gothic, Romantic, Tribal and so on – with complementary music, lighting and film from McQueen's catwalk shows.

It's an assault on the senses, so physical that it makes me feel like laughing, crying and screaming simultaneously. It makes me want to throw away every single thing I own and replace them only with things of real beauty. (It makes Evie want to go to Top Shop, immediately, and it makes my mum want to have a sit-down and a nice cup of tea at the museum café.)

It makes me realise that there are far more interesting and diverse ways of achieving a mind-altering state than Chablis. Music, art, theatre, dance, yoga . . . all those things I've neglected in favour of staying home drinking.

You do not need to be out of your head to blow your mind.

If only Alexander McQueen (who was born twenty-two days after me) had realised that, he might not have killed himself at the age of forty.

THE MONTH WHEN I START TRANSFORMING

WEIGHT LOSS

I had assumed that, while quitting drinking was going to be hard, a major bonus would be *skinniness*! Or, at least, less fatness. After all, one bottle of wine contains around 600 calories. One week's worth of wine (assuming a bottle a day) is 4,200 calories – two whole days' worth of recommended calorie intake.

Sadly, it doesn't seem to be that simple. I did, quite quickly, lose the puffy face and the wine belly got less pronounced, but the scales weren't moving much. As always, I'm not alone. I know from all the emails I get and blogs I read that most 'enthusiastic imbibers' find that the weight doesn't miraculously fall off.

Why? Why? Why? Where's the fairness in that?

As far as I can tell there are two main reasons. The first is that, after years of pouring in liquid calories that have to be metabolised by the liver before it can process anything we eat, we have rather messed up our metabolisms. Our bodies are not 'finely tuned engines' but are totally overlubricated. When we quit it takes time to adjust course, a bit like turning around a supertanker. Can I liken my arse to a supertanker? Oh yes, I think I can.

The second reason is that so many of us turn to sugar to help with cravings. Sugar gives us the same dopamine hit that alcohol did, which is why it's also addictive. Plus it's *comforting*.

Hell, we deserve a bit of a treat given all this bloody *denial.* During the first few weeks I'd often consume slices of cake larger than my own head.

The issue of 'cross-addiction' is well recognised. The under-lying problem we addicts have is an inability to deal with emotions, feelings, situations, *life in general,* without a prop. Until we've dealt with that deep-seated issue, we will go for the easy option and replace one coping mechanism with another. Food is the obvious one, because it mimics the hand-to-mouth motion of drinking (and smoking).

Funnily enough, looking back, I realise that my alcohol consumption really took off in my early thirties, after I managed to quit my at-least-twenty-a-day cigarette habit. I also gained a stone in weight. In my twenties my hands and mouth were far too occupied with smoking to eat or drink too much.

That Pavlovian reaction is deeply ingrained. Whenever I get the familiar squirming knot of anxiety in my stomach, which, thank goodness, happens much less frequently now I'm sober, I still feel the need to shove something in my mouth. (I'm going to resist the opportunity for a crude joke here because I am a *grown-up.*)

Interestingly, this equation works both ways. According to obesityaction.org, a study of gastric-band patients showed that, because they usually hadn't dealt with the underlying issues that caused them to overeat, once they were unable to gorge on food they'd often develop other addictions, like reliance on alcohol. So the alcohol addicts become sugar addicts, and the sugar addicts become alcohol addicts. It's like an addicts' version of *Freaky Friday* (without, I suspect, the same box office appeal).

I've been trying not to beat myself up about any of this. We *need* to be kind to ourselves, and to reward ourselves from time to time. But these 'little treats' can quickly add up. One slice of chocolate cake, a hot chocolate and two Beck's Blues is easily the equivalent, in calorie terms, of a bottle of wine. So I can see how easy it becomes to actually *gain* weight, rather than lose it, when you quit.

I do realise that it would be way more sensible to deal with anxiety by developing a cross-addiction to running or doing yoga, rather than sitting hunched up over my laptop grazing on chocolate-covered raisins and wondering why my wine belly isn't disappearing any faster.

Anyhow, the amazing news is that, after weeks – months – of seeing little progress on the turning-into-a-skinny-goddess front, the weight finally seems to be *falling off!* Since Day 1 I have lost a total of ten pounds. Two and a half inches off the waist and wine belly, and three and a half inches off the butt. I weigh less now than I have for FIVE YEARS!

The difference is, I think, partly a matter of time, and of my metabolism evening out (the supertanker turning around), and partly that I've started to pay attention to what my body is telling me. I spent decades drowning out my body's natural responses. It said 'Yikes! That drink is a poison! What are you doing to me?' I said 'Shut up and have a Nurofen!' It said 'I'm not hungry, I've just been drugged and dehydrated.' I said 'Be quiet and have a bacon sarnie.'

I feel terrible about what I've put my body through for so long, and feel it's now time to show it some respect. So I'm *listening.* I used to eat for all sorts of reasons – because I was cross, bored, hungover or drunk. Now I eat when I'm hungry and stop when I'm not. God, that sounds like toddler-level nutrition, but, spookily, it's totally new to me. And it's working, despite the fact that I'm still having my treats – the hot chocolates, cake and alcohol-free beers.

I know that outward appearances shouldn't matter, that it's

what's inside that counts, but there are few feelings better than taking all the size fourteen clothes to the charity shop. *Hello all you lovely size twelves, haven't seen you for a while. Fancy an outing?*

As if in a bid to scupper my new waistline, Evie is baking cupcakes for the end of term bake sale. Having accepted some time ago, when she caught me trying to palm off some cleverly distressed Marks and Spencer's cakes as my own handiwork, that she didn't have a mother who was an enthusiastic baker, she has learned, at the altar of Mary Berry, how to do it herself. The problem is she uses every single bowl and utensil in the kitchen. I walk in to a scene of utter devastation. Every kitchen surface is covered in icing sugar. It looks like there's been an explosion in a cocaine factory.

Evie takes one look at my face, then wags her finger sternly at the half-empty packet of icing sugar.

'Now you just sit there,' she tells it, 'and think long and hard about what you've done.'

MIRRORS AND PHOTOGRAPHS

I'm reading Irish Mammy's blog. She says *'The last few months of my drinking I felt invisible and old and that that was how I was going to feel till I died.'* This strikes a major chord with me, as I have felt increasingly invisible over the last decade.

Long ago I'd resigned myself to the fact that I wasn't going to be troubled while walking past building sites any longer, let alone find people turning to stare as I walked into a party (unless I'd accidentally tucked my skirt into the back of my knickers). I guess that's inevitable. But, on top of that, I deliberately *made* myself invisible . . .

I was painfully aware that, while my life was seemingly fairly perfect, it didn't stand much scrutiny. Anyone who looked a little more closely would probably see it all falling apart round the seams. I'd scoot in and out of the school gates in the morning as unobtrusively as possible, in order to avoid having to make conversation with a hangover. Ditto school gates in the afternoon, in case it was obvious I'd had a glass of wine at lunchtime.

As I became increasingly overweight, bloated and puffy, I avoided wearing anything much other than stretch jeans and black. My ideal garment would have been Harry Potter's invisibility cloak. My aim when dressing for a party was to not wear anything that would *draw attention*: to my wine belly, my rapidly expanding arse, or to me generally.

I couldn't face shopping for anything new as I didn't have the confidence any more to know what looked good (or less bad), and couldn't face buying anything in a dress size that I was desperately hoping was temporary.

Part of my quest for invisibility was the careful avoidance of mirrors. I would hate it when a mirror snuck up on me unawares. I'd suddenly be confronted by my image and think 'When did my mother get so fat . . . Yikes! It's me. Look away you fool, before you're turned to stone.'

If I knew a mirror was coming I could *prepare*. I'd suck my cheeks in, angle my head to avoid double-chinnage and pull in the belly. Evie calls this my 'scary mirror pose', and says it looks nothing like me.

The only thing I hated more than mirrors was *photos*. Only photos of me, obvs. I could look at photos of the children for hours. Until the age of around thirty-four (when Evie was born), there were *loads* of photos of me. See Clare partying, Clare hugging John (and his predecessors), even Clare on various beaches *topless*!

Last ten years? Barely a single picture. I've been as merciless as Herod, erasing all unwanted images in their infancy. Thank God for digital technology! One click and ppppfff . . . gone. So, our last decade of family albums feature John, the heroic single father of three. Or they would if photo albums hadn't been one of the activities that went by the wayside in favour of *drinking*.

But now I feel like a butterfly creeping slowly, slowly out of its chrysalis. I've started to realise that I don't want to be invisible any more. I want to be *seen*. I still don't have the confidence (or the cash!) to go on a big shopping spree, but I'm reaching into the depths of my wardrobe and pulling out more and more of the 'optimistic' clothes that have been loitering there for up to five years.

The 'optimistic' clothes are the ones in bright colours and bold prints that you buy slightly too small, on a day when you're feeling buoyant about the new diet. Inevitably, a few days or weeks later, reality bites savagely, but you can't face admitting defeat by taking the newly purchased garment to the charity shop, so it stays there for years, taunting you for believing that failure wasn't inevitable.

Anyhow, I'm at the supermarket with Maddie. We've finished the shopping and paid up, so I wheel the laden trolley towards the lift. Maddie stands on tiptoes, presses the button, with great ceremony, and the doors open. I envy her being at the age when even pressing a lift button is a huge excitement and wonder when I lost the ability to be thrilled by little things.

The lift is already occupied by a lady with a trolley, so I move to the side to let her out. She's a fair bit younger than me, slimmer and well turned out. The sort of person I like to think I am. But I'm not.

She moves to the side too.

Slowly it dawns on me that the lift is empty. The back wall is mirrored. I'm looking at myself! That moment of realisation makes everything, all the hand-wringing, white-knuckling and weeping over the laundry, worthwhile. There are few things in life better than being able to look into a mirror and like what you see.

So, I've declared a momentary truce with mirrors but I'm still not sure about photos, because, having unpacked the shopping and collapsed in an armchair with a celebratory Beck's Blue, I scroll through Facebook and discover I've been tagged in one.

Philippa, the friend who sent me the three-month coin, had come over to the UK for a visit recently and arranged a reunion for a gang of us who spent our teenage years living in Brussels. We'd all been at boarding schools in England, and at the start of each school holiday would meet up at Dover, where we'd catch the ferry for the five-hour journey to Ostend, then the train on to Brussels. By the time our parents collected us from the station at the end of the journey, we'd be reeking of Stella Artois and duty-free Marlboro Lights and, released from our various bastions of single-sex education, high on pheromones.

Despite the reunion being a picnic in the rain (how classically English is that?) I'd had a *ball* that day, catching up on all the news since we'd last met up about a decade ago, and meeting everyone's children. But in the photo (which I didn't know was being taken) I look utterly miserable.

I realise – horror of horrors – that I have *a grumpy resting face.* Yikes!

I spend the rest of the day trying to train my mouth to turn up even when I'm just 'resting'. And, when I'm walking down the street I make an effort to *smile at people*. Sometimes they think I'm a total nutter, but generally people *smile back*. Genuinely smile. And after just a few hours of doing conscious SMILING, I'm feeling great, although my underused cheek muscles are complaining about this impromptu workout, and the children keep looking at me suspiciously.

Kit has a history exam tomorrow, so we spend the evening re-enacting the Battle of Bosworth with a selection of Maddie's soft toys. King Richard III is played by a giant panda, Henry Tudor is a fluffy bunny and the turncoat Lord Stanley is a rather fetching pink unicorn.

I'm surrounded by happiness, cute animals and magical creatures. I'm spreading the love.

 DAY 134

MINDFULNESS

Alcohol addicts often talk about having 'monkey brain'. It feels like we have particularly *active* minds, constantly whirring, analysing, criticising and worrying. Or perhaps everyone has minds like that, but other people are just better at dealing with them.

I used alcohol to shut my head up. It felt like booze was the only way to stop me agonising about the past or stressing about the future. After running around all day, with my internal dialogue driving me crazy, I'd sink into an armchair, pour a large glass of wine and – after a few good glugs – relative peace. (Until about 3 a.m., when I'd be woken up by the monkey brain chanting a litany of self-loathing, taunting me for my lack of willpower.)

When I stopped drinking, one of the things I missed the most was that 'dimmer switch' or volume button. Which is where mindfulness, an ancient Buddhist practice, comes in. *Everybody* seems to be talking about mindfulness, which is being touted as the miracle cure for pretty much anything. And mindfulness is, apparently, a healthier way of silencing the monkey brain for long enough to give yourself a break.

I do some research on the internet and download a mindfulness meditation. I've never tried meditation before, but how difficult can it be? The children and the husband are all still slumbering upstairs, so I sit in my favourite, battered leather armchair next to my ancient, but trusty, Aga and press play on the download (eighteen minutes long).

There's lots of breathing. Lots of *paying attention* to the breathing, and to what the breathing feels like.

This is all somewhat scuppered when the terrier gets over-excited by discovering me sitting down with an unoccupied lap and decides to join in. Now I'm paying attention to the feeling of being licked by a puzzled dog with dubious oral hygiene. I'm sure Gwyneth Paltrow doesn't have these problems.

You will find thoughts wandering in . . . No shit Sherlock. Mine go something like this: *How long have I been doing this for already? Any minute now the troops will start appearing for breakfast. I'm hungry. What happens if I stop concentrating on the breathing? Will I stop breathing? Arrgghh. I'm going to die. Surely Jon Snow isn't really dead? How long have I been doing this for already? I've got stuff to do. I've got to write my blog and take the dog for a walk before they wake up. Was that someone waking up? Perhaps Jon will come back to life at the beginning of the next series. Must order next box set. I'm hungry. How long have I been doing this for already? Why are all my thoughts so shallow? Shouldn't I be thinking about global warming or world peace? Which topics disturb Angelina Jolie when she's meditating?*

Ten minutes in and I'm seriously stressed. I think I'm too British for this meditation malarkey. Frankly, it makes me feel like a bit of a plonker. But I don't want to give up on the idea of mindfulness, so I go back to the research. Surely there must be another way of being 'mindful' that doesn't involve having to spend eighteen minutes *breathing*?

I discover that mindfulness is very similar to the psychological concept of 'flow', that feeling when you are totally lost in an activity, and the time seems to fly by – you're almost in a trance. You're not worrying about anything because you are totally focused on the present moment. That's 'flow'. It's also 'mindfulness'.

So, to achieve a state of mindfulness, you don't need to learn to meditate (hurrah!) – you can just choose an activity you love and give it your *full focus*. Pay proper attention to what you're doing, how it looks, feels, sounds and smells and don't let your mind wander.

The activities that ex-addicts tend to choose range from yoga and gardening to cooking, knitting, art, dog walking or fishing. There are even several best-selling colouring books called *Colouring for Mindfulness*, or similar. You pick whichever activity you're most likely to be completely *absorbed* by. If any pesky worries creep into your mind you're supposed to notice them, then *get rid of them*. (This process is known in mindfulness circles as 'whack-a-mole' after the arcade game.)

The idea is that after half an hour you'll have achieved something (baked a cake, weeded the garden, caught a fish – whatever), but you'll also feel great – relaxed, calm and peaceful. Without the drink.

Thinking about all of this, I realise that my addiction to

reading and blogging is totally about mindfulness, about complete focus and losing track of time. When I'm absorbed in a great book, or I'm furiously typing on my laptop, I'm not thinking about anything else at all, I've sedated the monkeys (humanely) and given my brain a break.

So, having patted myself on the back for conquering mindfulness without having to do anything new, John and I head off to a friend's summer party in a trendy new restaurant in Chelsea. I drink my (organic) elderflower cordial and, despite still feeling a little bit 'off' and self-conscious, manage to meet a handful of new people (which I wouldn't have bothered to do in the old days) and crack a few good jokes.

One of the problems with drinking endless elderflower cordial as props, added to a pelvic floor that's coped with three pregnancies, is that you spend an awful lot of time on the loo.

So, I'm sitting there, in a dark cubicle, taking the opportunity to check my texts in case there's a message from the babysitter, when I hear the door open and two sets of high heels clatter towards the basins.

'Did you hear, Clare's quit drinking?' says Thing One. I stop breathing. I'm rooted to the loo seat. I try to make myself breathe in and out (quietly). This would be a terrible, and undignified, place to die.

'Clare *Pooley*? Blimey, she's the last person I'd expect to give up the booze!' replies Thing Two.

'I know, right. A bit extreme, don't you think? A bit—'

'*Boring!*' completes the other. They snigger. I want to dive through the door and stab them both with my mascara wand. Or, I think as I look down, a bacteria-laden loo brush. Even better.

'That's her off my party list!' shrieks Thing One.

I sit there, for what feels like hours, waiting for them to both go to the loo, wash their hands and leave. I'm there for so long that the automatic loo decides to *flush itself* while I'm still on it. It's the final indignity.

I don't even notice that I've been crying until I catch sight of myself in the mirror and see my panda eyes. I repair the eyes as best I can and walk out into the party, my greatest fears confirmed. Boring. A social outcast. A figure of gossip.

I'm trying to put faces to the voices I heard, but resist the urge to comb the crowd searching for them. I just want to go home. I find John and give him the *emergency evacuation* look. I've had enough of parties. I've had enough of being sober. I've had enough of being *me*. I just want to stick my whole head into a vat of wine and forget about it all.

As we leave, (by car, still a thrill), John says to me, 'You are amazing!'

'Why?' I ask, assuming he's referring to the fact that he now has a free chauffeur. But no. He elaborates:

'Al came up to me as he was leaving and said "Hey, John, your wife is *on fire* tonight!"'

HA! Take that, Thing One and Thing Two. I'm not boring! I'm no longer invisible, but actually ON FIRE!

I am Katniss Everdeen (without the murder of teenagers).

RUNNING

Today is the first day of the summer holidays. Seven weeks. It's not started well, as I have to explain to Maddie that most of her tadpoles have died in the heatwave. Poor little tadpoles who never made it into frogs.

Before I can warn her, she peers into the tank. 'Oh look, Mummy! They must have grown their legs really fast and hopped off already! I hope they've found somewhere nice to live. Smiley face.' (Bizarrely, she's recently started speaking in emoji.) I say nothing. Perhaps they did just grow up really fast. Who knows?

I'm excited. No school runs. Lots of adventures – beaches, ice cream, surfing, lie-ins, movies and expeditions. But I'm nervous too. Seven weeks of trying to find different ways of keeping Evie, Kit and Maddie off the computer. Arbitrating sibling disagreements (aka trying to stop them beating each other up). Cooking hundreds of meals that at least one of them will turn their nose up at, at every mealtime. Constant tidying, washing, suncream-applying, nose-wiping and manner-correcting . . .

. . . all without anything to 'take the edge off' at the end of the day. And with no time for myself with blogs, bubble baths, long dog walks or any of my other 'displacement activities'.

But it has to be better than doing all of the above with a hangover. Then letting them run wild from 5 p.m. onwards while I get stuck into the vino. Then shouting at them because I'm slightly drunk and cross. I'm starting the holidays with bags of energy. I weigh under eleven stone for the first time in years. I'm (relatively) relaxed and even-tempered. I can be the perfect mum! (Yeah, right.)

Last night John and I celebrated the end of term with date night. We grabbed a quick bite to eat (I've found that I can't hang around in restaurants for too long without a glass, or five, of Sauvignon Blanc), and then went to the movies.

We watched the new Terminator movie. John's choice, obviously. I wanted to see the Amy Winehouse biopic.

As always, the first twenty minutes of the film is really

stressful. This is because one of John's money-saving tricks is to pay for cheap seats, then go and sit, as if accidentally, in the VIP seats with the extra legroom and comfy armrests. I then wait in fear of the valid owners of our seats arriving, at which point we'd have to do the 'walk of shame' back to our cheap seats in the row behind.

The film was pretty much like the last Terminator movie, just with even more confusing time travel. (People going backwards, then forwards, then both simultaneously. Even sober it was tricky to follow . . .) What I did love, however, was the lead female character – Sarah Connor.

Sarah Connor (mother of the future leader of the revolution) is played by Emilia Clarke, who is also my favourite heroine – Daenerys Targaryen (Mother of Dragons) – in *Game of Thrones*. As I was watching Sarah Connor, I was imagining her getting a little stressed about the responsibility of saving the future of mankind. What if she'd decided to sink a bottle or two of vino instead of kicking ass with a machine gun? She wouldn't have been much of a match for a shape-shifting terminator from the future then, would she? Unless she was planning to bore him to death.

Imagine if the fabulous Katniss Everdeen had a few vodkas to take the edge off the nerves before entering the Hunger Games arena. She wouldn't be half as handy with a crossbow. A few hours in and there'd be cannon fire and her picture beamed up in the sky. End of series.

What about Ripley in *Alien*? If she'd decided to quench the anxiety a little with a few drinks before heading out with the flamethrower she'd have had aliens popping out of her stomach before she could say 'Open another bottle, will you?'

The conclusion to all of this is obvious: strong, kick-ass, aspirational women *do not drink*. They don't need to be drugged to save the universe. They have better, more important things to do. They know that alcohol will just *hold them back.*

I decide that while I may be (only just) closer to fifty than forty, I want – *I deserve* – to be a *strong woman.* In mind *and* body. I've quit the booze, and now I'm going to get back to my fighting weight. I'm going to get serious about running. I'm going to take up yoga and get strong and flexible. And then I'm going to change the world. (I might just have a sit-down and a quick cup of tea before I get started.)

So, today I am going *running.* When I say *running,* I really mean a combination of running and walking. And anyone more interested in veracity than being supportive might actually say *jogging* rather than running. But, hell, it's a start.

The terrier is in shock. He's used to me ambling along, checking emails, making phone calls and chatting to passers-by, while he wanders off having a good old sniff and marking the territory. Now if he stops for a bit he has to sprint to catch up with me.

I wouldn't say that I'm *enjoying* the whole thing yet. Once or twice I get a fleeting glimpse of 'runner's high' – the endorphin rush I've been chasing for years at the bottom of a bottle – but on the whole it's *really hard work.* I don't think I'm built for speed; I'm more of a Robin Reliant than a Ferrari. By far the best bit is crashing, sweaty and breathless, through the front door and announcing loudly to my bemused family, 'Morning all. Just been for a run,' before collapsing into my favourite chair with the newspaper.

DAY | 4 | 4

RELAPSE REMEMBERED

I am in Scotland with the kids.

John needs to return to his homeland on a regular basis in order to stride up heather-coated mountains in a skirt without underpants (yes, it is true what they say about Scots), shoot things (at the appropriate times of year), do silly dancing and eat deep-fried offal. He is scared that if he leaves it too long between visits he will turn into a sissy (English person).

As usual, we do the pilgrimage in two parts: part one involves me driving for nine hours north with a car packed to the gills with all our stuff, Evie, Kit, Maddie and the dog. Part two involves John following a few days later (important business to finish in the office, obviously) on the train, reading the papers and sipping gin and tonics.

The last time I made a serious attempt to quit drinking was two years ago. I made it to about six weeks sober, then did the long drive north. I know now (having spent whole days on Google) that people often crack at the six- to eight-week mark – it's when the pink cloud disperses to reveal 'the wall'. Back then I was unaware of this.

So, two years ago, all was fine until about eight hours into the journey. Evie, Kit and Maddie started fighting. Proper yelling and pulling hair. I suspect teeth were involved. I lost it and started yelling too. The dog spotted some sheep (he's a Fulham dog – cashmere jumpers he's familiar with, actual fleeces on legs . . . not so much) and started barking madly. Then, to cap it all, the police closed off the only road over the Cheviots due to a road traffic accident. We took a diversion and got horribly lost.

By the time we arrived it was late, I was exhausted and fed up and everyone, including me, was crying over something. I told myself that I really, really, *really* deserved a glass of wine. I found a bottle in a cupboard, opened it, and within about an hour and a half it was empty.

The next day I felt *awful*. After six weeks sober my body was screaming for mercy. I had no desire whatsoever to drink again. *Ha ha!* I thought. I have managed to reset the system. I am a *normal drinker*. I can let rip from time to time, then have absolutely no interest in continuing. Well done me.

And I didn't drink again. For a week. Then I drank a couple of glasses over dinner with family and patted myself on the back as I refused a third. Look at me: *moderation in action!* I didn't drink again for five days or so. You know the story. A month later I was back to drinking every day, more than ever.

So this time round I was nervous. I can't remember ever having done that journey, with all the packing, unpacking, driving, traffic jams, refereeing, etc. etc. without a bucket of alcohol at the end of it.

Until today!

Yes, I was frayed when we got here. No, the solitary Beck's Blue that I'd packed didn't hit the spot. BUT a few hours later and the children are in bed, I've had a hot bath, lit the fire (I know it's July, but it's *Scotland*), made a hot chocolate, unpacked the laptop and I'm doing great. The only sounds are the ticking of the kitchen clock, the tapping of the keyboard and the crackling of the embers.

And, even better, I'll wake up to the glorious landscape, stillness and fresh air, with a clear head and bags of enthusiasm. Another 'first' ticked off.

I type up my relapse story on my blog and invite my readers to do the same. Within minutes there are comments saying

Yes, me too! And the link to my blog is shared on several other sites as women (and some men) everywhere remind themselves that *one drink* never is one drink. Not for us.

DAY |1|5|2|

PACKING AND BONDING

Back in London and packing again, this time for our annual trip to Cornwall. Three weeks of sun (we hope), surfing and sandcastles. And it strikes me that part of the reason I'm so excited is that I have, relatively speaking, very few drunken associations with Cornwall.

My father's family are Cornish, so I've been going every year since I was born. I did a fair bit of drinking there, obviously. I've done a fair bit of drinking *everywhere!* But the drinking memories are totally overwhelmed by loads of sober ones.

Hot chocolate and doughnuts on the beach after surfing. Catching crabs in rock pools. Hide-and-seek in caves. Long, wind-blown cliff walks. Building walls of sand to stop the tide coming in. Picking blackberries and turning them into pies and crumbles. Flying kites. Frying sausages on the beach. Finding hidden coves. Spotting seals. Riding bikes. Paddleboarding. Water skiing. Ice creams. Cream teas. Cornish pasties. Swing ball. Frisbee. Building dams. Floating boats down streams. Sandy toesies. Burnt nosies. Brown paper packages tied up with string. (Oops. Wrong list.)

Last year a lovely American friend of mine came to meet us on our regular beach with her family. She's in fashion. She turned up wearing Jimmy Choo strappy sandals and pastel silks, perfectly made up and coiffed, dressed for the Hamptons.

She was horrified to find us in wellies and waterproofs, sheltering from driving rain in a cave, crazy hair matted with salt water and faces windburnt. We looked feral.

Cornwall reminds me that the best things in life don't need dressing up for. They are both free and priceless. And sober.

I have some holiday shopping to do, so I take Kit and Maddie to Westfield shopping centre, the local temple of consumerism where all self-respecting west London mothers go to worship on a regular basis.

Despite the fact that Westfield is only ten minutes' drive away I have only ever been there for the restaurants and movies. I've never before hit the shops. The truth is that for more than a decade I haven't really been interested in shopping, apart from for the children. It's no fun if you're feeling fat and generally hating yourself. I only shopped online, and mainly for stuff that wouldn't *stand out*. Ideally in black.

But now I'm feeling rather different. For a start, I'm nearly a stone lighter. I'm a *medium*! (I always hated buying anything in LARGE.)

So I leave Kit and Maddie in the children's play centre and . . . go a little crazy. I buy a top from Reiss (justification: it's white, it'll go with anything). I buy new trainers, a running top and capri pants from the Nike store (justification: the more you spend on a new hobby, the more likely you are to keep it up, and even if I get fat again, the shoes will still fit). I buy new underwear and nightwear from Calvin Klein (justification: sorry, there are some things I don't share, I'm not a Kardashian).

By the end of this splurge I feel HIGH. I'm light-headed. My pulse is racing. I feel *intoxicated*. I sit down with a coffee and google 'shopping addiction'. (I wonder how many people have googled that one from Westfield.) It turns out that shopping releases endorphins and dopamine, just like drugs and alcohol.

It is quite common for alcoholics to quit drinking and take up excessive shopping. There's even a Shopaholics Anonymous with a twelve-step programme.

I pick up the kids and leave Westfield feeling horribly guilty and sort of *hungover*. But, hell, I have a really cool pair of trainers.

We stop on the way back to collect Evie from a new friend's house. I've never met her mum before today, but I like her instantly. I can see us becoming friends.

'Cup of tea?' she asks, 'or a glass of wine?'

It's six thirty. A perfectly reasonable time for a glass of wine.

'Ooh. Tea, please,' I reply. (Obviously.)

I can see the disappointment in her eyes. Not because she's a drunken lush and desperately wanted to open a bottle (I can tell that look by now), but because of what it says about me.

I miss alcohol (and cigarettes) for their ability to create an instant bond. The 'tea or wine' test – in my book – was a way of telling what sort of person you were dealing with. I often used to employ the test with potential new friends. Those who replied 'Wine' were, I decided, the fun ones. Grown up when required, but always young, wild and reckless at heart. The 'wine' responders were my crew. My posse.

Cigarettes were the same. I've made some of my lifelong friends huddling in a garden at a party, trying to get the Zippo lighter to light in the wind, or when banished to the smoking section of an office, restaurant, train or aeroplane. (Remember those days?)

When I replied 'Tea' to the new friend, she thought 'Responsible, sensible, straight . . . dull.' *And that's not me!* I desperately want to shout *Don't worry, I'm NOT a cup of tea person, I'm a large glass of vino person, I'm a let's go wild and let our hair down person. I'm a to hell with it all person. But you'd better not open the wine, unless you want to haul me out of here at 2 a.m. after having heard my full life story and seen my comedy version of a cabaret striptease.* But I didn't. She'd have thought me crazy, and Evie would never have forgiven me.

What I miss by doing this all by myself, by not doing AA, is a *new posse.* And ex-drinkers are, in many ways, the best posse of all. People of extremes. People who've *lived a little.* People with tales to tell.

And that's me, me and my online crew.

THE MONTH WHEN THE UNIVERSE
SENDS A SIGN

ARRIVAL

It's time to leave for Cornwall!

I get up at the crack of dawn and spend several hours packing, trying to cram everything into our (not large) car and still leave enough room for three children and a dog. This isn't easy as I've bought enough Beck's Blue to sink a battleship. I don't know if Beck's Blue has yet penetrated such a remote corner of the world and want to Be Prepared. Luckily I squish it all in and don't have to choose between leaving behind the beer or a child. Not quite *Sophie's Choice*, but awkward, nonetheless.

I do the drive down in horrible traffic on my own (John, as usual, is following on by train after a day at work). Everyone seems to be heading for the coast, and the M5 resembles a car park rather than a motorway. We're all hot, tetchy and tired.

Then, finally, we turn off the A30 and on to the North Cornish Coast Road and I can feel the tension leaving my shoulders. Even the air smells different – of heather and salt. We play the usual competition, seeing who can be first to see the sea and shout 'Icanseethesea! Icanseethesea!'

After another half-hour of tiny Cornish lanes and terrifying blind corners, we arrive at our little cottage. Then I have another hour of unpacking while simultaneously dealing with three overexcited children.

Arriving at a holiday destination pulls every trigger there is:

149

stress (tick), exhaustion (tick), celebration (tick), reward (tick), anxiety (tick). BUT I have planned ahead! I am an expert at this game! I have a chilled Beck's Blue waiting for exactly this moment.

What I hadn't counted on was there being NO SODDING BOTTLE OPENER! What kind of holiday cottage doesn't provide a bottle opener?! I turn the cottage upside down. The children are hollering to go to the beach. I'm a woman possessed. I look like . . . AN ADDICT! (Who'd have thought it?) Or a crazy poltergeist, opening and closing, then reopening, every drawer and every cupboard.

I've obviously lived a sheltered existence as I have no idea how to get the lid off a beer bottle without an opener. I try everything, and only succeed in hurting my hands. In the end, I go into the tiny walled garden and smash the top off on a stone. Needless to say, beer goes everywhere, leaving me with two gulps of liquid, lots of foam and broken glass and smelling like a brewery.

It strikes me as ironic that, however badly I was addicted to alcohol back in the day, I never resorted to smashing bottles like a lunatic.

The kids and I walk down a narrow footpath, across a field, over a stile and through a dark, tangled copse down to the beach. As the sun sets, we sit on the rocks and eat Cornish ice cream, watching the waves crashing, with hypnotic regularity, on to the sand. Bliss. The vast Atlantic Ocean and three weeks' holiday stretching out in front of us. I watch some reckless teenagers tombstoning off the cliff into the choppy waters below, and the dog – in a hilarious display of hope over experience – trying to catch a seagull.

Later, the kids are in bed, windblown, exhausted and happy, and the dog is fast asleep, his legs twitching as he dreams of finally getting the better of those birds. I'm snuggled on the windowsill in my pyjamas, looking out at the stunning, wild, wet and windy landscape and listening for the sound of John's taxi. He'll be fresh as a daisy after a relaxing train journey with a good book and a half bottle of vino. But I forgive him as he should, as instructed earlier today, be carrying a bottle opener. If he isn't, I'm not letting him in.

BLACKBERRY PICKING

I've read a lot about the link between problem drinking and depression. They are so intertwined that it's often impossible to tell which came first; do we drink because we're depressed, or are we depressed because we drink? In fact, it can work like a downward spiral, sucking us in, like a spider down a plughole.

Yet again, it's down to the interaction between booze and dopamine. If you're feeling down, a drink *does* help to lift the spirits by giving you a dopamine kick but, as I now know, do this often enough and your brain reduces the amount of dopamine it produces naturally to compensate. This means that *without alcohol* you will feel depressed. Then, when you drink, the dopamine produced just takes you back to normal levels. In other words, you start to feel – because it's true – that only alcohol makes you happy. *But* it was alcohol, that false friend, that caused the problem in the first place.

To be honest, I don't think that I was depressed when I was drinking. I just felt flat. A bit *bleurgh*. Like all the colour had been leached out of the picture, leaving it sepia. But because it happened so gradually, I hardly noticed.

But now, especially down here in beautiful Cornwall, it feels like the knobs have been adjusted and we're back in glorious technicolour. The old brain has turned up the volume on the rusty dopamine producers and I don't need the booze to feel high.

I'm walking up a narrow cliff path with Kit and Maddie. They're bounding up the steep, uneven steps like little mountain goats, while I puff along behind them, desperately trying to keep up and cursing all those missed gym classes.

On one side, there's a steep drop down to a relatively calm, Tiffany-blue sea; on the other a tangle of heather, gorse and brambles. I'm scanning the sea for the black heads of seals, and the children are searching in the bushes for blackberries.

There are, it transpires, way more blackberries than seals. They've put a few in the bag (blackberries, not seals), but even more are smeared over their hands and faces. I pretend not to notice and imagine the crumble we'll make later. I can smell the sticky, tart blackberries and the sweet, crunchy topping. Custard or clotted cream? One of life's eternal dilemmas.

I see a woman walking towards us. I smile at her. I'm pretty sure that the sweet old lady is admiring my great parenting. Healthy, outdoor fun with the kids. And aren't they gorgeous, all windswept and dressed in Boden? Well done, Clare. Try not to look too smug!

As we pass each other she looks at Maddie shoving another blackberry into her purple-stained mouth.

'Dogs pee on those, you know,' she says.

She took my happy balloon and pricked it, the miserable old crone. Which made me think: do you want to be the person smelling the crumble, or the one seeing the wee? Because I'm smelling the crumble, and it's only now that I realise how much time I wasted looking for wee.

We meet up with John, Evie and the terrier on the beach. Since the tide is in we decide to play Poohsticks. This is no ordinary Poohsticks, it's the Pooley version, which, obviously, involves no moderation of any sort. Rather, it requires a lot of shouting (and barking), running, and a smidgeon of strategising and backstabbing.

You need three drinking straws in different colours, one for each child. (We send Maddie into the pub to get these because she's seriously cute and no barman can say 'no' to her. Just as well she doesn't order a vodka . . .) You then drop the drinking straws into the fast-flowing stream way up by the car park and run *really quickly* back to the beach, quite a way down the hill.

The stream flows under the road, and pops out through a bridge on to the rocks above the beach. We station a lookout at this point to check progress, and to make sure nothing's got stuck. There are two more lookouts lower down the stream as it tumbles over rocks, down mini waterfalls and round whirl-pools. Eventually, the stream reaches the sand, and one of the straws (usually Kit's, because he cheats) is declared the winner.

Who needs the Caribbean when you have three plastic straws and a Cornish stream? The simplest things are the best, and really do not need artificial stimulants to make them any better.

DAY | 1 | 6 | 2 |

FEELING THE WHOOP

Saturday morning in bed in Cornwall. We've now been here a whole week. The sun is shining and I can hear the sounds of Kit and Maddie getting up. (It's a small cottage. If anyone burps anywhere we all know about it.) I've been thinking about what's made this holiday, so far, different from previous years, when effectively the formula's been exactly the same (I'm obviously a creature of habits – good ones and bad ones). It struck me that the main difference is an absence of *restlessness.*

Throughout the drinking years I often wanted to be *somewhere else.* The only times I felt completely at peace were when I had a drink in my hand (which, increasingly, was quite a lot of the time). Almost as soon as I'd start one activity, I was considering what to do next. Rather than concentrating on the moment (mindfulness), I was already focusing on the future. I called this 'planning'. Now I see that it was, actually, restlessness.

There is a biological reason for this feeling. When we are addicted to something (nicotine, narcotics, alcohol, whatever) the reduced base level of dopamine in our brains means that any short period of time without our drug of choice makes us feel depressed, edgy and *restless.* We feel like something is missing – we're not complete. Which is, in fact, the case, as we've created an imbalance, a *hole,* in our neurochemistry.

So, however much we try to relax, to be in the moment, our subconscious (the wine witch) is whispering *Is there any wine in the fridge? Do you need to go to the shop? Haven't we been at this play centre/playground/funfair long enough? It's definitely time for a drink. Don't just sit there – do something about it!*

In previous years, with the kids on the beach in Cornwall, by 5 p.m. I'd be feeling angsty. I'd be hurrying everyone along, packing up, yelling eventually, making sure that we were back home in time for 'me time'.

But this year, as low tide has got later and later, we've adjusted our timings. We've been, literally, going with the flow – getting up later and going to bed later. Staying on the beach until 8 p.m. to make the most of the surfing, having sandy burgers on the rocks for supper and watching the sun go down. And I haven't wanted to be anywhere else at all.

That's one of the best gifts of sobriety: peace.

As soon as the tide's out far enough we all go down to the beach to surf. We battle through the waves in our glistening wetsuits, jumping over the breakers, tasting the salt on our lips and feeling the sun on our faces. I catch a big wave just right. As I hurtle towards the shore I look to my left, and there's Evie, grinning like a maniac. I look to my right, and there's an equally euphoric Kit. And I let out an involuntary Whoop. This is not an odd English euphemism for farting. What I mean is that I find myself accidentally yelling 'WOOHOO!'

Now, I am a jaded, middle-aged bird who has lived rather too hard for too long, so I cannot remember the last time I did an involuntary Whoop. For the last few years, not even getting plastered and throwing some shapes on the dancefloor made me Whoop. There was always a nagging voice (however much I tried to drown it out) saying *You'll pay for this tomorrow.*

Not only had the drink lost its power to make me Whoop. It also took the Whoop out of pretty much everything else. Feeling hungover, and counting the hours until the next drink, are very much Anti-Whoop activities.

And, you know what? Life is too damn short not to Whoop.

DAY |1|6|5|

THE GLUMS

This morning I've hit a sudden patch of The Glums. I've become so used to skipping around like an unbearably chirpy Pollyanna that this dark patch has floored me. Overnight, my setting seems to have switched from half full to half empty (ironic, really, as I've never knowingly left a glass half full *or* half empty). I've gone from being whoopy to weepy.

It could be hormonal. It could be the dreaded PAWS. It could just be a non-specific bad mood.

I run through all the reasons I have to be happy (in addition to the biggies like good health, happy children and lack of unmanageable debt): we are on holiday in Cornwall – one of my favourite places in the world. Evie, Kit and Maddie have declared it one of the best holidays *ever*. I have croissants baking in the oven and, against all odds, I have found a shop that sells Beck's Blue. I think they must have ordered it in error, because when I took a six-pack to the till they looked at me as if I were crazy and said 'You do realise this is *alcohol-free?*'

But still there's a grumpy voice pointing out the negatives: it's raining, and the forecast for the week is terrible. It's a holiday for everyone else, but I still have to prepare at least two meals a day (for a fussy, unpredictable audience who have been known to greet a meal they loved the previous week with eye-rolling and retching sounds), run the washing machine daily and the dishwasher twice a day. It's been more than a decade since I had a holiday with room service. Kit behaved so badly in a local inn yesterday (the usual argument over vegetables) that we had to leave, and I may be too embarrassed to ever return, and I was so busy typing my blog with one finger on my iPhone that *I burned the sodding croissants*!

I'm trying not to infect the rest of the family with the black cloud following me around, so instead I unleash my irritation with the non-specific grump on my blog and, a few hours later, I find a comment from Ulla, a wonderful reader from Denmark, who shares a story about one of her favourite childhood memories.

Her mother suggested a swim. 'But it's raining!' young Ulla replied (I imagine her with eyes as deep and blue as the fjords, and blonde hair in plaits, wearing a red gingham pinafore). 'So what?' said Mum (who, in my clichéd imagination, looks like Meg Ryan), 'we're going to get wet anyway!'

And, you know what? She's right. To quote a Facebook meme: *Life isn't about waiting for the storm to pass, it's about learning to dance in the rain.* The more we react to adversity by holing up and hunkering down (whether or not we're drinking) the more scared we get next time. Our world gets smaller and smaller. However, if we run out into the storm, if we turn it into an experience, if we actually *start dancing*, then next time we'll be braver. We'll know we can do it. Our world gets bigger and more filled with promise.

So, thanks to Ulla, we all don our wetsuits and head to the beach, slipping and sliding down the footpath, which has turned into a quagmire. It's late in the day, so the sun (what we can see of it, struggling through the storm clouds) is low, casting long shadows on the newly exposed sand, washed clean of all the footprints from earlier in the day.

We have the beach pretty much to ourselves, unheard of in August. The tide's going out, leaving huge calm pools of water among the rocks. We dive in, and I lie there in the drizzle, floating on my back feeling like Momma seal (or Sea Cow, perhaps?) surrounded by her cavorting cubs. The moment is nearly ruined when Kit asks his father 'Where's Mummy?'

'She's been beached!' he replies. Hilarious. Not.

I look up and watch the clouds clearing in the sky and feel the clouds clearing in my head. I've proven to myself that I can dance (and swim) in the rain, and hopefully I've made some memories that, like Ulla, my children will never forget.

Last year, on a rainy day like this one, I'd have opened a bottle of wine and spent all afternoon sneaking surreptitious top-ups from the fridge, then yelled at the kids, gone to bed feeling dissatisfied and grumpy and tossed and turned all night.

I'm back on form. Floating on the Happy Pink Cloud.

DAY |1|7|0|

MAKING AMENDS

My parents have joined us in Cornwall. This brings back vivid memories. It was in Cornwall last summer that my mother told me, kindly and gently, that she thought I was 'drinking too much' and that I needed to lose some weight. She said that she was particularly concerned about the link between alcohol and breast cancer, as she had breast cancer five years ago and didn't want me to go through the same thing.

I was obviously aware that she was right, on both counts, so you'd think I'd thank her for her maternal concern, consider it rationally and decide to take action, thereby leading to where I am today. Wouldn't you?

Hell no! I yelled at her big time. I threw all my toys out of my pram. I made her cry. I called her interfering, cruel and a hypocrite. I stomped off to my room clutching a goblet of vino and spent the rest of the week mainlining clotted cream and making snide remarks about Attila-the-fun-snatcher, and such-like.

She hasn't said much about the fact that I've not had a drink for nearly six months. Understandably, she's a little nervous about broaching any personal subjects around me. I'm wondering how long it will take, and what she'll say. If anything, ever. My dad thinks I'm on some kind of fad diet and keeps banging on about my new trim(mer) figure, bless him.

I write, in passing, about last year's hissy fit on my blog.

The thing I've learned about the sober blogosphere is that it's a really *nice* place. We're all very accepting and non-judgemental people (who are we to judge, after all?). I have admitted to some terrible things on my blog and yet everyone tells me it's perfectly okay, that they've done far worse.

So it's a bit of a shock when several readers call me out on my behaviour towards my mum. And they're totally, completely right. I have, they tell me, to apologise. Yikes.

I have to confess that the thought of saying sorry hadn't even crossed my mind. Isn't that awful? We don't really do 'talking about emotional stuff' in my family. In fact, I wonder whether the 'stiff upper lip' thing is part of the reason the British are so renowned for drunkenness. We need some way of dealing with the emotions we feel unable to display or discuss.

My reaction was: that was twelve months ago. Water under the bridge. It's obvious that I'm sorry and she was right – look at me! A stone lighter, and nearly six months sober – I clearly took it on board . . .

But saying sorry is the right thing to do. It's good karma. It's what we teach our children. And I know, from my kids, that a belated apology usually means more, and is more thought through, than a knee-jerk one at the time.

One of the cornerstones of AA is 'making amends'. In order to achieve freedom and serenity you need, they say, to make peace with the past. The eighth of the twelfth steps reads: *We made a list of all persons we had harmed, and became willing to make amends to them all* (the steps aren't exactly snappily written). So, I've been trying to find the right time to say sorry. I keep putting it off. It sticks in my throat. I'm fighting against years of conditioning.

Eventually I corner my poor mum in the kitchen.

'I've been meaning to say something to you,' I blurt out. She looks startled. Like a hedgehog in the headlights. As if I've triggered an emergency trip switch in my brain, it switches into inappropriately humorous mode as I remember one of Kit's favourite jokes: *Hedgehogs! Share the hedge!* I force my brain back to the matter in hand.

'When you told me last year that I drank too much and was too fat I was horrible to you. I made you cry. But you were right, and I'm sorry.'

'Gosh, I'd forgotten about that,' she says (probably fibbing), looking stunned but rather . . . chuffed. 'I'm sorry if I was a little blunt. But look at you now! I'm so proud of you – what willpower. You really don't want to turn into a slob.'

(I'm aware that my mum hasn't got a handle on the real issue and that her major concern was me 'letting myself go', but I don't think that matters.)

We hug. We cough in a rather embarrassed fashion. We carry on chopping vegetables, side by side, our knives hitting our boards in comfortable synchronicity, and change the subject.

But I feel a weight, that I hadn't even realised I was carrying, shift off my shoulders. And I think I made my mum really happy.

'Making amends' is about more than saying sorry – it's about putting things right. But I know that, as far as my mum's concerned, quitting the drink (and, as a result, losing the weight) is all the reparation she wanted.

So, all is good with the universe.

The only blot on the otherwise cloudless horizon is that Mum keeps creeping up on me when I'm on the laptop and, as I'm inevitably reading or writing about *booze*, I end up slamming the top down and looking shifty. She's now convinced that I'm having an affair.

An affair? When would I have the time? Or the energy? For the last eight years, since I quit working, I haven't even been able to go to the loo without someone asking where I am and banging on the door after a few minutes. How on earth would I be able to escape for long enough to *have sex*?

THE DOLPHIN

In her extraordinarily powerful eulogy to her dead husband, Sheryl Sandberg quoted a Jewish prayer: *Let me not die while I am still alive.* That's what drinking does to us. We kill ourselves slowly, drop by drop, glass by glass, bottle by bottle, when we should be living. We drown ourselves in booze, and bury ourselves under layers of flab.

In most of the drinking memoirs I've read, the authors

describe how drinking stopped them growing. To move forward as human beings we have to properly experience life in the raw. We have to learn to meet with triumph and disaster and treat those two imposters just the same.

When we drink, we don't do that; we just hide. Rather than our horizons expanding, our world shrinks. If we don't stop, it gets smaller and smaller until we've lost everything except the bottle. AA have a saying that describes this perfectly: *Alcohol gives you wings, then takes away the sky.*

That's just how I felt. Despite hanging on to the important things (so far) – my family and my home – the sky was closing in on me, and I'd lost myself. I was slowly dying while still alive.

But now, after nearly half a year of introspection and building myself back up, brick by brick, I feel like I'm standing on the edge of something. Now I can see the horizon and I have – for the first time in years – a sense of possibility, instead of hearing the clang of doors closing ringing in my ears.

I don't know what's going to happen next, but *something is.*

Today we're taking a boat trip along the Cornish coast. Bear in mind that this is not the Caribbean or the Mediterranean, it's the Atlantic, so we're dressed in head-to-toe oilskins and life jackets.

As we're waiting for the other passengers to board (the boat seats sixteen, plus the skipper), I look out across stunning Padstow Bay, listening to the call of the gulls, and think how far removed this is from my usual life. Then I hear Kit say, 'Hello Eric.'

'Who's that?' I ask him.

'You remember Eric, Mummy. He was in Mr Evans' class with me.' Eric's mum turns around and gives me a little wave.

Not so far removed from normal life at all. It turns out we're holidaying in Fulham-on-Sea.

We're a way out from shore, crashing through the waves, and I do something I haven't done since I was about ten years old. I ask the universe for a sign (yes, really). I say: *If my life is about to change in miraculous ways then send me a dolphin.*

Five minutes later and there's an effing dolphin swimming alongside our boat. *I kid you not.* Flipping Flipper! He's so close that I can see our boat reflected in his glossy, black eye.

So, watch this space, because I've wasted an awful lot of time, and it's my turn now.

SMILE AND THE WORLD SMILES WITH YOU

I've always loved the lead-up to September. It's a time of fresh starts. New, brightly polished school shoes. Well-stocked pencil cases. Catching up with old friends, and making new ones. Clean slates. Days getting shorter; shadows getting longer. The last, languid gasp of summer.

Going sober can seem very lonely much of the time, especially in the summer. It's easy to feel like the only black sheep in a flock of white. (Hang on. Surely we should be the white sheep in the flock of black?) Or the solitary lemming shouting 'How about heading away from the cliff, folks?'

But now, in these last few days of August, I feel like I'm swimming with the tide again, not against it. Everyone is putting the Pimm's back in the cupboard, preparing to get back to work and muttering about cutting back and getting fit.

So, I'm smiling a lot, and I realise how true the saying 'Smile, and the world smiles with you; cry and you cry alone' is.

We alcohol addicts do a lot of crying alone. We gradually become more and more isolated. We don't trust ourselves when we go out. We like drinking alone because there's no one to judge us. It's comfortable. We get fewer invitations, because even if we don't get inappropriately drunk, we tend to be a bit boring and self-obsessed. (We don't realise this at the time, obviously!) We repeat ourselves. We don't listen.

Back in the early nineties I read a much-talked-about book: *The Celestine Prophecy*. I don't recall a huge amount about it now, but I vividly remember the author talking about two types of people: *radiators* and *drains*.

He said that 'radiators' are people who radiate positive energy. They attract other people like bees to a honeypot. When you leave their company you feel much more upbeat and energetic than you did when you arrived. At the time *I knew* that I was a radiator. A happy, positive, glowing love bunny who everyone wanted to know.

'Drains' are the opposite. They are energy suckers. You spend time with them and you leave feeling *exhausted*. Much as you may love them and care about them, you just have to protect yourself and try not to spend too much time with them.

That's what alcohol does to us. It turns us into drains. Little self-obsessed bundles of misery. Do you remember the Snoopy cartoons? Whenever a character was miserable Schulz would draw them with a little black cloud above their heads? That was me. I just didn't see it. You don't get to that point over-night. It creeps up on you so slowly that you don't realise it's happened.

So I guess it shouldn't surprise me that things don't change straight away when you quit. Sometimes the changes are so gradual that you only see them when you look back and realise how far you've come. But slowly, slowly the clouds have dissipated. Gradually, I've stopped sucking all the energy down the plughole and started doling it out again.

Yesterday I was in Marks and Spencer buying a new, fluffy bath towel (cost: two bottles of vino). I hadn't bought a new bath towel for TWELVE YEARS! I chatted away to the cheerful cashier about the ups and downs of the school holidays. As I left she said 'It's been a *real pleasure* serving you today.' And, you know what? She wasn't just reading from the manual, she really meant it!

Then I took the dog for a walk. I passed a traffic warden writing out a ticket for some poor sod. Traffic wardens are not known for their geniality. But this one looked up at me, grinned and said 'Have a great afternoon!'

Same day, I got an email from a lady who I'd employed to do a small job for me. She wrote '*I believe in angels, and I think you are one of them.*'

I have a relatively new friend (she's known me for longer sober than drinking) who's been having a terrible time. She told me last week that I'd made more difference to her life in recent weeks than anyone else.

The combination of these big and little things made me realise, suddenly, that *I'm back to being a radiator*! I'm smiling, and the world is smiling with me.

I'm a much smilier, more chilled mother too. This time last year, very nearly seven weeks into the school holidays, I was going loopy. I was desperate for some time to myself. I was grumpy with the kids and doing a lot of yelling. I was grumpy because I was often hungover from the night before. I was grumpy because life wasn't working out the way I'd expected it to, and I was grumpy because I didn't like myself very much. But the children wouldn't have known any of that. As far as they were concerned, I was just cross with them. Their conclusion was that Mummy didn't really like spending time with them. They suspected that she'd rather be somewhere else. They weren't entirely wrong.

Now I'm no longer drinking, I'm on the same wavelength as the children. And spending time with them is a revelation. I see the world through their eyes. I see the magic in a tray of muffins rising in the oven, the suspense in a game of Cluedo (at least for the first six games) and the humour in a burping competition.

Getting three children under the age of eleven out of the door on time is hard work. In the old days, I would ask, plead, then shout (a lot) until they were all dressed and ready to go. I'd then be all stressed out and cross in the car, silently counting the days until school started.

Not now. I'm chilled. I'm in the zone. So, I say to the kids 'If anyone wants to go bowling they have to be dressed and ready by the door in fifteen minutes. Or we can just stay home. I'm easy.' I sit back with a copy of *Grazia*. Ten minutes later and they're all standing in a line, ready to go. Why on earth didn't I think of that strategy before?

We get in the car and sing to Coldplay's 'Viva la Vida' all the way. By the time we're on the fifth rendition, I realise that (finally) Gwyneth Paltrow and I have something in common: we both want to consciously uncouple from Chris Martin.

As we're queuing for our lane we have the usual discussion about our bowling 'handles' – the names that will go up on the electronic scoreboard. In a wave of confidence and optimism I decide on SUPERMUM.

Kit, who is not renowned for his spelling, fills out the form and hands it in. As I take my position, bowling ball in hand, ready for my first throw, I look up at the screen. There, for all to see, is my chosen name: SUPPERMUM.

Straight back down to earth and back in my place. One stray consonant and I've been demoted from superhero to purveyor of children's catering. Great.

THE MONTH WHEN I GO VIRAL

DAY |1|8|3|

HALF A YEAR

In the beginning, I counted in hours. Then days. Obsessively. I totally understood the maxim *One day at a time.* If I looked any further ahead than one day I panicked. *What? No more wine ever again? Can't compute. Overload . . .*

But now the days are flying past before I can count them. In fact, I totally forgot that, as of yesterday, I was SIX MONTHS SOBER. I forgot! Who'd have thought it?

Now I realise that you use 'One day at a time' until you no longer need it. It's there to stop you worrying about for ever (which, in the words of Prince, is *a mighty long time*) until you can cope with it.

And now, it seems, I can. Now, after six months, I can truly see myself never drinking again. It doesn't scare me. At all. It's liberating. Exciting. Miraculous. I'm not, I hope, being smug, or overconfident. I'm totally aware how easy it is to fall off the wagon and end up back at Day 1. I read stories about people like me doing just that all the time. I also know about the ups and downs. This time next week I could easily be a shivering wreck again.

But, the point is, right now *I am no longer scared. Or miserable. Or feeling denied.*

And today I can celebrate, because it is, finally, the start of term. Once I've dropped the children off I have a list of accumulated chores as long as my arm, but I'm sure I can fit in time to eat a giant slice of cake, listen to *Woman's Hour* on Radio 4 and maybe even read *Grazia*. Heaven.

Getting three children up on time and ready for school is a bit of a trial after seven weeks of laziness. Although we didn't leave the UK, it feels like we have major jetlag. We've been thrust into a new time zone where the day starts at 6.30 a.m. rather than 9 a.m.

It's total chaos as I try to track down Kit's new school shoe that the dog has decided to hide for fun, comb the knots out of Evie's hair and 'un-inside-out' Maddie's tights.

Somehow, with a combination of cajoling and threatening, I get everyone into the car, including the dog, who's looking forward to a brisk, long walk that doesn't involve his three siblings whining about stopping for snacks, or the loo, or to catch a rare Pokémon on *Pokemon Go*.

Not only do we arrive on time, but we're *early*! That's a first. No one else is here yet. I manage to get a parking space right outside the school gate. I really am an A* mother.

Slowly, the penny starts to drop. Three pairs of eyes swivel in my direction and Kit pipes up, 'Where is everyone, Mummy? Are you sure this is the right day?'

I use my phone to access the school website. Sure enough, we *are* early. Twenty-four whole hours early. School starts tomorrow. Bugger. I spot the deputy head, in casual jeans and jumper, heading towards the gate. I don't want him to witness my giant cock-up.

'Duck, children!' I yell as I dive down. They don't move, they just stare at me in the patronising manner that only under-twelves can manage.

'Why are we here, Mummy?' asks Maddie. 'Did you get the day wrong?'

'No, no, no,' I reply. 'I thought that, after such a long break, we should all do a *trial run*. And I'm thrilled to say you all did *really well*! Tomorrow's going to be a doddle! So, as a special treat, to celebrate it being the *last day of the holidays* I'll take you all to the movies.'

Bang go the chores. And *Woman's Hour*. And *Grazia* and the long dog walk. I'll just have to double up on the cake.

I get the children into bed as early as possible because school really does start tomorrow, and I snuggle up in bed with a hot chocolate, typing away on the blog about how it feels to be six months sober.

I write about how I'd thought that giving up booze would mean missing out, and yet the only things I've lost are the negatives, like the feeling of nagging anxiety, self-hatred and lethargy. I've lost the wine belly and the hangovers and I've killed the wine witch.

I've written about those major changes endlessly, but there are lots of little things too. So, I decide to write a list. I love lists. I've been writing a list of my desert island discs for about twenty years waiting for Radio 4 to call me up. (Unsurprisingly, my 'luxury item' used to be a case of Chablis. I need to find a new one now.)

I type *SMALL THINGS I'VE LOST*. Then add: *fear of cashiers, breath freshener, three o'clock in the morning, room spin, muffin top and Nurofen.*

Within minutes I start getting replies from some of my readers: *clinking recycling bags, drunken texts and unexplained bruises*, they suggest.

Yes! I reply, *plus dodgy minicabs, late-night fridge raids, unexplained rage, missing the end of movies, slurring and stained lips.*

More and more readers join the party, adding: *jokes about 'Mummy's wine', wardrobe malfunctions, googling 'Am I an*

*alcoholic', night sweats, make-up on the pillow and closing one
eye to read straight.*

I haven't had so much fun in ages.

DAY | 9 0 |

ALCOHOL—INDUCED RAGE

I keep coming across stories in the newspapers about celebrities getting into trouble due to fits of rage. Funnily enough,
it's never the teetotal ones and there's usually alcohol involved.
The most common incidents involve throwing mobile phones
at support staff, yelling at air stewardesses, being carted off
planes and losing it over inadequate catering arrangements.

Needless to say, I love reading these stories, because all of
us big drinkers have, in slightly less dramatic ways, had incidents of alcohol-induced rage. I remember (as, sadly, do many
of the other guests) throwing a glass of wine at my husband
(the wine *and* the glass it was in) during a row over a taxi
booking at a friend's wedding in France. Luckily, my aim was
terrible, so no lasting damage done, but sometimes these fits
of temper can have real consequences.

Years ago, when I was in the high-powered job (with the bar
in the office), I had two large glasses of wine with a colleague
at lunch. When I got back to my desk I found an email from
a very important global client asking for a number of unnec-
essary changes to the edit of the new TV commercial we'd just
shot. I fired off a reply in (drunken) high umbrage, calling him
a Neanderthal nincompoop who was obviously unable to appreciate a work of true artistic genius. This email became famous

and made me a heroine in the creative department, but it got me fired from that client's account and could easily have cost me my job.

According to my research, alcohol narrows our focus of attention, giving us tunnel vision, meaning that we become unable to take mitigating circumstances, other people's feelings or potential consequences into account if we're provoked when drunk. This means we can react violently in circumstances that we would ordinarily have shrugged off.

Also, because alcohol lowers our inhibitions, we are more likely to end up in dangerous situations, leading to potential confrontation. We get a dangerous, and false, burst of confidence. The problem is exacerbated by the fact that we are less able to process information properly and are, therefore, more prone to imagining insults (*he looked at me the wrong way, Your Honour*).

Since I quit drinking I haven't lost my temper once (well okay, maybe once or twice, but definitively not a lot). I am Zen-level calm.

Which is why events this evening come as a bit of a shock.

I'm in bed, about to drop off. John's in the bathroom. As he closes the bathroom door I hear a *whuuumph!* as the wet towel I'd recently picked up off the floor and hung up hits the floor again. Needless to say, John (who must have heard it too) pays no attention and climbs, nonchalantly, into bed.

I sit bolt upright in bed and yell 'THAT'S IT! I'VE HAD IT WITH THE TOWELS!'

John looks totally taken aback. Rabbit in headlights. There's no stopping me.

'I PICK UP YOUR TOWELS! I PICK UP EVIE'S TOWELS, KIT'S TOWELS AND MADDIE'S TOWELS. IF THE DOG USED TOWELS I WOULD HAVE TO PICK THOSE UP TOO! NO

ONE ELSE IN THIS FAMILY EVER PICKS UP A TOWEL. IF IT WEREN'T FOR ME THE WHOLE HOUSE WOULD GRADUALLY FILL UP WITH TOWELS UNTIL WE ALL SUFFOCATE UNDER WHITE FLUFFY TOWELLING!'

As I pause for breath, John puts his hand on my arm (very brave, as I am considering biting it off), and says – very quietly – 'Clare, this isn't about the towels, is it?'

I stop and think. It strikes me that while I am, obviously, and righteously, cross about the towel situation, the truth is that I am *always* cross about towels. But a dropped towel won't usually make me go stratospheric.

Evie is away on a school trip. I'm not going to see her for a whole week. The longest I've ever been without her previously is three days. I miss her. That's why I lost it.

Had I had a few drinks, I would never have realised this. I would have ignored John's intervention, which would only have increased my fury. I would have moved on from the towels, and on to my other pet hate – the way everyone leaves their dirty plates and cutlery *on top* of the dishwasher rather than inside it. I would have accused John of being a terrible husband and we both would have gone to sleep upset and angry with each other.

So, quitting alcohol doesn't make the occasional bouts of irrational rage go away, but it does help you to stop, get a sense of perspective and realise that *it's not about the towels.* Or the dishwasher. Or the catering arrangements. And that has to be better for our sanity and our relationships.

But I'd still love to know how to get anyone else in my family to *pick up a sodding, sodden towel once in a while.*

DAY | 1 | 9 | 9

SMELL

One of the strangest things about the sober journey is how the benefits just *keep on coming.* Some happen straight away – like losing the puffy face, and ditching hangovers – some more slowly. And, gradually, I've noticed that I *smell* much better. Actually, rephrase that, I *can smell stuff* much better.

(In fact, I probably *do* smell better too. I expect I often smelled of stale wine, seeping through my pores. Or sweat, after hours tossing and turning at night. Or toxic breath. Yuck. Enough already.)

I checked it out, and, apparently, drinking lots of alcohol does, over time, damage the part of the brain responsible for your sense of smell. Who knew?

I hadn't noticed losing my sniff-ability. It must have happened very slowly. But your sense of smell is totally tied in with your sense of taste. And I *had* noticed that my taste buds had dulled. I'd started adding chilli flakes to pretty much everything to give it a 'kick'. I'd even swapped my regular Heinz ketchup for the chilli version (yes, there is one! Kit picked it up once by accident and had steam coming out of his ears).

Next time you're at a dinner, watch who's adding loads of seasoning and condiments to their food – bet you it's the big drinkers. Now I can eat a simple tomato, basil and mozzarella salad, and it's like a massive taste explosion party in my mouth. That's all good. Great, in fact. But there are downsides to an improved sense of smell . . .

. . . A mouse has died somewhere in my cellar, the afore-mentioned Pit of Despair. I can't find it. (I can't find *anything* down there among all the old wooden tennis rackets, broken lamps, cables that went with long-obsolete electricals and cassette tape players that John refuses to throw away 'just in case.' 'In case of what?' you may well ask. Well, quite.) But wafts of death float up the stairs on a regular basis, making me want to vomit.

I look back at the research I did on feng shui when I was going through my sober decluttering phase (which never reached as far as the cellar, obviously). It strikes me that DEAD MOUSE has to be really tragically bad feng shui. Way worse than a picture hanging over your bed, an untidy entrance (snigger), or other feng shui cardinal sins.

I wonder where it died? Perhaps it's in my finance corner (which would explain a lot), or – even worse – my relationship corner. Yikes. Poor John.

I google 'dead mouse feng shui'. Nothing. So bad it's *not even considered.* What I did find, though, was a few mentions of dying plants and flowers. Apparently, it is *not good* to have any greenery in your house that isn't perfectly healthy as it creates the feeling that *your house is where things go to die.*

Bloody hell. If dead vegetation is so bad, what would feng shui say about my rotting rodent?

If I were still drinking I would probably be blissfully unaware of my feng shui car crash and the stench of decomposition invading my kitchen. But then I would have been unaware of pretty much everything else too. Now I've woken up and I can truly smell the coffee. And the mouse.

To delay returning home to the aroma of death for as long as possible, the children and I stop at the ice-cream van, which is parked outside the school gates, capitalising on the Indian summer. I order four 99s (one with additional strawberry sauce), and the ice-cream man does a comedy double-take.

I have to confess that I know the ice-cream man fairly well. I've bought so many ice creams and lollies from him over the years that if he sees me out and about on my own during the day he stops his van and offers me a freebie.

'Hope you don't mind me asking,' he says, 'but have you lost, like, *loads* of weight?'

'Err, yes, I have actually,' I reply.

'How did you do that?' he asks, by which point *everyone* in the queue is listening.

'I quit booze,' I said.

'Just that?' he asks, somewhat incredulously. 'No diet or anything?'

'Nope. Just the alcohol. Goes to show how much Chablis I was drinking. Ha! Ha!'

'Ha! Ha! Ha!' go all the other mums in the queue. If only they knew . . .

As I'm sitting in the car eating my ice cream up I scroll through my SoberMummy in-box and come across this email from one of my favourite readers, Jane, complaining about the stress of the new term. She says:

I get fed up with the endless school requests, usually sent the day before.

'Please send your child in wearing yellow for Roald Dahl day'. I don't have four effing yellow T-shirts! 'Please send your child in tomorrow wearing a pirate costume'. Thanks for the notice! Not to mention the mummy WhatsApp groups. 'Who would like to help me run the name-the-bear stall?'

I think I am getting cynical in my old age, but some of those PTA mums just need to get stoned and have sex.

I laugh so much that I spray vanilla-flavoured Mr Whippy all over the windscreen, just as the head of the PTA walks past.

DAY |2|0|4|

FRIENDS

One of my biggest concerns when I quit drinking 204 days ago was that I would lose all my friends. After all, who wants to hang out with a *teetotaller*? And, indeed, one of the areas of sober life that I haven't yet got to grips with is socialising.

I still find parties a bit odd. Funnily enough, I no longer find myself drawn like a magnet to the bar. I'm happy with a Diet Coke. Deliriously so if they serve a virgin mojito. But I do feel a bit 'scratchy'. Like I'm on the outside looking in. It's as if everyone else is in on a secret apart from me.

On the upside, I always get to drive home. I don't have to worry about slurring, accidentally insulting anyone, constantly having to queue for the loo or banging into furniture. I don't wake up the next morning feeling like death and dredging the memory banks to see what I have to hate myself for and where the strange bruises came from. And parties *are* getting easier, but they're still a work in progress.

I realise now that the mistake I made was to assume that most socialising has to happen at parties, or, at least, in the evening. Looking at my diary this week, I have a social event *every single day*. At least one. But I only have one drinks party. The rest are mid-week lunches with girlfriends, coffee and cake dates and long rambling dog walks. And – you know what? This type of 'socialising' is completely transforming my friendships.

When I relied on parties to catch up with friends, I found that you would only ever chat to one person for fifteen minutes. Tops. And you'd only cover the basics. Plus, once I'd had a few drinks it was *all about me, me, me.* Even if someone did give me some details about their own lives I'd forget them.

Party conversations in my neck of the woods revolve around the same general topics: children and schools. Especially the eleven-plus exams. To tutor, or not to tutor? Which/how many after-school activities to arrange. Gripes about the nanny/au pair. Then there's the dreaded house price and home improvement conversations; the problems with builders, the next-door neighbour's triple-decker basement dig-out. *Side returns* (which you won't have heard of unless you live in a Victorian terraced house). Where you're going on holiday is another favourite which doubles as an opportunity to boast about the second home, and the children's prowess at skiing/French/scuba-diving.

The other big conversational topic is gossip. I was a big fan. There's nothing that we people with dark, festering secrets love more than hearing about the imperfections of other people's lives. I especially loved tales of anyone deemed to have an addiction issue. Yay! I'd think. See – I'm not that bad. And even if I am, at least I'm not the only one. But this endless, mindless chitter-chatter, one-upmanship and gossip is bad for the soul. It's like a real-life version of Facebook, all show and no substance. And it doesn't nourish friendships.

I remember when I was a teenager, and in my early twenties, I used to spend hours with girlfriends discussing the *meaning of life.* We knew each other inside out and back to front. We'd exchange hopes, dreams and fears ad infinitum. Then, for the last decade or so, we'd just meet up at parties and spend ten minutes talking about whose au pair was secretly shagging their husband, and whether it made more sense to do a basement conversion or develop the attic.

But now, I might not be so brilliant at parties, but *almost every day* I spend an hour with a girlfriend. We talk about stuff that matters. I listen. I remember. I send them a text wishing them luck on the day of a big job interview. I take round flowers when they're not feeling well. I'm starting to be a *good friend again.*

I'd completely forgotten the truth that, with friendships, as with life, you get back what you put in. If you see your friendships as merely a source of idle gossip, then you can't rant and rave when it transpires that that's all you are to them.

The question I really should have asked myself isn't 'Will I lose all my friends?' but 'How on earth do I have any friends left?'

DAY |2|0|9|

THE OBSTACLE COURSE

After nearly seven months sober I'm starting to feel like a bit of an expert. I've read around thirty books on the topic, spent hours googling and reading blogs and, most importantly, have lived through 209 days of it. Every day I get comments on my blog and several emails from readers asking for advice, or just wanting someone to talk to who understands.

What I find most difficult is reading the stories of women (and some brave men who venture into my little corner of the blogosphere) who do the first few days *over and over again.* They do four days sober, then back to day one. They manage ten days next time, then go on a bender. Three days. Four days again. Ad infinitum.

I get it! I really do. I've been there. And you do just have to keep persevering until one day it sticks. But now, with the benefit of (more than) six months of hindsight, I just want to grab them in a big bear hug and yell 'Nooooo! You're doing the hardest part again and again, without ever making it to the good bits!' And the problem is, the longer you spend wallowing around in those early dark days of despair, the more you manage to re-enforce the idea in your subconscious that that's what sobriety is all about – hardship and denial.

There's another email in my in-box this morning from a lady in exactly that position.

How can I get past day three? I'm just so exhausted with it all. I'm completely useless. It's too hard.

So I write a post, for her and for everyone else like her. I call it The Obstacle Course and it goes like this:

Imagine you're standing in a field that you've been in for a long, long time. Initially it was beautiful – filled with wild flowers, friends, sunshine and fluffy bunnies (maybe the bunnies are a bit too much? But, hell, I'm going with it).

But, over time, it's got more and more miserable in your field. There are still some sunny days, but there's an awful lot of rain, and some terrible thunderstorms. You keep thinking the flowers are growing back, but they die before they bloom. The bunnies are few and far between.

Then you start meeting people who tell you about another field, not too far away. They've seen it. Some of them live in it. It's everything your field used to be, if not more so.

And they appreciate it so much more because they've seen what your desolate home looks like. They used to live there too.

'Hey, come and live with us!' they tell you, because they're not mean and selfish. They know that there's plenty of room at their place for everyone, and they genuinely want more friends.

You really, really want to join them. But there's a hitch. There's a huge great obstacle course in the way. You can't see the whole course, only the obstacle directly in front of you. And you can't see the promised land on the other side. You have no idea how big the course is, how long it takes to get through it, or whether you're up to it. But you know that you can't stay where you are. It's only going to get worse. So you take a leap and throw yourself at the first obstacle.

Initially it's not too hard. You've got bags of energy and enthusiasm. But, after you've been over a twelve-foot wall, through a leech-infested, waterlogged ditch, and dug under a fence with your bare hands you're exhausted. Fed up. You have no proof that this place even exists. You have no idea if you can ever make it that far, and you're desperate to go back to somewhere familiar, where you're not so tired, and cold and scared . . .

. . . so you go back to your field. And initially it's great to be home. The other people stranded there welcome you back with open arms and tell you that the alternative field doesn't really exist. You're comfortable. You know what you're dealing with. You think you can see the sun coming out and a bunny in the distance.

But you were fooling yourself. There are no bunnies left any more. The thunderstorms come harder and harder.

Eventually you throw yourself at the twelve-foot wall again. You brave the leeches again. You dig the tunnel. You make it to the fifth obstacle this time before you go back to the beginning.

You go back because you have no proof. You don't know how long it takes. You don't know if you can do it. *You're exhausting yourself by doing those first few obstacles* over and over again. *It's just* too hard.

So, if that's you, then listen to this. Because I do know. I am going to say it really loudly: **IT DOES EXIST! IT'S EVERY BIT AS GOOD AS YOU'RE HOPING. IT TAKES ABOUT 100 DAYS TO BE ABLE TO SEE IT, AND ABOUT SIX MONTHS TO GET THERE. YOU <u>CAN DO IT</u>.**

The truth is that the hardest bit of the obstacle course is the beginning. So you really don't want to keep redoing the wall, the leeches and the digging. Once you're through those, the other obstacles get easier, and they're further apart. And you get stronger, and fitter and more able to cope.

One thing to look out for is 'false summits'. Sometimes you think you've got there. You've seen no obstacles for ages, and you think THIS IS IT! Only to be confronted by a whopping great wall. (See the chapter on PAWS.) But by now you know how to scale those suckers. It's no biggie. You almost start to get a sense of achievement from making it to the other side of each one. After all, a field with no challenges at all in it would be a little . . . flat and feature-less.

So, my fellow adventurers, pack up your bags, say goodbye to your field, throw yourself at the obstacles and KEEP ON GOING! Do not look back until you get to the end!

I press 'publish' before I can change my mind. Maybe it will help someone. Perhaps they'll all think I'm slightly unhinged with my talk of rabbits and leeches and twelve-foot walls.

But then something extraordinary happens. All over the sobersphere people are talking about my field of bunnies. The link to my post is shared over and over again by people saying *read this. It will really help.* And people *are* reading it and saying *I want to get to the field of bunnies,* and then *I <u>will</u> get to the field of bunnies.*

I've gone viral. Well, maybe not entirely viral, but at least a minor bacterial infection.

THE MONTH WHEN IT ALL GOES TITS-UP

HELLO MOJO. WHERE THE HELL HAVE YOU BEEN?

We're going to a really big party tonight. It's a friend's Significant Birthday, and it looks like he's gone to town. The theme is *Game of Thrones* and the invitation, which arrived two months ago (probably by raven), was written on parchment with a wax seal.

In the 'dark drinking days' I probably wouldn't have gone. You see, it's in the country. Over an hour by car down the motorway. Going would have involved either one of us not drinking (not possible), hiring a driver to take us there and back (horribly pricey, on top of the present, costumes, babysitter, etc.) or finding somewhere to stay locally (even more expense, plus a real hassle). Back then, parties made me think of my heroine, Dorothy Parker (an alcoholic), who, at one New York speakeasy she frequented, was asked by a bartender 'What are you having?'

'Not much fun,' she replied.

But, now I'm sober, I thought *Wow, that looks amazing. I'll drive. If we leave by 12.30 a.m., we'll be back by 1.30 a.m. No problemo.*

I dress up. I root through the Wardrobe of Past Lives and Shattered Dreams, and come across a boned corset with lace arms and huge feathers round the neckline (I told you I had a wild past). I add a new, slinky black skirt and high boots, and a waist-length hairpiece (also, for some long-forgotten reason, in my wardrobe). Hello, Catelyn Stark!

As I'm now *one and a half stone* lighter than I was seven months ago, it all fits. And I look *slim.* No more wine belly. I wouldn't describe my stomach as a pancake, but it's certainly no more than a gentle hillock, an easy incline for the slightly unfit, occasional walker. Just in case I'm imagining things, I get the tape measure out again and, sure enough, my waist has gone from 36" to 33", my belly from 41" to 37" and my hips from 43" to 39". That's pretty incredible!

I'm so excited that I take a picture and, before I can change my mind, stick it on Facebook. This is significant. I don't think I have *ever* posted a picture of *myself* on Facebook.

John is looking grumpy, as he always does before a party. He wants to stay home and watch the rugby. I dress him up in a rather musty-smelling old (fake) fur coat I've dug out from the Pit of Despair, a crazy black wig and a plastic sword belonging to Kit. He looks like a cross between Jon Snow (which was the intention) and Monica Lewinsky (which wasn't). I realise that I am going dressed as his stepmother, which seems a little inappropriate, but in the *Game of Thrones* anything goes.

John drives us there, and I have a quick peek at Facebook. By the time we arrive I've had around fifteen comments saying things like *Looking HOT Mrs P!* Hot? Really? Me? But this means that, rather than slinking into the party, already half a bottle down, and heading straight for the bar (like the old days), I STRUT INTO THE MARQUEE! SOBER.

There are, I realise, actually *two* huge marquees, decked out with medieval paraphernalia. Goblets, thrones, huge banners, furs, velvets and dragons. There's snow, ice sculptures, White Walkers and wildlings. There's a dwarf (obviously), jesters, flame-throwers and a lady with a large snake (not a euphemism).

My rediscovered mojo and I have a blast.

Now, my local friends, who see me regularly, haven't commented much on my transformation. The changes have come gradually. Slowly, slowly. But most of tonight's guests haven't seen me for over a year. *I have never had so many compliments in my life!* (Except on my wedding day, when I did look genuinely spectacular, thanks to an army of professionals, a hugely expensive dress and a crash diet.)

I'm described as 'skinny' (which I'm absolutely not, but everything is relative, and I am wearing fabulous corsetry) at least ten times. A teenaged daughter of a friend says she hadn't recognised me. 'Oh, I've lost a bit of weight,' I say. 'Well yes, but *your whole face* has changed!' she replies.

I talk to everyone I know. I remember their names, and the names of their children (sounds simple, but an impossible feat when drunk, I always found). I throw some shapes on the dancefloor. (Dancing sober! Great fun! Who knew? The only problem is that a few hours in, without the anaesthetising effects of booze my feet are hurting so much that amputation feels like the only sensible option.)

While I'm dancing, wildly, surrounded by some great friends, I hear two women talking on the edge of the dancefloor. They're shouting at each other so they can be heard over the loud music booming from the speakers beside them. I'm transported back three months in time. *I know those voices.* It's Thing One and Thing Two. I look over at them and muster a smile.

'Hi Clare!' says Thing One. 'I think I might join you on the dancefloor.'

'You should,' I reply, 'after all, you can't let yourself get *boring* in your old age, can you?'

At half past midnight, I drive home, listening to the BBC World Service, John snoring, drunkenly, in the passenger seat, knowing that I'll wake up tomorrow tired but happy. In my own bed. Remembering a great night, when I insulted no one, managed not to do anything rude or embarrassing and redis-covered my mojo.

And, just to make it a perfect day, John's going to have a hangover . . .

DAY |2|2|0|

ALCOHOL AND PARENTING

I'm not a great parent. I was astounded when they allowed me to walk out of the hospital with a helpless, newborn baby twelve years ago.

'Where's the instruction manual?' I wanted to shout. 'I have no idea what I'm doing here! I'm an amateur!'

They say it takes a village to raise a child. And in the old days you would be surrounded by parents, grandparents, aunts, uncles and siblings who would all help teach you, and your offspring, how to do the growing-up thing. These days we are much more geographically spread out. We don't have the same support network of older, wiser advisors.

We muddle along, confused by the conflicting advice of the 'experts', like Gina Ford and Supernanny. We rely on our girl-friends (who are also making it up as they go along) and smug, self-righteous strangers on the internet.

Just as we start to feel like we're getting good at the whole baby thing, we suddenly have school-aged kids, and a whole new set of challenges. As we start feeling a bit more able to cope with those, BAM – they grow a foot and a crop of pimples and become smelly, hormonally challenged *teenagers*! It's no wonder we need a good glass (gallon) of vino at the end of the day.

It's only now that I see what a useless parenting prop alcohol is . . .

Putting the children to bed this evening, I realise that my house is now *peaceful*. Nobody shouts. This is a major change from a few months ago. When the children were small, I would get them into bed by 7 p.m. The bedtime routine was pretty exhausting – tea, bath, milk, nappies, stories, cuddles, etcetera, times three. But then I could sink back into an armchair, with hours of 'grown-up time' stretching ahead of me.

As the children grew up, however, bedtime got later and later, and wine o'clock crept earlier and earlier. My evenings would go something like this:

5.30 p.m. – children all home from various schools and after-school activities. Pour glass of vino while making kids supper.

6.30 p.m. – pour second glass of vino while trying, in vain, to get them to focus on their homework.

7.30 p.m. – pour third glass of wine while getting them in and out of bath and ready for bed.

By this time it would be around 8 p.m., and I'd be trying to do bedtime stories and get supper ready for the husband while getting more exhausted, frazzled and – let's face it – mildly drunk. The combination of tired, stressed and tipsy would lead, inexorably, to SHOUTING!

By the time John was back from work (at around 8.30 p.m.) I'd be yelling at the three children in rotation, desperate to get them into bed as quickly as possible so I could sit down with the husband and share a(nother) civilised bottle of vino with dinner.

But one thing I've now learned about bringing up children is that the only real way to teach them is by example. You can't tell a child not to swear, then swear like a trooper around them. You can't teach them manners and kindness if you don't display them yourself. If you show them that alcohol is necessary to have fun and to relax they'll believe it. And if you yell all the time then so do they . . .

So we did not have a peaceful house. I would yell, and the kids would all yell. At each other. At me. At their father. The mornings involved just as much shouting as the evenings, as I'd be tired and grumpy, and the getting-ready-for-school routine was all just a bit much.

But now I don't *mind* that the children aren't going to bed until 9 p.m. I *enjoy* having the extra time with them. We spend ages over stories. I teach them how to cook while getting supper ready for John. We chat about our days. I'm not constantly trying to *get rid of them.*

And mornings? I love them! I wake the children up by saying 'Wakey wakey! It's another glorious day!' I sing. I am punchably chirpy. I hardly ever shout any more. And if the children ever do, I say, very quietly, 'Please don't shout. We don't shout in this house.' And I am not being hypocritical.

If the children play up on the school run, I don't yell at them, I just park outside the school gates, wind the window down, sing loudly to whatever chart song is playing and add appropriate 1980s hand movements. This causes howls of anguish from the back seat as they desperately try to pretend that they've never met me before. (They get their revenge by shouting loudly in shops 'My mummy's forty-six!')

I am still very much a work in progress as far as parenting goes, but I have, at last, created a home that feels happy, relaxed and *peaceful.* It's still sometimes very noisy, but that's because we're laughing and dancing to bad disco music.

If anyone was ever foolish enough to ask me to write a

parenting manual, the very first page would say: *Put down the vino. It is not your friend. Alcohol and children mix like oil and water. The wine witch is not Mary Poppins . . .*

REGRETS

Often I hear people say that they are *grateful* for the years, decades even, that they lost due to alcoholism, because it made them who they are: stronger, more compassionate, more enlightened. And I think *'Really? Grateful?'* Now, if God had found it in herself to make me one of those irritating people who can have a glass of vino and then *genuinely* not want a second one (or the whole bottle), *then* I would feel grateful.

I was thinking about this when, over the weekend, we went to the movies to see *Everest,* a fabulous film about the death of eight climbers near the summit of Everest in May 1996. One of the climbers that day was an American doctor called, rather appropriately, Beck Weathers. He'd taken up mountaineering as a way of coping with debilitating bouts of depression.

When a terrible blizzard struck as the climbers were descending the mountain, Beck was left for dead by his fellow mountaineers. They believed that there was no way he would make it down the mountain alive. Beck remembers 'dying', but when the sun rose he saw a vision of his family in front of him. Beck was almost totally blind by this point, unable to feel his hands or face, one arm frozen over his head, and he hadn't eaten for three days or had any water for two.

Despite this, Beck managed to stagger and crawl back to the

nearest camp where, a second time, he was left alone by his fellow climbers in a tent to die. Again he refused to do so, and was eventually airlifted off the mountain by helicopter.

After watching the film, I read an article written by Beck himself in the *Mail on Sunday* about his experience and his life after Everest. He talks about how he lost both his hands. Then, he was sitting in a chair back home when a chunk of his right eyebrow fell off. Later, he walked down the hall and his left big toe broke off and went skittering away, followed, a while afterwards, by his nose.

You would think, wouldn't you, that Beck would feel a bit bitter? About losing so many crucial body parts. About being left for dead by his friends, not once, but twice. But no. Beck says: *Would I do it again? The answer is yes, even if I knew everything that was going to happen. I traded my hands for my family and my future. It is a bargain I readily accept. For the first time in my life I have peace. I searched all over the world for that which would fulfil me, and all along it was in my own backyard. I am a blessed individual. Even better, I know it.*

Beck *is grateful*! This made me feel incredibly humble. I still can't go as far as gratitude, but I do find that I have no regrets. Which is why I'm currently dancing around the kitchen singing along with the incomparable Edith Piaf to 'Non, Je Ne Regrette Rien'.

I'm reminded of one of my father's favourite stories. It was 1962. He was twenty-four years old, handsome (so he says), hugely talented (so everyone says), and had just been posted to Brussels by the British civil service. One evening, Dad was offered a theatre ticket by a colleague who was stuck in the office and couldn't go. It was a show at the Théâtre de la Gaîté (which was later turned into one of my favourite nightclubs, it's probably now a luxury apartment complex).

Dad knew nothing about the show, but he did know that the theatre always served a carafe of wine and a cassoulet for every theatregoer to accompany the performance (there was a wooden ledge running in front of all the seats that served as a table). Given that he was a bachelor and unable to even boil an egg, a free meal was too good an opportunity to miss.

Dad tucked into his dinner, rather hoping for a Moulin Rouge type of spectacle with lots of long legs, perky bosoms and feathers. Instead a raddled old lady stepped on to the stage, alone, and walked up to the microphone. He started to regret his decision, and to plan an early exit. Then she opened her mouth and started to sing. Only my father could end up seeing the legendary Edith Piaf *by accident*!

I look up Edith on Wikipedia. She was an alcoholic. She died less than a year after Dad saw her sing. And she wasn't the old lady he remembers. When he saw her she was *forty-six years old*. Exactly the same age as me.

Edith had a tragic life. Her mother abandoned her at birth, and she was brought up in a bordello by her grandmother and a bevy of prostitutes. Edith was blind for four years of her childhood. At seventeen she had her own daughter, Marcelle, who she abandoned, just as her mother had done to her.

Marcelle died of meningitis aged two. It is rumoured that Piaf slept with a man to pay for her funeral. The love of Edith's life died in a plane crash in 1949, on his way to meet her.

Given all of this tragedy and heartbreak, it's hardly surprising that Edith became addicted to alcohol and morphine. Despite three attempts at rehab she couldn't beat her demons. She died – at the age of forty-seven – from liver cancer.

In memory of Edith, I vow to have no regrets. Regrets can haunt you. They can paralyse you, and stop you moving forward. That's why 'making amends' is so fundamental to AA. I cannot regret a decade, or more, of my life. A lot of it was a great deal of fun. I had three wonderful children, and managed, somehow, to do a half-decent job of getting them through early childhood. My past got me to where I am now, and that's a pretty good place to be.

Funnily enough, it's not the things I *did* that I regret, but the things I *didn't do.* I'm haunted by the thought of what I might have done with my life if I hadn't lived so much of it anaesthetised.

I loved my years at university. But one moment still bugs me. It was the end of my first year. I had Part One exams coming up. I was loitering in the quad, probably with a cigarette in one hand (I was always smoking in those days), and plastic cup in the other (ditto, drinking). A couple of my fellow students turned to me and said 'Hey Clare, it's all kicking off in Berlin. They're tearing the wall down – piece by piece. We've found cheap tickets and we're going to join in. You coming?'

I was tempted, but I was broke. I had work to do. I said no. *I missed the chance to take part in a seminal moment of history.* I swore after that day, after I'd watched the television footage of the people destroying that hated monument, that I would never again fail to seize the day. And yet I've done it over and over and over again. The days just slipped through my fingers like grains of sand. But no more. Next time a wall comes down I'm going to be there.

I'd imagined that Edith's last words, as her liver killed her in a final act of revenge, would have been 'Non, je ne regrette rien.' They weren't. Her last words were 'Every damn thing you do in this life, you have to pay for.'

DAY |2|2|7|

I NEED HELP

My mum's first words when I pick up the phone are 'I'm afraid I've got some bad news.'

I feel sick. Ever since the call five years ago when my mother told me she had breast cancer, I've dreaded calls that begin like this.

'Go on,' I say, thinking *Stop, I don't want to hear this.*

'It's your aunt. She has breast cancer. It's aggressive.' I'm immediately overwhelmed by a maelstrom of emotions: relief that my mum is okay but devastated for my aunt. We discuss all the practical things – the diagnosis, what next, how everyone is coping – when all we really want to do is shout *Why, why, why? How is that fair?* My lovely, kind and selfless aunt who's never done anything to deserve this.

Unlike me. Which is when another thought starts niggling in the back of my mind: *one close blood relative with breast cancer is unfortunate. Two* (my mother and her sister) *starts looking like a pattern.* I'm furious with myself. THIS IS NOT ABOUT ME. This is about my beloved aunt, and here I am worrying about *myself.* But, once I've hung up the phone, that thought just won't go away.

So, just to shut it up, to allow me to concentrate on how I can best help my aunt, I go upstairs to the bathroom and take off my top and my bra. Now I've read all the endless articles and heard all the advice about checking your boobs regularly, and I do. I'm sure I must have done so no more than a month or two ago. In fact, I know I did, because I remember feeling

199

an odd twinge in my left boob recently, so I'd given it a good old prod and not found anything untoward.

But this time, as I work my way carefully round the lefty I swear *I can feel something.*

STOP IT. YOU'RE IMAGINING THINGS. YOU'RE GETTING HYSTERICAL.

I walk over, topless, to the bathroom mirror and look at myself. This is not something I do often. After breastfeeding three children it's just not a wise idea. Either my mind is playing tricks on me, or there's a distinct *dent* in the bottom of my left boob, right where I thought I could feel a lump. I have become oddly asymmetrical.

I start to panic. I feel sweaty and clammy and I think I may have stopped breathing. I keep checking lefty. There's nothing there – it's fine. No, wait, there is. I'm going to die.

I have the strangest sensation, as if I'm looking at myself from a different place, or a different time, and I think *This is a moment you are never going to forget. This scene, with you topless in front of the bathroom mirror staring at your strangely misshapen boob. It's the point where everything changed.* It strikes me, somewhat inappropriately, that if this image is going to be seared in my memory for ever, I should at least have cleaned the bathroom, which is a jumble of kids' toothbrushes and pastes, first.

I feel like I've turned around the telescope through which I view my life, and I've gone from gazing at wide horizons to everything being reduced down to a pivotal pinprick. I can't breathe. I'm being suffocated by a surfeit of significance.

I need to do *something* to stop myself going crazy. I can't call John – it would make it all too real, and I don't want to worry him unnecessarily. I can't call my mum – she has enough to deal with right now.

More than anything else I want a drink. I know it would magically take the edge off the fear. One or two drinks and I'd calm down, think logically, realise that I'm making a mountain out of a molehill, a cancerous tumour out of a small, benign cyst.

I go down to the kitchen. There's no wine in the fridge, but there's a half-full bottle of vodka in the cupboard. I pour a glass and stare at it. So innocuous, looking just like a glass of water, and yet, in that glass is numbness, calmness, a magical alchemy that will make all of this go away.

Then I remember Sarah Connor, Ripley, Katniss Everdeen and the Mother of Dragons. These are the kinds of moments that you can't run away from. You have to stand your ground and face them. Get your flame-thrower out and fry them to bits. Clear-headed and sober. This is when you need to be a grown-up.

So I don't turn to the booze, I turn to the experts.

I ring the GP, my clammy fingers slipping on the keys, to ask for an appointment. There aren't any available – obviously. I weep at the receptionist. I tell her I've found a lump and I'm terrified. I wait for her to tell me not to worry, to assure me that the doctor will see me straight away, given the circumstances, and tell me that I'm *absolutely fine.* She totally ignores my snivelling neediness (maybe I'm the fifth overemotional middle-aged woman with a breast lump on the phone this morning?) and gives me an appointment for Monday – *four days away.*

With shaking hands, I open up my laptop. I log on to my blog and I type the title of a post: I NEED HELP, and all the time I'm typing, I have Edith's last words going round and round in my head: 'Every damn thing you do in this life, you have to pay for'; followed, surreally, by the soundtrack of *Fame* – 'and right here's where you start paying'.

DAY |2|2|8|

WAITING

Just like the early days of not drinking, I wade my way through each hour like trudging through quicksand. Whenever I'm not with the kids I'm googling. *Breast cancer or cyst? How many breast lumps are cancerous? Indentation in breast. AM I GOING TO DIE?*

I'm constantly prodding poor old lefty, checking that I'm not just imagining it all. Is *the lump* getting bigger? Is it soft and squishy (a good thing), or hard and knobbly (not good)? My poor old boobs haven't received this much attention since the teenaged disco years, and back then they were a completely different kettle of fish (can one describe one's boobs as a kettle of fish?), all pert and exuberant and devoid of strange indentations.

Having not told anyone IRL (as the kids would say) what I'm going through, the blog is my lifeline. I've had loads of comments from women all over the world, holding my hand, wishing me luck. *I've had the same thing,* many of them say, *it was fine! Eight out of ten breast lumps are benign. It's our age. It's hormones. You'll be okay. You've helped so many people – nothing bad is going to happen to you. We're thinking of you. We're praying for you.*

I'm too on edge to eat, so I'm surviving on coffee and Beck's Blue (I've drunk six of them today). While the thought of getting totally lost in a bottle of vino is still horribly tempting, I know that allowing myself to ignore the situation is not a good idea. This is something I have to deal with. I need to be strong. I need to be sober. I repeat those words like a mantra. One thing the last seven months has taught me is that there is no problem in life that cannot be made worse by alcohol. Thank goodness for the children and their familiar routine, which keeps me away from the internet research and self-examination for hours at a time.

My other distraction technique is planning the service for my funeral (standing room only, lots of people weeping). It's like a more morbid version of my old game of deciding on my desert island discs. Strangely therapeutic.

John gets back from work. Relatively early – there's a first.

'Why didn't you tell me?' he says. He's read my blog.

I cry. He hugs me and tells me it's all going to be fine. I get tears and snot all over his smart work jacket. He gives me the same statistics – it's terribly, terribly common. Most lumps are benign. (He's obviously been googling too.)

I know I know I know. And the terror *is* beginning to lift a little. It's all going to be okay. My mum and my aunt were in their seventies when they got breast cancer. I'm only forty-six. I'm fit and healthy. I'm never sick. I've not been to the GP for *years* apart from with one or other of the kids. This is just a salutary reminder that we should never take anything for granted and to make the most of every minute. It's a well-timed wake-up call, and next week everything's going to go back to normal.

By way of distraction, I go to town with family supper. Evie, Kit and Maddie get into the spirit of things while laying the table. We have our wedding china and the – rarely used – silver cutlery out, plus a whole candelabra.

The five of us sit down, and I realise that the empty sixth place is occupied by a malevolent ghost – *the lump,* sitting there, laughing at me for thinking I could make him go away. So, to misquote Leonard Cohen, I tie him to the kitchen chair,

I break his throne and cut his hair. Then I forget about him.

The children have momentarily suspended hostilities and are being nice to each other. Kit even eats some vegetables. I'm drinking the inevitable Beck's Blue (I should buy shares). John's drinking red wine.

Then Kit leans across the table to grab something (probably some ketchup to hide the taste of the aforementioned vegetables) and he accidentally . . .

. . . knocks John's glass of red wine right into my face.

There's a stunned silence (a most unusual event in our house). I sit there with a whole glass of fine Tuscan Barolo dripping off my nose and all over my hands. I fight the instinct to lick my fingers.

'Well, that's really not very fair, is it?' I say as they all fall about laughing.

Positive thought for the day: if I have to have both boobs lopped off, then perhaps they can do a reconstruction and give me *pert ones*!

DAY | 2 | 3 | 1 |

VISIT TO THE GP

I'm feeling strangely calm. I know that the GP will give me lots of reassuring statistics and tell me she's ninety per cent sure it's all going to be fine, but best send me for some checks *just to be on the safe side.* I just have to get through the next couple of hours and then I'll feel much better about the whole situation.

Only that's not how it goes.

When I lived with the trainee doctors after leaving university, our favourite TV programme was *Casualty*. We'd watch all the opening scenes and lay bets with each other on who was going to die this week. Based on the reaction of my GP, had I been watching this consultation on an episode of *Casualty*, I'd have given my character no more than a few months to live. Sorry love, you're not going to be in next week's episode. Don't give up the day job.

She doesn't give me any reassuring numbers. She doesn't tell me it's all going to be fine. She looks rather concerned. She says 'I'm rather concerned.' She doesn't like the feel of my lump (which, it turns out, isn't in my imagination), she doesn't like the 'family history', she doesn't like the dented boob.

The damn woman doesn't even ask me how much alcohol I drink. The only bit of this consultation I was looking forward to was being able to say *nothing. Not a drop.*

'Most breast lumps are benign, aren't they?' I say, feeding her the script.

'Mmmm,' she says, not meeting my eye and tapping away on her keyboard, 'I'm giving you an urgent referral.'

'So when can I have an appointment?' I ask, feeling sick.

'It'll take three weeks,' she replies. THREE WEEKS? ARE YOU KIDDING? I THOUGHT YOU SAID URGENT?

My allocated ten minutes is up, and I leave clutching my referral letter, which contains descriptors like 'craggy' and 'tethered' (which I know from my internet research are *not good* adjectives), and feeling like I've been hit by a bus.

I get home and pour it all out on my blog. Then, a couple of hours later, my phone rings. It's my friend Sam. I haven't seen her since our lunch when I was celebrating 100 days. It feels like a lifetime ago. I make a superhuman effort to sound cheerful.

'Hello, gorgeous! How are you doing?' I trill, like a hyper talk-show host who's trying too hard to reverse her falling ratings.

She cuts to the chase. 'Clare, you know I put you in touch with my friend Jenny who needed some help with quitting the booze? Well she called me after reading your blog this morning. I know what's going on. Let me help.'

I start sobbing.

'I'm going to make some calls, then I'll phone you right back.'

And you know what? Within a couple of hours later she's fixed me an appointment with one of the best boob guys in London, which, it transpires, John's work insurance will pay for. It's tomorrow.

'It's all going to be fine,' she says. And maybe it is. But if it isn't, at least it'll be not fine *quickly*. And I am so very grateful to my amazing friend, who didn't just call with platitudes but actually did something immensely helpful, and I'm so grateful to my blog, which allowed my silent cry for help to be heard.

DAY |2|3|2|

THE CANCER CLINIC

If you ever have the misfortune to have a breast cancer scare, then try not to do it at half-term, when the kids are all at home wondering where on earth Mummy has gone. I would also suggest avoiding Breast Cancer Awareness Week.

Now, Breast Cancer Awareness Week is, obviously, a wholly good thing *unless*, as in my case, breast cancer is something you're trying desperately hard not to think about. I'm aware already! Painfully so! I do not want to see your irritating pink ribbons and perky pink balloons everywhere I go, nor do I want to find 'My breast cancer hell' stories in every magazine I pick up, when I'm trying to take my mind off the whole damn thing. Grrrrrr.

My wonderful mother is looking after the children at home while John and I are at the cancer clinic, which means I've had to tell her about *the lump,* so she's now supporting a sister *and* a daughter.

We're in the waiting room, and I'm distracting myself by looking around at my fellow patients. There's one sporting a cheerful headscarf. She has no eyebrows or eyelashes. Another one has a very short, curly hairdo. There are a few terribly smartly dressed ladies reading magazines who look as if they've just popped out in their lunch hours for a routine, non-stressful, boob check and a couple of women like me looking, frankly, terrified.

The walls of the clinic are covered in paintings of 'soothing scenes'. This irritates me even more. Do they really think that a cancer diagnosis would feel any better because you get to look at a *waterfall*?

'CLARE POOLEY?' booms the receptionist. It's time to face the music.

We're ushered through to Mr Big's office. This man has dealt with hundreds of thousands of potentially dodgy breasts. He is, they say, a genius. He explains that he'll do a quick examination, then I'll be given an ultrasound, mammogram and, if necessary, a biopsy. Before we leave here today we will know, in broad terms, what we're dealing with.

I go behind a curtain to strip off while John, Mr Big and the nurse wait, then Mr Big cops a feel. I am, I tell myself, in great hands. Literally. I'm not expecting any prognosis at this point, that's what the mammogram and ultrasound are for, so I'm utterly and completely floored when after a matter of seconds he says, with no preamble, as if he's just got all his numbers and is declaring a BINGO, 'It's breast cancer.'

Fuck.

I guess he doesn't have the time for much of a bedside manner, and the nurse is obviously used to this kind of situation as she rushes forward with a box of tissues and a sympathetic face. But I don't cry. I'm far too stunned for that. I just feel numb.

John and I go back to the waiting room. I say nothing, just sit there staring at the paintings of effing beaches and sunsets. John reads the paper. I kid you not. He's turning the pages and everything. I want to yell at him 'Don't you care that your wife and the mother of your children MIGHT DIE?!? Why aren't you wailing and crying and cursing God?' But I'm far too British, and I know that he cares, deeply, and that this is just his way of dealing with things. BUT I STILL THINK HE'S AN ASSHOLE.

Mr Big, with just a few words, has sucked everything out of my world, leaving a vacuum. All the thoughts that usually swirl around my head (*Does Maddie need new school shoes? What am I going to cook tonight? Brexit! Did I pay the gas bill?*) have disappeared, leaving just me and my malignant tumour. I wonder if they'll ever come back, or if my tumour will just expand and expand and fill up everything with its malevolent mass.

I go for the mammogram, where they squish my boobs one at a time into a machine that resembles a giant sandwich toaster. I'm never going to be able to make a cheese toastie again. Then I have an ultrasound, which is just like one of those prenatal checks without any of the joy. Finally, they plunge a whopping great needle into my boob to remove some cells for biopsy.

Once I'm off the end of the conveyor belt I'm called back

into see Mr Big, who tells me that he was, of course, absolutely correct in his initial diagnosis. (Ooh, isn't he clever?) I have breast cancer. As far as they can tell, it is early stage.

The breast nurse takes over and does lots of empathy and reassuring statistics. *Ten years after diagnosis eighty per cent of breast cancer patients are still alive. There's no sign yet of any spread to your lymph nodes. You probably won't need a mastectomy, just a lumpectomy. We have a cold cap treatment so you might not lose your hair. Do you have any questions?* Yes! Hundreds!

'No,' I say.

'You'll need to come back for your biopsy results in a few days' time, at which point we'll be able to discuss your treatment plan in more detail. In the meantime, why don't you go home and have a stiff drink?'

Oh ha bloody ha.

I don't remember how we got home. No idea. I do remember trying to communicate to my poor mother that *all is not okay,* while simultaneously reassuring the children that *everything's perfectly fine and Daddy and I have had such fun on our special mid-week date.*

As soon as I can, I escape with the laptop and log on to my blog. There are about fifty messages from amazing women all over the world, checking in on me, waiting for the news that it was, as expected a cyst, a fatty lump, something benign. I tell them that it isn't. But I also tell them that I have *no desire whatsoever* to drink. One of the only things I can imagine that's more terrifying than a cancer diagnosis is a cancer diagnosis with a hangover. The only thing worse than a sleepless night prior to my next appointment would be a sleepless night with the alcohol horrors thrown in.

There's nothing better than facing your own mortality to

make you realise that you don't want to blot out a *single minute* with alcohol, or to waste another morning feeling below par. I'm sure that the reason I'm able to remain (relatively) positive rather than being horribly depressed is because I am sober.

Then, in order to cheer up myself and my readers, I write a list of seven reasons to be positive:

1. I have one of the best consultant breast surgeons in the country.
2. They are pretty sure that it is STAGE 1 (or early stage 2, as my lump, at around 2cm, is on the borderline of both) – which, as cancers go, is a *very good one to have.*
3. One of the best ways to ensure that you don't get breast cancer, or (in my case) don't get it again, is *to not drink alcohol.* And I've ticked that one off already.
4. Next time someone annoys me by grilling me as to why I'm not drinking I can say *because it doesn't go well with chemotherapy,* which will really shut them up good and proper.
5. The recommended way to deal with cancer treatment is to take it *one day at a time. Baby steps.* Stay in the moment – don't look ahead. Face your emotions. And after the last (nearly) eight months I have a postgrad degree in all that stuff.
6. What better way to support my aunt during her cancer treatment than to *join in?*
7. I have the support of a fabulous family, and the constant distraction of three amazing kids who can always make me smile.

So, I tell them, please don't feel sorry for me, just do me a favour and think *If Clare can stay sober while having part of her boob hacked off, then the rest blitzed with lasers and soaked in poison, then I jolly well can too.* (And make sure you check your boobs regularly. My quick once-over when I heard about my aunt's diagnosis probably saved my life.)

Forcing myself to be upbeat on the blog, and the resulting wave of love and support that envelops me like a giant virtual hug, makes everything seem much better.

I can hear a gale blowing outside. The temperature seems to have dropped several degrees over the last few days. Winter is coming. As I try to fall asleep there's one thought plaguing me: *That sodding dolphin lied to me.*

DAY 2 3 4

SPREADING THE WORD

I've still told very few people that I quit drinking seven months ago. If you stop smoking you shout it from the rooftops and everyone congratulates you and treats you like a hero. Quit drinking and they think you're odd, and treat you like a leper.

However, I've discovered that getting breast cancer is way better in the sympathy stakes (although not so good in other ways, obvs). Even though cancer isn't exactly something you *choose* to have, you're immediately defined as brave and coura-geous. Ironic, as I'm actually terrified, and if I could turn tail and desert the field of battle then I absolutely would.

I've told a small handful of close friends and family about the diagnosis in person, but I really can't face having to do that conversation over and over again; nobody enjoys it. But, at the same time, I don't want to leave the jungle telegraph to do the work, to have everyone whispering about me in the school playground and avoiding me because they don't know whether I know that they know.

So I write a group email. I make it matter-of-fact and upbeat. I tell everyone what's happening and ask them to remain totally positive and normal in front of the kids (who, at this point, are blissfully unaware of the whole situation). Then I send it to all my good friends, the children's form teachers and the mums at the school gate.

Then, I decide that if I'm going to have to deal with this one, I may as well milk it. Yesterday I got a parking ticket. I always – on principle – fight parking fines. I rarely have a leg to stand on, but that's beside the point. So I sit down and write to the local parking authority:

Dear Sir/Madam,
re: Parking Contravention Notice XXXXX
I do apologise. I accidentally parked in a bay that was temporarily suspended. I misread the date on the sign. It was entirely my fault, and I put your people to some trouble having to tow my car to an adjacent bay.
However, the reason for my mistake was that I had just received a cancer diagnosis and my head was all over the place. I realise that this does not mean you should cancel the fine, but – if you were to – it would restore my faith in humanity.
Should you wish to verify my story, please do call Mr Big at the London Breast Clinic.
Go on – make my day. I could do with some good news.

Kind regards,
Clare Pooley

Now I'm on a roll. I open an email from the PTA asking if I'd run one of the stalls at the school christmas fete (which John calls the fete worse than death). I do this every year. I've done hot dogs, tombola, the book stall, meet Father Christmas, you name it. It's a lot of work, and every year I think *maybe someone else could do it this time.* So I send a reply.

> *Many thanks for your email. I'd love to help out, but I'm afraid I'm a bit up to my eyeballs at the moment dealing with breast cancer. I'm sure you understand, and I wish you the very best of luck with the fete.*

Every cloud has a silver lining.

 DAY 2 3 5

MRI

Two days after the breast cancer diagnosis and it's started to sink in. To distract myself, I take Evie shopping on the King's Road. I'm doing fine until we pass one of my favourite shops. It's a boot shop that has been there for about thirty years. It always has kick-ass cowboy boots in the window and it's – quite brilliantly – called R. Soles. (Say it out loud.)

Now R. Soles is gone. Boarded up. And I suddenly feel unbearably sad. Evie (who still knows nothing about the whole cancer thing) can't understand why I'm weeping in the street over a boot shop closing down. She's mortified. (At the age of eleven there's no fear greater than one of your friends happening upon your mother having a breakdown on a busy street in

Chelsea and posting the damning evidence on Instagram.) But, obviously, it isn't about the boots.

Now I have to go back to hospital for an MRI scan. None of this is as simple as it sounds, as it involves finding someone to look after Evie, Kit and Maddie, who are still in the middle of a two-week half-term. John's taken a half-day off to hold the fort at home, but that means me going to hospital by myself.

I can already see the next few months requiring more of the endless juggling, favour pulling and passing the poor kids from pillar to post, when all they want is their mum to be there, as usual, acting normal.

The MRI scan basically involves lying on my front with my boobs in two giant buckets (made for better endowed ladies than I), then being pushed into a tunnel resembling something out of *Star Trek*. I have to lie still for forty-five minutes, so I close my eyes and try to sleep, but it's so noisy it's like trying to snooze in the middle of a motorway or building site.

As I sit on the tube on my way home, a giant wave of general *bleurgh* hits me. Will I ever get to see the end of *Game of Thrones*? I feel like a whoopee cushion without its whoop. Silent tears start dripping down my face. This sort of behaviour in the country that invented the stiff upper lip is generally not acceptable, and is likely to get you arrested or sectioned. Luckily, the general code of conduct on the tube is to *ignore everything and everyone. Pretend you haven't seen it* (whatever 'it' is).

(I once saw a man on the tube dressed in a pin-striped suit, expensive, brightly polished brogues and carrying a leather brief-case, during morning rush hour. He'd obviously been on a bender the night before as he'd gone green. Everyone sitting around him was looking nervous. Eventually he put his briefcase on his lap, opened it, vomited into it, closed it again and carried on as normal. No one said a word).

So here I am, weeping on the tube, being ignored like the vomiting banker, and the wine witch is having a field day: *No one would blame you if you had a drink! It's **medicinal** for f***'s sake. When you quit you never expected **this** to happen . . .*

I really, really need a drink. I need to take the edge off. I need to escape for a while. I need to give myself *a treat*, and since I've completely lost my appetite, chocolate cake just doesn't cut it any more. But, at the same time, I know that I need a drink like a hole in the head. Because just one drink wouldn't even *begin* to hit the spot. It would be a whole bottle. And then it would be a whole bottle every day until this has all gone away, which – even in the best-case scenario – is months into the future.

And there's nothing that breast cancer likes more than alcohol . . .

So, I use the old 'early days of sobriety' trick. I have a warm bath and go to bed early with a hot chocolate and a crappy novel. But, after months of sleeping like a log, I'm now becoming reacquainted with my old friend: 3 a.m.

I've been awake for hours fretting about my meeting with Mr Big for the MRI and biopsy results later today. I just don't want the news to get any worse. The MRI could show more tumours growing in my boobs. The biopsy could reveal a horribly aggressive strain of cancer that is dividing and multiplying like crazy. I go on some breast cancer support forums, which quite quickly convince me that *I am going to die and my children will be motherless.*

Googling, I decide, is not a good idea. So instead I check my SoberMummy email account. There are lots of incredible emails sending love and support and wishing me luck. Then I find an email from Elizabeth. Elizabeth had mailed me a few weeks ago saying this:

I'm drinking a bottle of 12.5% red wine a night and would love to be one of those 'normal' one glass with dinner people, but I'm an all or nothing girl. When I smoked, I smoked thirty a day. Now I haven't touched a cigarette for eleven years but I have another crutch in red wine. I will stop one day and I read your blog every day. So please don't stop blogging because one day will be day one of never again.

And now there's another email from her. I open it up and start to read:

I have just read today's blog and I really feel for you. I know exactly what you're going through. I found a lump when I was forty-two (sixteen years ago) and it turned out to be cancer. What I can tell you is that the waiting is far worse than anything you have to come. The not knowing, the terrifying scenarios that play in your head every single second of the day far out-terrify the outcome. I don't know what else to say, because whatever I say won't help while you are in this horrible fog of doubt. All I can tell you is the truth. You are going to be fine. I know this because (a) I've been there and (b) I'm a nurse :-)

I am just one of so very many people thinking of you because you have done so much for so many. If anyone deserves good luck it is you. Keep dreaming your dreams because there is a future for you and your lovely family and this is just a blip in that wonderful future. Dolphins never lie.

And those incredible words, from someone I've never met, mean more than I can possibly express.

DAY 2 3 7

'MUMMY'S GOT CANCER'

So, here's the scoop: I have a 22mm, grade 2, lobular invasive carcinoma. On the upside, I only have *one* tumour – righty is completely clear, and there's nothing else in lefty. Grade 2, while not as slow-growing as a grade 1, is a damn sight better than a ferocious grade 3. I'm also HER2 negative and ER and PR positive, which means I can be treated with the wonder drug tamoxifen. My lumpectomy is scheduled for a week's time, and shortly after that (once they have the results of the lump and sentinel node biopsies) I'll have meetings to discuss chemo-therapy and radiotherapy.

As far as they can tell, the cancer's not spread anywhere else. If it does go beyond the breasts and the lymph nodes, it's known as 'secondary breast cancer', or Stage 4 breast cancer, and if I've got that I'm toast. It's incurable. They're sending me for a PET scan on Monday 'just to be sure'.

So, today I have a day off the tests, but I have an equally terrible chore ahead. Empathetic Breast Nurse has insisted that we tell the children I have cancer. They are, she says, bound to overhear a conversation otherwise and will panic. If we're not upfront and honest with them from the beginning they will always worry about what else we're holding back.

I have to take Evie to the orthodontist today to talk about getting her teeth straightened, so I've said I'll tell her, leaving

John to tell Kit and Maddie (who at six and eight won't need as much information).

Somehow I get through the orthodontics consultation. The dentist gives us all sorts of detail about options, timings, costs and next steps – involving getting specialist X-rays done. I nod away like the organised, efficient mother that I am, and take in *absolutely nothing.* I have, literally, no idea what she's just said. Note to self: book appointment with another orthodontist in a few months' time.

On the way home, as we walk across the park, Evie's chattering away about school. I'm waiting for her to pause so I can take the plunge.

'Fun fact!' she says. 'My cookery teacher's a lesbian.' I just love the fact that something that in my day would have caused a total scandal has now been relegated to 'fun fact'.

'Good for her,' I reply. Then, taking a deep breath, 'Evie, you know I've been having a lot of meetings and appointments recently? Well, it turns out that I have a little lump in my boob, and it's cancer. I know you'll have heard about cancer and it sounds really scary, but what you should know is that talking about "cancer" is like talking about "a virus". A virus can be anything from flu to Ebola, and cancer can be an easily curable one, or a really nasty one. The good news is that Mummy's cancer is a *good one.* Breast cancer is really easily fixed these days and I have the most clever doctors on the case with the very best medicine. *It's all going to be fine.'*

'So, you're not going to die?' Asks Evie, in an uncharacteristically small voice

'Ha ha ha ha. Goodness, no. How could I possibly do that and leave your father in charge? Don't be ridiculous. Do you remember that time we got stopped at passport control and they asked him what Kit's birthday was just to check that we weren't travelling on forged passports, and Daddy couldn't remember? Nope, there's no way I'm going anywhere!'

And I'm thinking *please, please God, let that not be a lie.*

'We knew something was up,' says Evie, who is a bright cookie. 'Kit, Maddie and I have been talking about it. We thought you were having another baby. We've been arguing about what to call her. I voted for Willow.'

Good grief. I'm not exactly happy about the cancer thing, but at least it doesn't involve nappies and breastfeeding. Or having to call a child *Willow*.

'How did it go back here?' I ask John when we get home.

'Surprisingly fine,' he replies. 'Kit wants to know if there'll be loads of blood and Maddie asked if we can keep the lump in a jar on the mantelpiece.'

The kids have gone to sleep, and I do something I swore I'd never do, and I swear I'll never do again. I sneak into Evie's room and find her diary. I want to check how she's *really* taken the news. I find the most recent entry. *Mummy has breast cancer,* she's written, *but she's got some great doctors and she's not going to die, so it's all okay.*

Phew. Job done.

DAY |2|3|8|

FRIENDS (AGAIN)

They say that a cancer diagnosis teaches you who your real friends are. It's true. Bizarrely, I haven't heard a peep from a couple of my oldest friends since I sent the 'I've got cancer' email. I'm sure it's not because they don't care, it's just that they don't know what to say, or that they're so scared of the whole C-word thing that they can't bear to think about it. In contrast, there are a few women who I barely know who have been extraordinary.

I called one of the class mums, Lucy, a few days ago to let her know that I might not be able to make a mums' night out. I tried really hard not to get overemotional on the phone as I've only recently met her, through our sons who are great friends. I failed. Ten minutes later and she was standing on my doorstep, having dropped everything and climbed on her bike in order to give me a big hug.

Then there's Harriet. Again, I don't know Harriet that well. We met when two of our children were at the same nursery school. But Harriet was one of the first people I told about *the lump* as her mum died of breast cancer, and something told me that she'd be able to help. She's been amazing. She calls or texts me several times a day, just to see how I am, or to make me laugh.

So, today, when I get to the point when I can't carry on pretending that *everything is okay* in front of the children, I call Harriet and ask her to meet me in the local park so I can have a good howl away from my kids and hers.

I've discovered that crying is incredibly therapeutic. I feel like a pressure cooker. The steam builds up and up until I'm about to explode, then I have a really good weep and it's like releasing the pressure valve. Nature's safety mechanism: far healthier than downing a bottle of vino.

I get to the park ten minutes early and stand there, weeping like a madwoman, watched by my bemused terrier. Out of the corner of my eye I spot someone waving at me. Oh bollocks. It's one of the school mums. I don't know her name, and I don't think we've ever spoken, but I know her by sight. I've always been a little in awe of this mum as she looks a bit like an ex-rock chick and, at a school where everyone calls their children names like Sebastian and Benedict, hers are called, quite brilliantly, Spike and Buster.

She's walking towards me with her dog, not having realised yet that I have mascara all over my face and am covered in snot and tears. I hastily wipe my face and distract myself with this thought: *If your children are called Spike and Buster, what do you call your dog?*

'Keith! Sit!' she says to the dog. Keith! That figures.

'Are you okay?' she asks, and I end up telling her everything. She gives me a hug and I have the feeling I've made a new friend. Jane.

As Jane and Keith head off towards home I spot Harriet walking towards me clutching a parcel.

'It's for you,' she says. I unwrap the box to find the most gorgeous leather-bound notebook.

'It's so you can write down everything the doctors tell you in your consultations,' she tells me, 'so you don't forget anything.'

Only a really great friend realises that there are few situations that can't be improved by great stationery.

DAY 239

DEALS WITH THE UNIVERSE

I had my PET scan today. They inject you with a radioactive fluid and then stick you in a CAT scanner. The doctor operating the scanner can then see any tumours in your body glowing on the screen.

My doctor is gorgeous. I try not to flirt, as being flirted at by a woman twenty years older than you, dressed in a hospital gown and slippers and with (at least one) cancerous tumour, must be a frightening ordeal. He hands me a CD-ROM.

'Give this to your consultant tomorrow,' he says, 'and best of luck with everything.'

I know he knows. He's seen *inside* my body. I'm desperately trying to read his expressions. Relief? Pity? Horror? Am I *riddled*? I have a fear of the adjective 'riddled', which has replaced 'gusset' as my least favourite word.

'Don't forget, you're radioactive for the next few hours, so don't go near any children. Or pets.'

So I go home, feeling like an evil version of the Ready Brek boy, and have to explain to three upset children – and a confused dog – that there will be no cuddles tonight.

I go to bed and, like I did when I was a child, and would promise to eat all my Brussels sprouts if Father Christmas would bring me a Sindy doll or a Girl's World, I do a deal with the universe.

Dear Universe,

If I find out tomorrow that my cancer is 'localised' and has not spread, I promise to:

1. *Never, ever envy the lives or possessions of other people. I will always remember that love, family and health are truly the most important things in life, and that if you have those you are utterly blessed.*

2. *Make the most of every day and every moment. To treasure every bedtime story, hug, family meal, shared joke – all those little moments that make life special.*

3. *Be the sort of mother, wife and friend who others can rely on in a crisis, the one they turn to first. To be their rock*

when they need one, as people have been for me. And I'll help my children to grow up strong and wise, so that they can look after themselves when I'm no longer here.

4. *Look after and respect my body. Our bodies are incredible machines, but they need us to keep them safe. I will never again fill my body with toxins and poisons (although chocolate is fine, and I'm not about to start posting recipes for kale smoothies).*

5. *Give back. I have spent most of my life focusing on ME. Through my blog, and through random acts of kindness, I will make sure that every day I give something back.*

But, if it's spread, and I'm told to put my affairs in order, then all bets are off, universe. I'll look up at you, cursing, from the gutter, empty vodka bottle in hand.

Only kidding.

I cheer up a bit when I discover that someone has found my blog by typing 'Real Mummy's Massive Tits' into Google. I don't imagine that my blog is what they were looking for. Then I find this from a lady in America:

Thinking of you every day SM. Just wanted you to know that my church prayed for your recovery on Sunday and we're not talking about a few dusty pews half full of elderly folk (no disrespect to old people intended!). This was a 200+ congregation, so get ready because I believe good things are about to happen. Hang in there. Jill.

I'm overwhelmed.

DAY |2|4|0|

THANK YOU

If someone had told me two weeks ago that I'd feel grateful for having a cancerous breast tumour I'd have thought they were crazy, but here I am thinking . . .

HALLELUIA! IT'S JUST ONE MALIGNANT BREAST TUMOUR!

The scan showed nothing else. It's not gone anywhere. Just sitting happily, minding its own business in the bottom left quadrant of the lefty. And as of Friday it'll be gone. Off to the lab in a jar. And I can get on with chemo (if they decide I need it) and radio, and blitz the hell out of any stragglers.

Since I can't have a glass of champagne to celebrate, I have bought two boxes of Matchmakers (one orange, one mint flavour), which I'm going to eat until I feel physically sick.

DAY |2|4| |

FAREWELL, FAITHFUL FRIEND

I'm feeling a little tearful tonight as I prepare to say farewell to a fair old chunk of my left boob. I'm exhausted, so, as it's Halloween, John has taken the children out trick-or-treating. As I wave off my little witch, pumpkin and evil scientist, I promise that I'll stay by the door to hand out sweets to visitors. As soon as they've gone I turn out all the lights and sneak up to bed, ignoring all the demons outside as I wrestle with the ones in my head.

The boobs have stuck by me, through thick and thin. They started life all perky and upbeat. The life and soul of the party, and massive attention seekers – rather like me. Then they got a bit battered by life, and by looking after three children. A little older and droopier, but still able to have a good old flirt when helped by a hefty bit of underwiring.

After tomorrow, they'll never look the same. Lefty will always be a vivid reminder of a battle fought and – I hope – won.

Thanks to knocking the vino on the head (nearly) eight months ago, I'm going into the operation fighting fit. My BMI is smack bang in the middle of the 'normal' range, and I can happily tick 'non-smoker' and 'non-drinker' on the pre-assessment forms.

But here's my guilty secret: *I'm really looking forward to the morphine.* A legitimate, medicinal purposes only, mind-altering substance. Now that's got to be a bonus.

To take my mind off the impending operation, I check my emails and I find this, from the lovely Elizabeth, the cancer-survivor-and-nurse who mailed me just after my diagnosis. She says

> We find the people we are meant to find, and, as a result, come tomorrow, when you lose a bit of boob, I'm going to give up my wine habit. It seems like as good a day as any to rid myself of a bad habit while you rid yourself of bad cells.

Go girl!

THE MONTH WHEN I TALK CHEMO

DAY |2|4|5|

RECOVERY

So, three days ago I was in hospital waiting for my lumpectomy. A lovely anaesthetist came over to discuss the operation. 'Then I'll start the anaesthetic, and you'll feel a bit woozy – like you've just had a couple of glasses of wine,' he explained.

I tried hard to look nonchalant. You're not supposed to look excited about being knocked out and operated upon.

'Once you've come round, the nurse will give you some oral morphine for the pain. Not too much, or it'll take you longer to get up and about and back home . . .'

After the nightmare two weeks I'd had, the idea of some 'obligatory' oblivion was incredibly tempting. Almost (but not quite, obviously) worth losing part of a boob for. An hour later, I was all gowned, stretchered and waiting to go in. The anaesthetist worked his magic. We were chatting away when suddenly I felt incredibly light-headed, and found it almost impossible to finish my sentence. It was like the middle bit of a great party . . .

. . . then I was in the recovery room and they were giving me a syringe full of morphine. And I was thinking: *Hello numbness. I remember you! Hello, nothing-really-matters, so good to see you. Waaay haaay pink, fluffy cloud, give me a hug.* All was well with the world. For the first time in weeks I wasn't scared. I was all wrapped up in a feather-light duvet of lassitude.

I went home a few hours later, told everyone, at length,

exactly how much I loved them, then slept like a log. Everything was hunky-dory.

Until now. When it isn't.

I go for a walk in the park, in my fetching American tan surgical support stockings, with Evie and the dog. I probably walk too far, so soon after an operation. Then a bird shits on my head. I kid you not. It's so big I think for a moment I've been hit by an acorn. Evie reminds me that it's supposed to be good luck, but it feels like the final indignity. And I remember the small print the anaesthetist had given me about the post-morphine blues. (I've never been one to dwell on the small print.) And I'm thinking: *Hello utter despair. I remember you! Hello irrational anger. Welcome back. Oh, self-loathing! You've shown up to join the party.*

Then, with total inevitability, the wine witch pops her head round the door and says *I have just the thing to take the edge off . . .*

Alcohol, morphine, it's all the same. What goes up must come down. I've moved on to paracetamol.

| DAY | 2 | 4 | 8 |

WHEN LIFE THROWS YOU LEMONS

I was a 'high-functioning' alcohol addict. I never (well, hardly ever) dropped a ball, my guard or (God forbid) my knickers. I kept the ship afloat pretty well on a bottle of wine a day. I now realise this was only possible because my life was blessed. I have a great marriage, happy, healthy children and active parents. We're solvent (most of the time), and relatively secure.

But sometimes life throws you lemons. Divorce, bereavement, a sick child, a major illness. Suddenly, out of the blue, your life can shift on its axis and never be the same again. And that's when the wheels start to come off and everything falls apart. That's when 'high-functioning' quickly morphs into 'low-bottom'.

I was thinking about this the other night. I woke up to find little fingers around my neck. Maddie had had a nightmare, and had crept into our room and snuggled into bed between us. I remembered being that age (very nearly seven), and the feeling that if you were with both your parents then *absolutely nothing* could harm you. It's like being enclosed in an impenetrable magic circle of security.

It reminded me that I am the leader of this pack. Chief Operating Officer. That utter certainty, that innocence of my children, is *totally in my hands.* If I fall apart then everyone falls apart, and, like Humpty Dumpty, no one will be able to fix them without the cracks showing.

If I had had to deal with cancer when I was drinking I know for sure that it would have been different: when I found *the lump,* instead of getting it checked immediately, I would – with the help of a few glasses of wine – have pushed it to the back of my mind for at least a few weeks. Alcohol gives us false confidence. And those few weeks could have made all the difference.

When I finally got the diagnosis, I would have gone on a bender. And being drunk (or hungover) makes us self-centred and unaware of those around us. I would have cried (a lot) in front of the kids. I would have ranted and raged. Then I would have disappeared into my room, feeling extremely sorry for myself, and not emerged for some time.

In one fell swoop I would have destroyed the confidence and security of my family. I'd have pushed Humpty Dumpty off the wall and mocked all the king's horses and all the king's men as they tried to put him together again.

Instead everything carries on as normal, around all the endless hospital visits – and it's that normality that's keeping me sane, and them protected. I hold everything in my hands, and I'm keeping it safe.

I post this on the blog, and I tell my readers:

You, too, are pack leaders. You are responsible for your cubs, your partners, your aged parents. One day, life will throw you lemons, and it's down to you to be strong enough to greet them with a sharp knife and a grater, not a large gin and tonic. Make sure you're ready. For them, as well as for you.

A couple of hours later the phone rings. It's John, calling from the office where, it appears, he has been reading my blog. He is outraged. He wishes it to be known that he is, in fact, Pack Leader, not me.

'Yes, dear,' I reply.

Feeling all positive and alpha female, I pluck up the courage to sneak a peek under the swathes of dressings at My Left Boob. It turns out that Mr Big is, in fact, as advertised, a genius. Lefty is very black and blue, but apart from that doesn't look terribly different (she was far from perfect to start with, to be honest). Given that they removed an ice-cream scoop-sized chunk of boob and sent it off to Imperial College as part of a student research programme (I kid you not) this is extraordinary. It looks like I'm not going to send small children screaming in horror from the bathroom if they catch sight of me in the bath. My potential career as a topless dancer may be buggered, but that I can live with.

So now I'm back on form, feeling perky, looking more perky

than I expected, and I have two weeks' R&R before my next appointment. I've got this covered.

 DAY 255

GOING BACKWARDS

The problem with having time off from all the endless tests and hospital visits is that, for the first time, I've had a chance to dwell, and I've had the strangest sense of going backwards, of déjà vu.

The cancer journey is so spookily similar to the getting-sober-journey that it's hard to believe the timing is coincidental. It feels like the last eight months have been a warm-up to the Big Event.

Like going sober, dealing with The Big C is a leap into the unknown. It's about learning to live, at least for a while, in a world of uncertainty and fear. You ride a roller coaster of emotions when you first quit drinking, taking you from the pink cloud to the wall and back again, and the last few weeks have been like that again – just more so. I lurch from feeling thrilled at just *being alive* to weeping uncontrollably when in parks with the dog (so the children don't see).

The tools I use to deal with all this are the same too. I take one day at a time. Baby steps. I try not to look ahead until I know I can deal with it. Like the early sober days, I find that I have to be kind to myself. Sleep in the afternoon for a while if I have to. Have hot baths. Eat cake.

And, like quitting the booze, I've discovered that finding a tribe is crucial. People like me who've trodden the path before me, and can let me know what's ahead.

I found my sober tribe online because I was too ashamed to look for a real-world one, but, funnily enough, confessing to cancer is way easier than confessing to an alcohol addiction, so I'm discovering a few local ladies – mums like me – who've been through breast cancer and out the other side and can tell me what lies ahead. I'm also using the Haven. It's a charity-funded retreat in Fulham for women with breast cancer. I'm meeting a former Macmillan nurse there this morning.

Bizarrely, in my previous life I was responsible for the Macmillan Cancer Support brand strategy, and all their advertising. It's hard not to imagine the Authors of Destiny sitting on some celestial cloud chortling and patting each other on the back at their clever use of irony.

Am I losing my mind?

DAY |2|6|0|

COMPLIMENTS

We overly enthusiastic drinkers tend to be extremely lazy when it comes to looking for a mood boost. We have one go-to default option: booze. Well, here's another one. It's way better for your liver, and your long-term mental health. Plus, it costs nothing: *pay someone a compliment.*

It's been scientifically proven that when we receive a compliment, our brains are flooded with serotonin, which is an amazing (free, legal and harmless) drug. It's the 'pride' drug, the 'status symbol' drug; the high-quality cocaine of the brain chemistry world. BUT, here's the spooky thing: not only does the compliment *receiver* get a serotonin hit; so does the compliment *giver.*

This process of giving and receiving flattery also builds a bond between the two, which raises levels of oxytocin in both, and it fulfils our positive expectations, which adds a great big shot of dopamine (that's the chemical released when you have your first glass of wine of the day).

So, all in all, what's not to like?

I'm thinking about this in the car, while listening to a piece on Radio 4 about Caitlin Moran (one of my favourite journalists). She's started handing out cards to creatively dressed strangers in the street that read *I want you to know, I really appreciate your look.* What an inspired thing to do!

Imagine you are a hormonally ravaged teenager with minuscule levels of self-confidence. You've spent hours in your bedroom trying on various outfits and posting pictures on Instagram to see which get the most 'likes'. Eventually you decide on the 'least worst' option. But ten minutes after leaving the house you *know* you've made an error. You're about to bail, or to walk into a party with the self-assurance of a gnat. Then a total stranger gives you a card saying *I really appreciate your look.*

Suddenly you stand a foot taller. You are Khaleesi! You enter that room like you're being *paid* to turn up. Then you pull the Year Twelve god you've been lusting after in remedial maths lessons, and you embark on the great adventure that is First Love. **sigh**

I stop at a traffic light. A guy on a pizza delivery bike ahead of me speeds off to the front of the queue. As he does so, a leather glove falls out of his pocket. A young bloke on the pavement spots this, runs into the road and picks up the glove. I half expect him to nick it (that's the kind of thing that normally happens in London). But no. He runs, at full speed (as the lights are changing), through the queue of traffic, taps the pizza guy on the shoulder and hands him the glove.

As the traffic starts moving, I pull over, wind down my window, and shout out to the Good Samaritan, 'You are a *truly great human being!*' then drive off. In my rear-view mirror I can see him grinning. I'm grinning. I can *feel* that serotonin, oxytocin and dopamine having a party in my head. It's made my day.

We take the kids out for supper at their favourite restaurant. We have a running family joke at this place, as the waiter always starts by offering us 'complimentary water'. (N.B. This is not super-generous. It's tap water. Of course it should be free.) When the water arrives, decanted into two large earthenware bottles, the children take turns picking it up and making it 'complimentary'. It goes round the table saying: 'Wow, Mummy, I LOVE that dress on you! So slimming!', 'Daddy, your hair is looking PLENTIFUL today!' and so on.

It strikes me that *every* meal should start with a bottle of complimentary water.

DAY 2 6 4

CONTROL FREAKERY

I am a bit of a control freak. This caused me all sorts of angst back in the drinking days, as when you're drinking (a lot), you are never totally in control. Even when you're sober, you can't control much of your life (as more and more time is taken up drinking, or recovering from drinking), your moods (which lurch from euphoric to suicidal), or your thoughts (as the wine witch has taken up permanent residence in your head).

And when you're drunk you're *definitely* not in control.

Just one or two glasses in, and all those good intentions go out of the window. You can't control how much you're drinking, what you're eating, or what you're saying and doing. A bottle down and you're hoovering up the calories, spilling all the secrets and dancing on the tables like a woman possessed (which you are).

So, actually, being *back in control* has, for me, been one of the best things about being sober. I know exactly how I'm going to feel every morning (perky), I have hours extra in the day to get things done and I'm generally even-tempered and level-headed.

I've taken this control thing to dizzy new heights. I have endless 'to-do' lists. I have a huge kitchen diary with everyone's movements detailed. I have a rota on the front door showing which child needs what to take to school, plus all the after-school activities, etc. Then there's the 'highlights board', which shows the week's main events – all colour coded.

At least that's how it was until recently.

One of the very irritating things about breast cancer (along with the hushed voices people use when they talk to you, the way some people just disappear out of your life and the preoccupation with death), is the TOTAL LACK OF CONTROL.

In less than three weeks the children break up for the school holidays. In four weeks it'll be Christmas. Usually I would be planning pantomimes, menus and expeditions and sifting through party invitations. But I don't feel able to plan, or commit to, anything because, until I know my chemotherapy schedule, I have no idea what I'll be able to do and what I won't.

I haven't updated the highlights board for ages, as it's just too depressing listing 'hospital visit' as the main event for the week. Then, once I start chemo, I'll lose control of my physical well-being, my appetite, my hair follicles – pretty much everything.

Tomorrow – finally – we're meeting the oncologist. I'm hoping that, once I've had this meeting, my life will feel slightly less like trying to juggle with jelly. In the meantime, I keep reciting the serenity prayer (I thought that this was written by Sinéad O'Connor, but it turns out it was penned by an American theologian in 1951, then adopted and popularised by Alcoholics Anonymous):

God grant me the serenity to accept the things I cannot change, the courage to change the things I can, and the wisdom to know the difference.

DAY 265

THE PROF

The Prof sits in a large, leather swivel chair, behind a huge great desk, looking at a massive high-tech screen that details the results of all my various tests. He looks super-clever and *powerful,* like a, much friendlier, Antipodean version of Blofeld. All he needs is a white cat to stroke. I consider suggesting it. Must be nervous.

He takes a piece of paper, draws a line down the middle and writes on the top of one side *positives,* and on the top of the other *negatives.* He starts with the positives, listing things like size of tumour (relatively small), aggressiveness (mine's a lazy bugger, apparently), type (hormone positive), lymphs (clear), etcetera. It's a fairly long list.

He then moves on to the negatives. He pauses, dramatically, like an *X-Factor* host about to announce who's in the final, over the right-hand side of the page, then says, 'Nothing'.

Nothing.

He says, 'If you were my wife, I would not give you chemo-therapy.'

I eyeball him. 'Do you love your wife?' I ask. Always check the small print.

'Oh yes.' He chuckles. 'You see, in your case, chemotherapy would improve the prognosis by *less than one per cent'.*

On that basis, it seems crazy to poison my body (yet again!) for three months, don't you think? Like using a sledgehammer to crush a grain of sand. I do need a course of radiotherapy (starting next week, I hope) and *ten years* of hormone therapy, but that's all (relatively) straightforward.

The Prof then goes on to ask me about my lifestyle, including how much I drink. I'm thrilled.

'Nothing,' I reply.

He looks shocked. 'Is that a lifestyle choice?' he asks. I confess that I had, in the past, drunk a little too much (John's trying not to snigger), so decided to pack it in completely.

'Very wise,' he says, 'liver disease is the next ticking time bomb among middle-aged professionals. We see it all the time.'

I bask in the self-satisfaction of the smug reformed character, and revel in the fact that I was, if obliquely, referred to as 'a professional'.

Then the Prof stands up and shakes us both warmly by the hand. 'I suggest you go home and crack open the champagne!' he says. Didn't I just tell him I don't drink?

So, things are looking up. I could be past the worst by the new year.

We're celebrating with hot chocolate and sex. Just to be clear, that's Noah and Alison having sex in *The Affair* on Sky Atlantic. *Loads of it.* Don't they ever get tired? Don't they ever want to just collapse on the sofa with a hot chocolate and a box set?

John presses pause, leaving Dominic West's naked buttocks hovering mid-thrust. I'm not complaining.

'Clare?' he says, in a worryingly tentative tone of voice. 'Has the whole *cancer thing* made you look at your life and wish you'd done anything differently?'

I'm stunned. John doesn't *do* questions like this. He's a man who thinks that asking if you take sugar in your tea is getting a little *personal.* I think for a short while.

'You know what?' I reply. 'There's only *one thing* about my life that I'd want to change.' He fixes me with a hard, somewhat nervous, stare. 'I haven't had enough room service.'

'Room service?'

'Actually, I'm being serious,' I say, seriously. 'You see, ever since Evie was born, nearly twelve years ago, every single time we've been on holiday we've done self-catering. And we've had some lovely holidays – Cornwall, Scotland, skiing – and we're very lucky. It's just that I'm still planning meals, shopping, cooking, loading the dishwasher, unloading the dishwasher, washing the clothes and cleaning up the mess. It's my same life, just moved to a different location. I would love to spend *just one week* having someone else doing all that stuff.'

John looks a bit perplexed, but I think I see a glimmer of understanding behind his spectacles. Maybe he's realising just what his life might be like if I wasn't there. I realise that this could be a once-in-a-lifetime opportunity, so I plough on.

'It would be particularly brilliant if that *one week* were somewhere with guaranteed sunshine, that doesn't require packing waterproofs and wellies. Maybe (dramatic pause) *an island.* Maybe *in the Caribbean.* (I'm on a roll.) Maybe we should book it *right now* for when all my treatment is over.'

And while John is still recovering from the unintended consequences of asking a personal question, I call my sainted mother and get her to agree to looking after the kids for a week in March. Then I google 'best places to stay in the Caribbean. Not too expensive' and pass John his (dusty) credit card.

A masterclass in seizing the opportunity.

Twenty minutes later, and I've booked us a holiday in Jamaica! We've been once before. Almost twenty years ago, when John and I had just started 'dating', we were invited by another couple – great friends of ours – to stay with their wonderfully eccentric cousin, Willy.

Willy was an artist. He'd emigrated to Jamaica, along with a bunch of other wild young things, back in the 1970s when the lifestyle to which they'd been accustomed – living in large houses with butlers, cooks and maids – became unaffordable in England.

Willy lived in a fabulous Jamaican Great House, up in the hills, but he, the house and the staff were becoming increasingly decrepit. When John and I lay in bed at night we could see the stars through a hole in the roof. Dead romantic, until it started to rain.

Willy was a wild and extravagant host. Over the years everyone who was anyone, from (allegedly) Princess Margaret and Marianne Faithfull to Fergie (the ex-royal, not the Black Eyed Pea) had been to stay. The days revolved around sitting on the terrace, drinking cocktails, planning the next meal and talking about life, the universe and everything with an endless succession of visitors, from famous reggae producers to eccentric aristocrats.

We'd get up late, and as it was practically noon, would start drinking Bloody Marys or Buck's Fizz pretty much straight away. We'd carry on drinking through the afternoon, and party into the night. By the end of the week I was only held together by the toxins. It took me at least a week to recover – mentally and physically – and I was young back then.

Do I regret it? Not a bit. Would I do it again? Hell, no. It'd probably kill me. This time I'm going to do Jamaica a different way.

John seems happy with the proposed destination, mainly because it allows him to use, liberally, his favourite joke.

'I'm taking the wife to the Caribbean.'

'Jamaica?'

'No, she's coming of her own accord.'

Funny the first time, but I suspect that by the time we get on that plane it'll be, like the elbows of the ancient jumpers he refuses to throw away, wearing rather thin.

DAY |2|6|8|

SOBERMUMMY'S PARTY SURVIVAL GUIDE

It's Thanksgiving in the USA and here, in London, the Christmas party scene is cranking into action. The whole of the sober blogging world has started to panic about how we're going to get through it all. My email in-box has exploded with mails from readers asking for advice and, after nearly nine months, and with several sober parties under my belt already, I really do think I can help. So I sit down at the computer, click on 'New Post' and write this:

> *HAPPY THANKSGIVING to all my friends over the pond. This post is in honour of you.*
>
> *It's the party season. And parties are often the most tricky thing about getting sober. I think it's especially hard for us because we, my friends, used to be* the party people! *That's*

what got many of us into this mess in the first place, isn't it? We were the dancers, the raconteurs, the life and soul, the last to leave.

But we didn't do it alone, did we? We always had our friend – the booze – with us. Until our best buddy turned on us, defriended us on Facebook and made our lives hell. Believe me, parties can and will be fun again. However, it's probably the area that takes the longest to deal with. So, in the meantime, here's SoberMummy's Party Survival Guide:

1. **Remember, you do not have to go**

   I am, generally, big on honesty. However, *in the early days of sobriety you do have to forgive yourself a few big fibs. It's obligatory. And the great thing about the party season is that it's easy to say 'Oh gosh, so sorry! I've already got something on that night!'* No one will think you're a sad loser. *They'll just assume you have invitations coming out of your nostrils. And you* do *have something . . . an appointment with series six of* Mad Men, *a slice of chocolate cake as big as your head* and a hot bath with bubbles. *So what if you miss out? It's one party season in the long, happy, healthy life that you have to come.*

2. **You do not have to stay**

   Remember those days when leaving a party was a real chore? You had to locate the host among the throng, find a taxi number, manage to type it into your phone while drunk, to sound sober to the receptionist so they wouldn't just hang up, and to look sober to the taxi driver so they wouldn't just bugger off etcetera . . .

   NOT ANY MORE! You can drive! Which means as soon as you're finding it too difficult you can just leave. *Don't* bother saying goodbye, as you'll just have to explain your-self. They'll all be drunk! No one will notice, or remember. Just slip away, patting yourself on the back for a job well done.

3. **Take time out**

Sometimes you don't need to leave permanently; all you need is a bit of Time Out. Go for a walk. Or just go sit in the loo for a bit (I believe you Americans call it The Bathroom, even when there's no bath in it).

4. **Fake it**

I think it makes it harder when you have to explain you're not drinking, so why put yourself through it? Just hang on to a glass that looks like it contains something alcoholic, and say nothing. No one will notice, they're all drunk – except the sober ones, and they'll salute you! (Note to self: we need a secret handshake!)

5. **Deal with the envy**

One of the problems with parties in the early days is that terrible urge to stab 'moderate drinkers' in the eye with your fork (or is that just me?). Yes, it is unfair that they can stand there quaffing away and you can't, but remember everyone has their shit to deal with. For a start, they may well be battling the wine witch themselves and envying you your poise and serenity. If not, there'll be something they're dealing with, because that's life. Maybe every time their husband asks them to pass the salt they're secretly thinking 'F**k off, you've ruined my life!' Maybe they have a child who's doing drugs, or a parent who no longer recognises them.

Nobody gets to our age without encountering something bad. *You got alcohol addiction. It's not the worst thing that can happen – you can beat it.*

6. *Watch the drunkards*

As the evening wears on, and you start getting a little bored, then see it as a nature programme:

'Here we encounter the drunkard, in their natural habitat. Watch their mating ritual. Standing too close. Spraying their mate with saliva. Swaying on their feet and laughing too loudly . . .'

Feeling smug isn't a nice quality. Nor is quietly sneering at people. But, hell, we have to get our kicks somewhere!

7. *Know your enemy*

The wine witch pulls out the big guns at parties, so be prepared. *If you know what she's going to say you can deal with it. Here is the classic:*

'Hey, it's a party! Just have the one. You can quit again tomorrow!'

We've been through this one many times, my friends. If you could 'just have one' you wouldn't be here, would you? You'd be reading a blog on 'perfect parenting for the mother of three' or 'quilting for beginners'. Play the tape forward: arm yourself with visual images of where that 'just one drink' has got you in the past. It's never pretty. If necessary, reread my post 'The Obstacle Course' while you're on the loo (in 'the bathroom').

8. *Pardon the turkey*

I was reading about the tradition (established by Reagan in 1987) of the American President giving a pardon to the

Thanksgiving turkey, who then gets to live out his/her life in turkey nirvana instead of being stuffed and served with cranberry and all the trimmings. Another issue with parties is that they can give us flashbacks of the dark drinking days. *You remember all your past misdemeanours, and often encounter those who* you have wronged. *Well, now it's time to forgive your inner turkey. That was then, this is now: move on.*

9. *Focus on the morning*
If things get tough, I always focus on the morning. Just think how brilliant you are going to feel the day after *the party, while everyone else is in bed groaning, and filled with regrets. That is your payback time. Your reward. And you'll have earned it!*

Please share this post as widely as you can for all the sober revellers out there, and HAPPY THANKSGIVING!

Love SM x

I press 'publish' and sit back in my chair, thinking that the last thing in the world I want to do at the moment is go to a party. I just want to crawl into bed and hunker down until January.

I'm a fraud.

THE MONTH WHEN I GET A TATTOO

RADIOTHERAPY

So, how does one celebrate nine months totally alcohol-free? Three quarters of a year!

I had been invited to a ladies' lunch in Edinburgh. I usually avoid the whole 'ladies who lunch' scene, but Princess Anne is the guest of honour at this one, and I've always had a bit of a girlie crush on Anne. She's so wonderfully down to earth and *horsey,* despite the whole 'my mummy's the Queen' thing. However, recent events conspired against me, and instead of being able to dine with royalty, I have my first session of radio-therapy.

I'm back to counting days. I have fifteen sessions over three weeks. Five days on, two days off.

Radiotherapy, it transpires, is a walk in the park compared to chemotherapy. (I feel almost guilty about not doing the chemo thing. I can't meet the eyes of the ladies in the wigs and headscarves in the waiting room. I imagine they're thinking *'Look at the imposter over there, with the whole cancer-lite thing going on. Hah! Call that a treatment programme!?! Wimp!')*

After a short wait, during which I read the same page of *Hello!* magazine seven times while taking in nothing, I'm ushered into a room that is dominated by this narrow bed fitted with arm restraints. It's like something out of *Fifty Shades of Grey* but, sadly, without Jamie Dornan. Then, two irritatingly pretty and chirpy radiotherapists spend an age getting me into

249

exactly the right position while they chat over me about the upcoming office Christmas party. Meanwhile, I'm topless, with both arms over my head, feeling like a spatchcocked chicken just waiting to be sprinkled with olive oil and herbs.

In order to line me up perfectly each time, they tell me I have to have two permanent tattoos – one on either side of the boob that tried to kill me. I'm quite excited about this. I've always secretly wanted a tattoo.

'Can I choose the style and colour?' I ask. I was thinking dolphins, as an homage to Sam Cam, another girlie crush.

'No. You get a blue dot, like everyone else,' they reply, missing a fabulous opportunity to upsell. 'Any more questions?' John had asked me to see if they had any advice on how to fix our broken microwave. Judging by their response to my inspired dolphin suggestion, I'm not convinced that this would go down well.

Finally, when I'm deemed to be perfectly in position, everyone scurries out of the room to hide behind very thick glass so as not to get anywhere near the horribly dangerous rays that are firing at me from close range. I'd quite like to bugger off too, frankly, but I'm not given that option.

So, I celebrate nine months of being sober with a massive blast of radiation to the bottom left quadrant of the left boob. Not the way I would have planned it, but – on the upside – my final session is scheduled for 23 December – just in time for Christmas!

I trudge home on the tube, clutching a pair of cashmere bedsocks that I've bought my aunt to keep her toes toasty during chemotherapy. I'm feeling a bit *bleurgh,* surrounded by revellers on their way out to Christmas celebrations. Everywhere I look there are people sporting flashing reindeer antlers and comedy Christmas sweaters. Every shop I pass is playing different Christmas music, creating a bizarre mash-up effect. Oh little town of Rudolph the red-nosed reindeer bells were ringing out for Christmas day.

Then, when I get home, I realise that I still haven't had a response from the council about the parking ticket I was issued about six weeks ago. This is a little odd, as whenever I've argued parking tickets in the past I always get a response – either positive or negative (usually negative) – within two or three weeks.

I go online and type in my Parking Charge Notice number. A message comes up saying **PCN NOT FOUND**. You know what this means? Some little angel in the local council read my letter, knew that they couldn't *officially* let me off, so they just *deleted me off the system.* With one or two keystrokes, one random act of kindness, they have restored my faith in humanity.

Council person – you rock. You are an amazing human being, and I hope all your wildest dreams come true.

DAY |2|7|7|

PANIC ATTACKS

I've always been an optimistic and happy person. I expected good things to happen to me, and – generally – they did. Then I got hit with the breast cancer and for the last six weeks I've been in shock – dealing with one day at a time, swinging from despair (*I'm going to die soon!*) to elation (*I'm not going to die yet!*) and back again.

But now, nearly two months on, the dust is starting to settle, and the reality of living the rest of my life *in remission* is starting to kick in. And it's giving me panic attacks.

I have always had the attitude that *if you don't have a temperature, and nothing's fallen off, you go to school.* I've always assumed that if you don't even *consider* the possibility of bad health, it won't happen. Mind over matter. Then I got proved wrong. And I can see how easy it is to lose that faith, and to start seeing the world as essentially hostile, filled with potholes just waiting for you to fall in them.

I spotted a new mole on Evie the other day. Instead of thinking *Oh look, a mole,* I thought *Aarrrggghh! Skin cancer! She's going to die, and she's only twelve!* I keep fretting (for no specific reason) that John will lose his job and we'll be penniless. I worry (with some good reason) that our house is falling down. And, obviously, I worry that the cancer will come back, that I will DIE (painfully and unattractively) and my children will be MOTHERLESS, until John gets seduced by a large-breasted, facelifted temptress who doesn't love them and spends all the remaining family money on HANDBAGS.

This is not like me.

I have, they tell me, so long as I take the right drugs, a ninety-two per cent chance of remaining cancer-free. Most of the time I'm able to focus on the ninety-two per cent. But, increasingly, I'm jolted by the thought that *I have an eight per cent chance of a recurrence, which would be incurable.*

I realise that there are two ways I could deal with the rest of my life. I could scream **WHY ME?** and see myself as a victim of some cruel universe, living the rest of my life in fear of the cancer progressing or returning, spending hours googling 'cures' and prognoses. I could turn my rose-tinted glasses into cancer-ridden spectacles and live half a life. I could reach for the booze as a comfort and end up like Haymitch after his victory in the Hunger Games.

Or, I could view this whole experience as a wake-up call. A reminder that life is precious, and that we need to make the most of every moment. I could see myself as a *survivor*. A kick-ass Katniss Everdeen, who comes away from the Hunger Games stronger and more fierce.

In the words of President Snow, the answer is *Hope. It's the only thing stronger than fear.* So, several times each day I realise that I'm standing at a crossroads, with the left path marked **FEAR** and the right marked **HOPE**. Every time I have to consciously make myself turn right. I hope that, eventually, choosing that path will once more become automatic. Every morning I tell myself that *I am not a victim, I am a survivor. Katniss, not Haymitch.*

On the upside, one fear I've completely lost is the fear of ageing. In my neck of the woods, people spend a fortune trying to look younger. I know many women who are unable to look surprised, or cross, or anything other than blank, bland, puffy and waxy. I used to spend hours fretting about bingo wings, turkey neck and *jowls*. But no longer. Because while I was going through the 'I'm going to die, imminently' phase, I discovered that instead of feeling sorry for old people, I felt jealous. Fist-clenchingly envious. I'd look at the wrinkles around their eyes and mouths and think *Look at the evidence of twice as many smiles as I'll ever smile.* I'd see them shuffling along cautiously and think *See how they've trodden twice as many paths as I'll ever go down.* I realised that the alternative to growing old isn't living for ever in our pert, healthy bodies – *it's dying young.*

The truth is that ageing is not so bad. Many studies have shown that people get happier and happier as they get older. Our forties are, apparently, our most miserable years, as we're run ragged by young children, ageing parents and trying to keep all the balls in the air.

And living life sober is not some form of terrible compromise either – *it's better. More real. More vibrant.* So, for the first time, I am completely at peace with the future. Getting older. Staying sober.

Because I have seen the real alternative *and it sucks.*

Before I go to sleep I play my new game of checking which Google search terms are leading people to my blog. Someone found me today by way of typing 'Mummy sex'. I'm feeling racy.

MARRIAGE

Fourteen years ago today I married John. And, miraculously, despite years of increasingly bad behaviour, followed by a rather dramatic and screeching U-turn nine months ago, he still seems to love me, wonky, radioactive left boob and all.

I count myself extremely lucky, as a recent study showed that more and more marriages are breaking down because of the wife's excessive drinking. It's thought to contribute to as many as one in seven divorces.

I can see how that can so easily be the case, and I get so many emails from women telling me that their husbands have given them an ultimatum: either the booze goes, or I do.

Looking back, I see now that alcohol was the root cause of most of our marital arguments. There were a few *spectacular* ones, like the Finnish wedding.

John had known the groom since the age of ten, when they were at school together in Scotland. They also spent a memorable year, after they graduated, living in St Petersburg, where

John learned to speak rather ropey, but extremely sexy, Russian.

The wedding venue was stunning – the bride's family summer house on the edge of a fjord, in the height of summer when, that far north, it never gets dark. At about 2 a.m. the light would get a little dusky, but a couple of hours later the relentless bright sunshine would return, determined to compensate for the preceding months of darkness.

We had a ball. Being just over a narrow sea from Russia, there was a vodka and caviar bar, which we made the most of, then a lavish wedding feast of reindeer, washed down with endless enthusiastic toasts of unpronounceable Finnish spirits.

At about three in the morning, the last coach was leaving for the hotel, half an hour away. John was having so much fun with the Finns in the sauna that he refused to come back with me.

They were all sitting in the heat, naked and sweating, while John sang 'Finns can only get better' (that joke must have worn thin after a while). Then they'd run at full pelt down a wooden jetty and dive into the ice-cold fjord.

I lost it. We had a screaming row, and then I sat on the floor of the bus (there were no seats left) telling all the bemused (and rather concerned) passengers at great length how John had never truly loved me and it was all over.

John managed to get a lift back in the boot of someone's car about an hour later. We both woke up, terribly hungover, at around lunchtime, having forgotten most of the detail of our very public meltdown, and couldn't understand why everyone was looking at us strangely and asking if we were 'okay'.

The vast majority of the alcohol-based arguments were, however, nothing like as dramatic as the Finnish one. Just the endless tetchy debates (when hungover) about who was going to feed the baby at 5 a.m., or take the toddler to a party where you'd have to clap and sing and *participate*. Then, after a few glasses of wine in the evening, the drunken fights (inevitably started by me) about who wasn't pulling their weight around the house, or with the childcare.

I'm sure that every married couple has these sorts of arguments, but the problems start when *the majority* of your conversations end up like this.

Marriage is like a piggy bank. Every time you do something nice, thoughtful or generous for the other person you put money into the bank, and every time you treat them badly, thoughtlessly or carelessly you take money out. If you're not careful, eventually the piggy bank is empty.

The other issue with drinking in a marriage is that excessive alcohol use leads to self-hatred, anxiety and depression, all of which make it very difficult to focus properly on your relationship, to top up that piggy bank.

Despite my dire predictions on the floor of that bus in Finland, John and I are still together, and I cannot tell you how grateful I am that I quit drinking before I drove him away. He is my best friend, my lover, my partner in crime. Only he could make me laugh through a cancer diagnosis and treatment.

Fourteen years ago, one of our friends read the poem 'The Owl and the Pussycat' at our wedding. That's how marriage felt to me. The two of us sailing off in our beautiful pea-green boat in search of the land where the Bong-tree grows. As a wedding present, I bought John a tiny but beautiful oil painting of the owl and the pussycat, clutching their honey and their money, under the stars, which hangs above our bath. And it has been like that. A journey, treacherous at times, often challenging, but thrilling and magical.

This morning John bought me wedding anniversary scrambled eggs on toast in bed. I started sobbing into the egg. He looked alarmed, assuming he'd done something terrible. But I was crying because I'm just so terribly grateful.

Not just for the egg. For everything.

DAY |2|8|5|

THE PSYCHOTHERAPIST

I've never had any form of counselling or psychotherapy. I'm far too British and 'stiff upper lip'. I'm very happy sharing pretty much anything with friends. But strangers? Oh no! (I realise it's somewhat ironic that I've now taken up blogging, and share everything with thousands of people I've never met.)

I remember being totally shocked when I first went to the USA, and every time I went into a shop someone said 'Hi! How are *you* today?' Initially I'd look over my shoulder, assuming they were talking to someone else, then bite back the urge to say, in very British, Roedean vowels, 'I'm sorry, but have we met before?'

The other thing that alarms me about the concept of seeing a psychotherapist is that it spells psycho-the-rapist. I mean, how off-putting is that?

But then, as part of my 'cancer care package' I've been offered six sessions of *free* psychotherapy. I've been married to a Scot for far too long to turn down such a good bargain, so today I turn up for my first session. Here's how it goes:

Therapist: So, Clare, how *are* you? (steady gaze)

Me: Fine, thank you for asking. How are you? (steady gaze back)

Therapist: No, Clare. How are you *really?* (hard stare)

Me: Fine! (slight bottom-lip tremble)

Therapist: No. How are you *really* really? (penetrating stare)

Me: (uncontrollable weeping)

I start to offload and, actually, it feels pretty good. Cathartic. Until I get to this bit:

Therapist: How do you feel about the possibility of your children losing their mother?

Me: (staring at box of tissues)

Therapist: Clare?

Me: I don't even consider it. (glare)

Therapist: But when you do consider it, how do you feel?

Me: I can't even let myself go there. (super-hard stare)

Therapist: *Why* can't you think about it?

Me: *Because they are way too young to be without their mother!* (more uncontrollable weeping)

(Pause)

Therapist: How did you feel when I made you answer that question?

Me: I hate you.

Therapist: It's good that you can be honest with me.

Really? Just wait till I get started . . .

Despite the spat over my potentially motherless children, I sign up for five more sessions. I explain that since my cancer diagnosis I've gone from being Little Miss Optimistic to Chicken Licken – constantly fretting that the sky is going to fall on my head, and the heads of everyone I love.

We are, apparently, going to use cognitive behavioural therapy

(CBT) to sort that one out. Plus, she's throwing in some mindfulness practice to try to keep me anchored in the present rather than fast forwarding to *certain, painful death and motherless children.*

So, I'm interested to read in the paper on the way home that a review published in the *British Medical Journal* yesterday finds that CBT is *as effective* a treatment for major depression as antidepressants. CBT is defined as 'a series of techniques that teach patients how to replace dysfunctional thoughts and behaviours with more adaptive ones, which can reduce distress and improve mood.'

It strikes me that that's exactly what I've been training myself to do in the nine months since I quit drinking. And it transpires that CBT is increasingly being used to treat alcohol dependency, by helping people to identify their triggers and develop new coping strategies.

I figure that I'm going to start the new year all physically fixed (ten months sober by then, and cancer-free – I hope). I might as well develop some really good emotional strategies too. That way, if the sky really does fall down again, I'll be ready to catch it with a bucket.

| DAY | 2 | 9 | 0 |

CHRISTMAS IS COMING

After the last two months, and with some help from psycho-the-rapist, I'm getting better at coping with anxiety and stress without drinking. I know that when the s**t hits the fan, you need a clear head, not one befuddled by booze, or hijacked by a hangover. But *I still miss it* when it comes to celebrating. In some situations, like when the Prof told me I don't need chemotherapy, eating a piece of cake just doesn't feel *adequate*. And Christmas is like that. Along with birthdays, it's the occasion when a Beck's Blue feels a bit *bleurgh*.

I have never done a sober Christmas. Even when I was pregnant I allowed myself (with my obstetrician's blessing) a glass of wine on Christmas Day. So, knowing that 25 December may be tough, I'm limbering up in preparation.

Step one *is being honest*, which means revisiting the Ghost of Christmas Past. When I think about drinking at Christmas, the glasses I remember are: the crisp, chilled white wine while wrapping the stocking presents on Christmas Eve, the glass of champagne while getting Christmas lunch ready and the full-bodied glass of red with the turkey.

(Even writing that list I can hear the wine witch whispering *Ooh yes. Go on. You could have **just those three**. That wouldn't be so bad, would it? For f***'s sake, you're celebrating Christmas, nine months sober AND getting over cancer!*)

But the trick is to force yourself to remember *all the others*. Because I wouldn't drink one glass while wrapping the presents, I'd drink a bottle. I'd often put the wrong presents in the wrong stockings, leading to bemusement the following morning as Maddie would find football socks, and Kit a Barbie. 'Ha! Ha!' John would chortle, 'Santa was at the whisky again last night!'

I'd wake up, as usual, at 3 a.m. and toss and turn, sweating and hating myself, until around 5.30 a.m. when the troops would pile in. Three children and a dog, brimming over with excitement and anticipation. Instead of joining in the joy of Christmas morning, I'd try to hide my aching head under a pillow, while panicking about preparing Christmas lunch for ten, on three hours' sleep and a hangover.

By 11 a.m. it would feel like we'd been at it for hours, and we'd open the first bottle of champagne (the only day of the year when drinking before midday is not only acceptable, but obligatory). By 1 p.m. I'd have drunk most of a bottle and lunch would be going seriously screwy. Juggling turkey, stuffing, five vegetables and gravy-making is testing at the best of times, and near impossible when drunk and knackered.

The children would be high on sugar and consumerism, and behaving terribly in front of grandparents, necessitating more alcohol to dampen the stress. Finally sitting down for lunch was a huge relief, requiring . . . a toast! Plenty of fine red wine, continuing well into the afternoon. After all – IT'S CHRISTMAS!

Final tally by the end of the day: two bottles? Maybe three? An afternoon and evening spent dozing on and off, and trying to ignore the children. A toxic night tossing and turning, and Boxing Day feeling like near death.

So, having made myself relive the *reality* of Christmas Past, I now have to find a way of really appreciating Christmas Present and Christmases Future. *Without the booze.* I decide to do some internet research and look up a self-help guru called Wayne Dyer to see what he has to say about Christmas.

Wayne talks (on drwaynedyer.com) about reclaiming '*what should be a time of appreciation, excitement, joy, and peace'.* That description sounds a million miles away from my usual experience of Christmas! Peace? Appreciation? Excitement? My feelings about Christmas would usually encompass *panic, trepidation, queasiness, exhaustion* . . . Peace? Definitely not. Apart from a fleeting moment when I'd just poured the first glass of wine of the day. Oh. There's the problem . . .

Intrigued, I read on. How, oh wonderful-Wayne-guru, can Christmas possibly involve appreciation, excitement, joy and peace – and no alcohol? Here's Wayne's mantra for *'rekindling the spirit of love, and living life to its fullest'* over Christmas:

1. *I'll let the holidays flow, rather than trying to make them fit into a fixed schedule.*
2. *I'll remember that people are more important than things.*
3. *I'll relax my expectations for myself and others this year.*
4. *I'm going to live in the present moment and enjoy each activity for itself instead of always thinking about what is ahead of me.*
5. *I'm going to approach the holidays with a sense of joyful anticipation and wonder, just like I did when I was a child.*

All easier said than done, but I've been repeating 1–5 over and over, hoping that it'll all sink in. It does rather go against all my natural inclinations. NO FIXED SCHEDULE? Are you kidding? NOT THINKING AHEAD? Nothing will ever get done!

I read Wayne's list out to the family. They snort with derision. 'Doesn't sound like Mummy, does it children?' says John, staring pointedly at my To-Do List and Holiday Planner. Well, I'm going to prove them wrong. No more blurring all the edges. No more wading through the days numb or hungover. Just joy, anticipation and wonder in glorious technicolour.

Tomorrow is the last day of the school term so, inevitably, for Kit's year there's a Christmas-themed dress-up competition.

'Kit, why don't you root around in the Christmas decorations box and find yourself some tinsel and baubles to wear tomorrow?' I suggest.

'But Mummy!' he wails, 'I want to go as a *chimney*.'

A chimney?!?

'It's not *fair*!' he declares, his protruding bottom lip wobbling. My children have a very well-developed sense of fairness. Woe betide anyone who treats one of them differently from the others.

'Darling, it's a bit late now to start doing arts and crafts,' I suggest. He starts welling up.

'But Maddie went to French day as the Eiffel Tower!' he replies, wiping his eyes with the back of his hand.

I realise the downside of turning into a Supermum. I have, accidentally, raised expectations. Bugger.

We get to the art shop just before it closes, then spend the next two hours constructing a chimney, complete with flames, hanging stocking and Santa's feet, while I repeat to myself, through gritted teeth, *joyful anticipation and wonder.*

DAY |2|9|1|

JOYFUL ANTICIPATION AND WONDER

I'm beginning to regret sharing Wayne Dyer's advice on coping with Christmas with the family. Whenever I get shirty with anyone, for totally messing up the kitchen, for example, John mutters under his breath *'relax my expectations of others'*, or *'I'll let the holidays flow'*. I think I may kill him.

The children are now on holiday. In the old days I would have created a crazy schedule – determined to make sure that *we all had a great time.* There would be panto one day, skating the next, soft play, trampolining, bowling, you name it. All fuelled by buckets of Sauvignon Blanc (me) and Haribo gummy bears (them), and costing a fortune. By Christmas we'd be on our knees.

This year I've planned very little. I've been (as Wayne suggests) letting the holidays flow rather than planning ahead. I have to confess that this isn't down to suddenly having discovered my inner Zen. I've been forced into the laissez-faire thing by the fact that three hours of every day (at least) is taken up by hospital visits (radiotherapy every day, plus check-ups). This requires a rota of extremely helpful friends, and John, covering childcare, and means that I've organised little else. And you know what? Here's a revelation: it really doesn't matter! It turns out that Evie, Kit and Maddie are just completely thrilled to be at home.

I walk into the kitchen after my latest blast of radiation and six eyes turn towards me as I'm asked 'What's the plan for today, Mummy?' (They know that I usually have *a plan*. Often with several subsections.)

I take a deep breath and say (with manufactured enthusiasm) 'We're going to the supermarket!' (It's the last day you can pre-order turkeys.) I expect dissent. Anarchy. But no! We all climb happily into the car and head off (to Waitrose, obviously, I may be 'going with the flow', but I'm not letting standards slip completely).

'Yellow car!' shouts Maddie from the back seat. I can't remember when the 'yellow car' game started. It is a game with no beginning and no end. The rules are simple: when you see a yellow car you shout 'yellow car' before anyone else does.

'Yellow car!' shouts Kit, right in my ear, making me jump.

Luckily, I think as I turn into the car park, people who shop at Waitrose tend not to drive yellow cars. I'm safe for the next hour.

Usually I'd avoid taking three children to the supermarket like the plague – far too stressful, and takes way too long – but today we turn it into a game. We do girls versus boy races. I give each 'team' a list of items and see who can bring them back to the trolley first.

Then I let them use the self-checkout machine. Yes, it takes hours. There are many 'unexpected items in the bagging area'.

It's quite possible that we didn't pay for something (or paid twice), and I seem to have ended up with *way* more chocolate than I'd officially authorised. But it doesn't matter. We don't have anywhere else to get to. We order the turkey. We buy some extra Christmas decorations, which we put up when we get home. I get my chores done *and we have fun.*

I realise that, with the right attitude, any activity can be festive and Christmassy. So, tomorrow's post-hospital 'Christmas activity': taking the dog to the vet for his annual inoculations! (I'm not sure that he's going to be seeing the 'joy and wonder' in that one – he has been known to bite the vet.)

DAY 293

WHO'S GOT CANCER?

I spend a fair amount of time each day sitting in the waiting room of the cancer clinic, so I've invented a game to stop myself getting bored. It's a little macabre, and I can't see Hasbro fighting for the copyright. It's called: Who's Got Cancer? You see, most people come in with a partner or a buddy. You know one of them has cancer, but not which one. Until the receptionist calls a name, and you see who responds.

Sometimes it's pretty easy to deduce. It's the one with the suspiciously luxuriant hair, but no eyebrows, eyelashes or arm hair, for example. However, sometimes it's really difficult.

I try very hard to NOT look like a cancer patient. I turn up as if dressed for the theatre (Shakespeare, not operating). I wear heels, cashmere and fur trim. It makes me feel better. Plus, I'm usually the youngest person there by a decade or two, which makes me feel additionally glamorous (if a tad *unlucky*).

Today a young couple walk in. They're both gorgeous. Radiantly healthy-looking. I'm bamboozled. Turns out it's him – poor sod. Testicular? Hope so – it's got good odds and, apparently, one ball can happily do the job of two.

The problem is that I suspect everyone else is playing this game too. I have a cold, but am trying desperately not to cough, because every time I do I can see someone thinking *Uh oh. Secondary tumours in the lungs (terminal). Or primary lung cancer (terrible odds).* All of us have become amateur medics, you see.

Then a middle-aged lady arrives. She's French, and has that effortless, Parisian chic. I assume early stage breast cancer (like me). She has her daughter with her, around twelve years old – the same age as Evie. Nice of her to come with her mum, I think. And she looks really cheerful about it, despite it being a precious day of the Christmas holidays.

As I watch surreptitiously, the daughter pushes up her sleeve, revealing a chemo cannula. I feel like I've been punched. You see, there is something way worse than having cancer treatment: watching your child have cancer treatment. I AM LUCKY.

(Listen up, angel of destiny. I'm taking this bullet for my family, so don't even think about pointing a finger at one of my children. Or John.)

What this game has taught me is that you can never tell what's really going on in people's lives. It's so easy to look at the perfect worlds of the people around you, at their Boden-esque Instagram feeds and Facebook pages filled with aspirational events and conquered milestones, peppered with thumbs-up and heart emojis, and wonder where you went wrong. And drink is a consolation, taking the edge off that feeling of dissatisfaction, of unfulfilled potential, of stuck-in-a-rut-ness.

But the truth is, *nobody's life is perfect.* You never know who's dealing with a life-threatening illness, a sick child, a parent with dementia, a job that bores them stupid or a partner they secretly despise.

A friend told me that after her parents got divorced, her mother told her never to take the 'life-and-soul' couples at face value. She said that the reason they're always at every party, always having fun, is that they can't bear being alone together. She knew because that used to be her.

So I'm going to stop envying other people's lives, and start living my own. *Really living it.* Because, like the grit in the oyster that forms a pearl, it's the imperfections in our lives that (eventually) make us strong, unique and beautiful. So long as we deal with them, and don't just drown them out with buckets of vino.

DAY 2 9 7

IT'S FINISHED!

Yesterday was my final session of radiotherapy. If I could liken myself to a microwave oven (and right now I think I can), this is the moment at which I would be going 'PING!'

I'm now a bit sore (as if I'd fallen asleep on a very hot day with my left boob poking out from my bikini – which, funnily enough, I did quite often back in the drinking days), very tired, and one side of my torso is hotter than the other (weird, right? or, actually, weird left in my case).

Apparently, at some American clinics they have a huge bell in the waiting area, and when you've finished your cancer treatment you get to ring the bell and everyone cheers. I really, really wanted a bell to ring. Instead, I showered the nurses with chocolates, gave them all a hug and told them I never wanted to see them again. (Given the forced grins, I suspect they've heard that one before.) Then I walked out into the winter sunshine, feeling simultaneously elated and weepy.

And all I wanted to do – desperately wanted to do – was to get utterly trashed. I wanted to drink *at least* a bottle of wine. I wanted to talk nonsense with John. Laugh. Cry. Have drunken sex. Make everything fuzzy, walk into the furniture, then pass out on the sofa.

Instead I went shopping. I spotted a sale on in Zadig & Voltaire, and bought a charcoal and gold T-shirt, an Alexander McQueen-inspired scarf and a crimson sweater with black sequinned detailing. Rock-chick clothes, not sober-person-cancer-victim clothes. An easy fit in *medium.* Whoop whoop.

I went home, then we dropped in on some friends for mulled wine and mince pies (I took my own Beck's Blue), watched two more episodes of *The Affair* and went to bed sober – as always.

And today? I woke up guilt-free – the only hangover from yesterday being some new clothes.

I figure that every year there are bound to be a handful of days when it would be really, really good to get drunk. But what about the other 360? Because, in my case, one doesn't come without the other. Plus, it strikes me that it's a bizarre reaction to have: I've got to the end of a horrendous two months. I am, as far as we can tell, cancer-free. So why not anaesthetise myself to the point of oblivion to celebrate? It's just a habit.

And now it's *Christmas Eve*! And, you know what? I'm not worried about Christmas itself at all. I'm *excited about it.* Because Christmas Day (unlike New Year's Eve) is about *way more* than drinking. It's about seeing the children's excitement when they bring in their stockings to show us in the morning (and Santa was *on form* this year), church, slap-up lunch, handing out and opening all the presents, charades, great TV, the Queen. It's got a bit of everything. Something for everyone.

I go to the supermarket to collect the turkey we'd ordered, and last-minute supplies. Our kitchen fridge is bursting at the seams, so I ask John to take the turkey down to the old 'over-flow' fridge we keep in the Pit of Despair.

I'm bustling away in the kitchen, unpacking shopping, and can hear John's footsteps on the old, wooden cellar steps. Then I hear this: 'Oh my God!'

'What? What?!?' I yell down.

'Do you promise not to panic?' he replies, using the phrase most guaranteed to cause panic. In trepidation, I walk slowly down the steps. Our cellar – filled with old filing, photos, memorabilia, hand-me-down clothes waiting for the children to grow into them, and anything that John can't bear to throw away (anything at all: he's Scottish) is two inches deep in water.

It transpires that the lead pipe (which must be at least 100 years old) connecting us to the mains water supply has cracked somewhere between our house and the road outside, and water is constantly pouring into our cellar.

We turn off the mains water supply. We spend the three hours we'd planned to be at Winter Wonderland with the kids mopping up gallons of water. We pile up all the soggy stuff to be dealt with *at a later date.* We call several plumbers, who laugh at the idea of a last-minute Christmas Eve call-out and point out that we'd require a digger and some major works in any case. It is going to be *very expensive* at a time when we have *spent all the money.*

But you know what? I'm totally calm. This time last year I would have yelled. I would have cried. I would have drowned my sorrows in several bottles of vino then yelled and cried some more. Christmas, I'd have declared, had been *ruined.*

Instead, we have created a temporary holding solution involving buckets and sandbags, which means that we can turn the water on for several hours at a time, so long as we empty the buckets frequently and do some furious mopping. Then we yell out 'Water's going off, so everyone go to the loo!' We fill the kettle and pots and pans with water and disconnect from the mains again to let everything dry out for a bit. Then we have a big hug.

It's not the way I planned Christmas Eve, but it's okay. It's okay because I am strong. And I am strong because I am sober, and because I know that there are worse things that can happen. This one's fixable.

But, because of all of this, I wake up on Christmas Day stupidly early (5 a.m.). I go down to the kitchen, which is lit by fairy lights. I can see the remnants of the glass of whisky, mince pie and carrot left in the fireplace for Santa and his reindeer. I'm waiting to hear the first sounds of Evie, Kit and Maddie checking to see if *he's been,* and showing each other what they've found in their stockings. I'm waiting for John to wake up and reconnect us to the mains so I can have a shower . . .

It's going to be a great day.

DAY 2 9 8

CHRISTMAS

At around 7 a.m. Evie, Kit and Maddie come down with their stockings. It appears that Santa chose particularly wisely this year. Well done him! And, for once, he managed to get all the presents in the right stockings – that's a first.

After breakfast, unable to hold the children back any longer, we gather round the tree to open a few of the presents. We didn't invite anyone to join us for Christmas this year, as we weren't sure how sick I would be. Usually we'd be hosting for a least ten friends and relatives, but this year it's just the five of us, so it's super-relaxed.

I've managed to persuade Evie to come to church with me. I think church should be obligatory at Christmas, especially in a year when you've quit booze, dealt with cancer and have an awful lot to feel thankful for. Sadly, the rest of my family are heathens and quickly jump at the option of staying home to prepare lunch while Evie and I 'get the God thing covered,' as John describes it.

I'm really keen to go back to the church where John and I were married, and Evie was baptised. It's the oldest church in London (St Bartholomew the Great), built in 1123 and utterly awe-inspiring, but it's in the City – on the other side of London. So we drive, through deserted streets, along Piccadilly, past Soho, through the old legal district and the new financial district, and into Smithfield.

The church is packed with hundreds of other people 'getting the God thing covered' – standing room only – and the service is beautiful, with a full choir, a procession past the crib and lots of carols. Then it's time for communion.

But what to do about the wine? I figure that it'll only be one sip, and, if it's blessed, then maybe it doesn't count? After all it's been transubstantiated! It's actually the blood of Christ, right? (Or is that only in Catholic churches?) So I have a good old gulp of communion wine. And, I have to confess, I enjoy it. That full, rich flavour, and that slight burning sensation in the back of my throat. Do you think I can rejoin the back of the queue and have another go? Once an addict, always an addict.

We get back in time for a slap-up lunch. I have a glass of alcohol-free wine (Torres Natureo), which isn't bad, and at least gives me the illusion of a 'special treat'. John has found a mini bottle of champagne and teeny-weeny bottle of port in M&S, who were doing a special (if rather depressing) 'Christmas for One' offer. I do hope he doesn't feel too hard done by.

There's more present-opening after lunch, except for poor Kit. Kit takes after his mum. He has a problem with moderation and, as such, attacked pretty much all his presents, in a flurry of overexcitement and hastily torn wrapping, in the morning, leaving him almost nothing left to open this afternoon. Then we play games and watch Christmas TV (along with regular sessions of bailing out water from the cellar) until bedtime.

And, you know what? Without the wine, it's so easy. No arguments, no stress, no self-hatred. Just fun, joy and gratitude. So, roll on next Christmas! Because, like everything, once you've done it once, it's never so scary again.

DAY | 2 | 9 | 9

GOING AWAY

I've been packing all day. At 3.45 a.m. we leave for Gatwick airport. We're off to Switzerland for a week's skiing. This is the holiday I thought I'd never get to take. I'd expected to be hooked up to the chemo machine, waving goodbye, bravely, to the rest of the family and watching my eyelashes fall into my chicken broth. But I'm going, and I can't wait!

While I'm running around getting all our things together, we discuss what we like most about Switzerland.

'Cheese fondue,' says Evie.

'Hot chocolate and those really cool icicles,' adds her brother.

'Skiing, durr brain,' says Maddie. 'What do you like best about Switzerland, Daddy?'

'Well, their flag's a big plus,' answers John, causing multiple groans and rolling of eyes.

In the 'old days' I would have found packing for the five of us to go away incredibly stressful. I'd have drunk my way through it, and left something crucial behind – like my underwear. This time I've been super-calm.

But, you know what? I'm a bit fed up of being calm, of being grown-up, of being *brave*. What I really want to do is to spend a week being childish. Silly. Overexcited. I want to throw snowballs, make snow angels, career down slopes and play practical jokes. I want to eat lots of chocolate and melted cheese. I want to toast marshmallows on the fire and swan around in a onesie. And the incredible thing is, as I sat here, writing that list, picturing all the things I want to do, none of the images in my head had me clutching a glass of vino.

Isn't that amazing?

THE MONTH WHEN I GIVE BACK

DAY $\boxed{3}\boxed{0}\boxed{4}$

A BRAND NEW YEAR

I wake up early on New Year's Day. A brand new day in a brand new year.

Last night, here in the picture-perfect Swiss Alpine town of Verbier, it started snowing. Fat flakes of snow, the first in weeks, illuminated against the night sky. The fireworks kicked off at around 6 p.m., and continued all night. Constant bursts of colour, the noise ricocheting off the mountains, the air filled with the smell of cordite (I love the smell of cordite in the evening).

There was a minor wobble when I discovered that the steaks I'd bought from the local supermarket for our special New Year's eve dinner were *horsemeat*. I try to be open minded, but still baulked at the ideas of feeding my family *Black Beauty* or *Champion the Wonder Horse*. All the local restaurants had been booked up months in advance and the fridge was bare apart from half a pack of eggs, but I found a tired old baguette left over from breakfast and whipped up some celebratory eggy bread, with extra ketchup. No-one cared.

At midnight we joined thousands of revellers, dancing to a crazy DJ, in the town square. There were people of all ages and hundreds of nationalities, speaking a variety of languages. Russian oligarchs rubbing shoulders with ski bums financing their ski season by washing up in the town's restaurants, united by their love of the snow and their desire to welcome the new year in with a bang.

I didn't need to drink to feel high. In fact, the boozed-up revellers, falling over on to broken glass and recklessly lighting fireworks into the crowd, were a great reminder that it's a good idea to be in control. At midnight, hundreds of people sprayed champagne over the heads of the dancers (I never would have wasted good booze like that in my day), so I still went home reeking of alcohol.

And the best bit? Waking up today knowing that, for the first time in recent memory, I can really enjoy the first day of the year. All sparkling new and filled with possibility. Starting as I mean to go on, not filled to the brim with toxins and regret.

The slopes are empty. Just me and my family, swishing our way into the future. We take the cable car up to the top of Mont Fort and look down across the four valleys. I'm standing at the top of a clean sheet of paper, blinding white in the new-year sun. Skis on, ready to write a new chapter in the unblemished snow.

I can't believe I'm here. Here with the people I love most in the world. Here with all my hair and the majority of two boobs. Here with no hangover. High in the mountains. High on hope.

GRATITUDE

I have to get everything packed up and cleaned, ready to move the family back to London, involving one taxi, one train, one plane and one car journey. We're due to get home around 10 p.m., and the kids start school at 8.30 a.m. tomorrow. (This time I've double-checked the date.) Added to which, I know that I'll be back to earth with a huge bump, dealing with the flood in our cellar, the extra pounds I've gained over Christmas, the annual tax return and *the biggie.*

'The biggie' is the fact that over the last week I've managed really successfully to forget about the whole *cancer* thing. I've hardly thought about it, after two months of thinking about little else. But now I have to get back to the reality of check-ups and starting a *ten-year* course of tamoxifen.

In the old days I would have boozed my way through a day like today. Not enough to get drunk, but to provide a constant blur and take the edge off all the stress. A glass or two while packing, one at the airport, one on the plane (more if I could brave the disapproval of the air hostess) and the best part of a bottle on returning home.

Not now.

Instead of drinking to keep me calm, I'm trying something else: gratitude. Apparently it's the new mindfulness. Loads of celebrities, from Arnold Schwarzenegger to Barack Obama, swear by it. Oprah insists that the 'gratitude diary' she's been keeping for the last twenty years is the most important thing she has done in her life. Twitter is suddenly littered with #gratitude (accompanied by sick-making pictures of minor celebrities doing improbable yoga poses in jaw-dropping locations, which would be more accurately described as #showingoff).

There's science behind it too. Psychologists have shown that gratitude is linked to better sleep, less anxiety and depression, sounder relationships and higher long-term satisfaction with life. Gratitude apparently makes us healthier as well, and Janice Kaplan, author of *The Gratitude Diaries*, believes that being grateful for our food can even make us thinner.

People who believe in the law of attraction and fans of the bestselling book *The Secret* take it even further, claiming that being grateful for what you already have will attract more good things into your life.

What's not to like?

So I give it a go. I take my list of all the things that are stressing me out, and turn it on its head. Instead of fretting about the journey, I focus on what a great holiday we've had. Kids back to school tomorrow equals more free time – yay! Thank goodness we found the mains pipe leak in our cellar *before* we went away and were able to turn the water off. A four-pound weight gain is *nothing* compared to the eight pounds I'd have gained over a boozy Christmas. Well done me earning (just) enough cash last year to qualify for a tax return. And, the biggie: thank you, thank you universe, for the fact that I'm currently (as far as they can tell) cancer-free.

And you know what? I do feel like a rather punchable Pollyanna, but IT WORKS! I go from dreading the day to feeling positively buoyant. Perhaps it's true that it's not happy people who are grateful, it's grateful people who are happy.

TAMOXIFEN

I've been taking tamoxifen for the last ten days. Only nine years and 355 days to go. Tamoxifen is a wonder drug, and is one of the main reasons why the recurrence rates for breast cancer have fallen sharply over the last thirty years. My cancer was fuelled by oestrogen, and tamoxifen disables the oestrogen receptors of any stray cancer cells, rendering them much more impotent. BUT it's making me feel really weird.

For the last few days I've had pretty constant low-level nausea. I'm exhausted. And my brain is totally fogged up. I have to try really hard to remember what I'm supposed to get done each day.

Last week I managed to totally forget Maddie's parent – teacher evening. I just didn't show. When I confessed, even Kit was horrified (he said *That's really BAD, Mummy,* and his standards are *low).* And it is bad! Entry-level parenting: feed children three times a day, make sure none of their limbs fall off and turn up (sober) for parent – teacher meetings once a year.

Then yesterday I was meeting a friend after the school run for a dog walk. I got halfway to school before I had the odd feeling that I'd forgotten something. *I'd left the sodding dog behind!* I had to do an emergency loop back home with Maddie yelling 'I'M GOING TO MISS RECORDER CLUB!' all the way.

I feel very much like I did for the first two or three weeks after quitting the booze. In fact, it's just like the early days of pregnancy. And that's when the penny drops. I had to stop using my regular contraception because the hormones would act like rocket fuel on any rogue cancer cells. Perhaps I'm up the duff!

But I've only taken a couple of *teeny-weeny* risks, and surely you can't get pregnant by accident at the grand old age of forty-six (nearly forty-seven)? I start to hyperventilate. Babies are, of course, a blessing. But I've been there, done that. I really couldn't start all over again with nappies and sleepless nights. Plus, you can't take tamoxifen when you're pregnant; it's very bad news for the baby, and see above re: hormones and rocket fuel. It's quite probable that a pregnancy would kill me, leaving three existing children motherless.

I can't face going into the chemist to buy a pregnancy test. They'd laugh at me (*ha ha, who do you think you're kidding,*

Grandma?), so I order a whole load of groceries I don't need from Ocado, just so the latest in digital display pregnancy tests can be delivered to my front door.

So, here I am, peeing on a stick while the children watch TV downstairs, praying madly like an errant teenager.

Three long minutes.

Then: *not pregnant.* (The actual words come up these days, not just a blue line, that's progress for you). HALLELUIA! Although, does that mean I get to feel like this for *ten whole years*?

Then I make a huge error. I google the side effects of tamoxifen. Exactly what the Prof had warned me not to do ('the millions of women worldwide who have no problems with tamoxifen do not bother posting on internet forums,' he'd said, with a stern stare and a wag of the index finger). There are hundreds of stories of women gaining two stone, going nuts and feeling awful, eventually ditching the tablets, having decided that quality of life is more important than quantity. Fifty per cent of women never finish a five-year course, let alone ten. Then this chilling statistic: one quarter of women taking tamoxifen will die from breast cancer recurrence within ten years anyway.

Well, that made for a good night's sleep. Not.

I'm hoping that this is temporary, and that after a few more weeks the side effects will settle down. I'm taking my own advice and focusing on *gratitude.* I am (as far as we can tell) cancer-free, and NOT PREGNANT. Hurrah!

DAY 326

GIVING BACK

I'm at the Haven again, the amazing support centre for women coping with breast cancer. They've offered me a free acupuncture session to help with the side effects of tamoxifen. (I have no idea how being turned into a human pincushion for an hour works, but it really seems to. Extraordinary.)

Anyhow, on my way out, I pass a lady coming in for her first consultation with the breast nurse. She has a gorgeous, strong face. She's younger than me, but she looks drained, as if someone had taken a giant vacuum cleaner and sucked all the joy and hope out of her life. Which I suspect they have. It reminds me vividly of how I'd felt turning up for my first consultation three months ago, and I desperately want to give her a hug and to say *It's going to be okay.* (I don't. The poor woman is coping with enough, and doesn't need to be suffocated by a mad stranger.)

I know the Haven will look after her. They'll talk her through her diagnosis and treatment plan. They'll offer her counselling, nutritional advice and complimentary complementary therapies like reiki, acupuncture, reflexology and massage. They'll invite her to join their self-help groups and yoga sessions, and they'll advise her on what government benefits she may be eligible for. But, most importantly, they'll listen, they'll understand and they'll make her feel less alone.

That's what they did for me. And I *really, really* want to give back . . .

Most of us 'overenthusiastic drinkers' find that, once we're out the other side, we have a real need to help people still struggling. It's one of the fabulous things about the sober blogosphere: you start blogging, and reading other people's blogs, to help yourself. Then you find that, over time, your blog starts to help other people following in your footsteps.

Giving back is also fundamental to AA. It's the twelfth of the twelve steps. AA (on alcoholics-anonymous.org.uk) state that *an alcoholic who no longer drinks has an exceptional faculty for 'reaching' and helping an uncontrolled drinker.* Bill Wilson (in *Twelve Steps and Twelve Traditions*) writes, *When the twelfth step is seen in its full implication, it is really talking about the kind of love that has no price tag on it.*

Giving back is not entirely selfless, though, as Bill points out: *Practically every AA member declares that no satisfaction has been deeper and no joy greater than in a Twelfth Step job well done.*

So now I discover that this need to give something back isn't just about quitting the booze. I think it's true of coming out of any major life change or trauma. And I want to give back to the Haven, to help those women following in my footsteps – and I have an idea.

I go home and log on to my blog. I start a new post and call it GIVING BACK. I tell my readers all about the Haven, about how they helped me and about the lady I saw going in as I was coming out. I point out to them that I don't make a penny from writing my blog and that reading it costs them nothing. Then I say:

If my blog has helped you, then please, please *will you do something extraordinary for those people who are doing something extraordinary for women who are having an awful time? It will be like a sort of global, interwebby, karmic circle, passing on the love.* And I set up a JustGiving page and ask them to donate (using any pseudonym they like) just a small fraction of what they would have spent on booze to the Haven, so that together we can change some lives.

At around midnight, as I'm heading off to bed, I check my

JustGiving page and am reminded again that ex-drinkers are some of the best, kindest and most fabulous human beings. My karmic circle of love has already, in a matter of hours, raised over £1,000! And the money is still pouring in, from all over the world. The Haven are a small charity, so that sort of cash makes a real difference. One thousand pounds will fund *two years' supply* of acupuncture needles, or twenty hours of counselling sessions for women who have just been diagnosed with breast cancer.

And, you know what, Bill was right. There is no joy greater than a twelfth step well done.

MONEY, MONEY, MONEY

Today is *a very bad day.* I have to file my tax return. Isn't it funny how the first 100 days of staying sober go *so slowly,* and yet the twelve months between one tax return and the next scoot by like a Russian athlete on steroids? I particularly resent the hours and hours it takes me to sort out all my tax paperwork and fill in the online forms, because my paltry income barely makes it above the tax threshold. Endless angst for a mere molecule, in a drop, in the vast ocean of HMRC's tax receipts.

I remember doing my return last year. I decided to 'celebrate' partway through with a glass or two of vino. Needless to say, that didn't help much. The other thing I remember about last year is that I *started* January, as per usual, with a bank balance of, approximately, *zero.* The excesses of Christmas had totally wiped me out. So, by the end of January I was well into my overdraft facility. By the time I'd paid the tax I owed, I was

£4,000 overdrawn. It took months (and begging the husband for an emergency handout) to get me anywhere near the black again.

My attitude to finances is very mature. I have two basic principles: (1) whenever you take cash out and your balance is displayed on-screen *close your eyes.* (2) Towards the end of the month, when you go to withdraw cash, *pray to the cash machine gods* and they will, hopefully, continue to provide.

But, as I prepare all the numbers for my tax return, wading through months and months of online bank statements, I notice an *incredible thing.* At the beginning of January this year *I was in the black. SOLVENT!* And, even more incredible: at the END of January I am in the black. STILL SOLVENT! (This won't be the case, obviously, by the time I've paid Her Majesty's Revenue and Customs.)

There is only one possible reason for this miracle (my income, from the small amount of brand consultancy and copywriting I do for friends from my kitchen table, is *down* year on year, not up): *I have saved a small fortune by not drinking.* Like the weight loss thing, it's happened slowly, slowly, drop by drop. So slowly that I didn't really notice it (plus I had my eyes closed). But, nearly eleven months later, I am approximately THREE THOUSAND POUNDS better off than this time last year. HALLELUIA! The sales are on and it's time to shop . . .

YOGA AND BUDDHISM

Addictions are often referred to as *maladaptive coping strategies.* The theory is that we human beings are not very good at dealing with the stresses and anxieties of everyday life, and, as a result, we find various ways of coping, many of which are *not healthy,* and can turn into addictions.

Even people who drink 'normally' often have their own maladaptive coping strategies, their own bad habits that they turn to as a stress release – overeating, self-harming, shopping, pornography, gambling, extramarital affairs, smoking, illegal, prescription or over-the-counter drugs, etcetera. All these behaviours have the same root cause.

The maladaptive coping strategy theory also explains why quitting alcohol is so much more complex a process than we expect, and why we so often fail. I imagined that my life would go on pretty much as normal, just without the booze. Now I realise that *not drinking* is the *easy bit.* The tough bit is dealing with all the emotions that are suddenly exposed to the light, as if I'd brutally ripped off a sticking plaster.

If we don't find new coping strategies we will, inevitably, pick up the drink again.

I used (and still do, to a lesser extent) alcohol-free beer as a new way of coping. And cake. Then, over time, I started to find healthier coping strategies: running, walking, mindfulness, hot baths, gardening, reading and writing. This is, I believe, the proper definition of *growing up*: being able to deal with whatever life throws at you without looking immediately for a fire exit.

But there's one coping strategy many sober people swear by and I've not yet tried it: yoga.

Now, I've done a bit of yoga over the years, with varying degrees of success and embarrassment (is it only me who feels the urge to fart during a sun salutation?), but, strangely, not since I quit drinking. Then I realised that, over the last few months, with all the stress of the cancer thing, all my muscles have become tighter and tighter. Everything is *clenched.*

One thing I miss about drinking isn't just the mental relaxation of those first few sips (gulps!) of wine at the end of the day, but the way you could feel your muscles relaxing – your jaw unclenching, teeth stop grinding and shoulders unwinding. It strikes me that I need to find another way of doing that – of physically ironing out all those knots.

So, I go to a yoga class.

I feel like a pillock. I do a lot of wobbling. Falling over. Going left when everyone else is going right, and admiring everyone else's handstands from a sitting position. (Especially the guy with the torso like a comic-book superhero who is balancing on *one* hand.) BUT I find that it's a wonderful way to stay in the moment and take my mind off any worries, and I come out feeling like I've been massaged for hours. Everything feels *looser.*

Inspired by all the chanting, and in a fit of enthusiasm for all things Zen, I decide to do some reading about Buddhism. Perhaps that's the way forward.

It turns out that Buddhists have key commandments that they live by: the five precepts. Number one is doing no harm to other living things. Two is not taking what is not freely given. Three is no sexual misconduct, and four is no lying or gossiping. And guess what number five is? *Refraining from intoxicating substances.*

Hurrah! I'm already one fifth of the way to enlightenment! (Note to self: need to work harder on the gossip thing.)

Apparently, the reason the fifth precept exists is that taking intoxicating substances leads to 'heedlessness', or 'carelessness' – the exact opposite of mindfulness. Plus, becoming intoxicated is very likely to lead to you breaking one or more of the other four precepts.

There is a parable from the Vinaya, which explains it

beautifully. A woman tells a Buddhist monk that he must either sleep with her, kill a goat or drink some beer. He chooses the beer, believing that it will do less harm than the other actions. Needless to say, he gets drunk on the beer, shags the woman and eats the goat.

And ain't that the truth?

PICTURE THE YOUNG YOU

A friend once told me that if she has to make an important decision (like whether to accept a marriage proposal or a new job), she looks at a picture of herself as a child, looking all fresh and innocent and smiley, and asks herself 'Would I want this for her?' At the time I thought she sounded a bit Gwyneth Paltrow, but now I figure I should give it a go.

I brave the Pit of Despair and find a picture of myself aged about ten. It's one of those formal school portraits. I had long, straight, dark hair pinned back with kirby grips, and a smile that displayed a mixture of milk teeth, big teeth and gaps. I was proudly wearing my HEAD GIRL badge (this was before the rebellious years, back when I was a frightful goody-goody), pinned to my pale blue, nylon, polo-neck jumper. I still remember how that jumper would make my hair stand on end with static electricity every time I pulled it over my head.

I look hard at that little girl, all sparkly eyes and unshakeable belief that the world held all sorts of possibilities, just waiting for her to come and grab them. And I think *Would I want her to drink a bottle of wine a day? Would I want her to waste all that talent and enthusiasm for life in an endless cycle of getting over the hangover and waiting for the next drink?* I let her down, that little girl. And now I have to make it up to her.

So then I think *What did she LOVE back then? What made her heart race faster?* (Apart from Ben – the HEAD BOY. I wonder what happened to him.) And the answer is *words.*

I spent hours and hours reading. Hiding under my duvet with a torch, well past my official 'lights-out' time. I often had four or five books on the go simultaneously. I read and reread my favourites until they fell apart. And I wrote. A diary, and lots of stories. A poem I wrote at about that age was a runner-up in a WHSmith writing competition.

By the time I got to boarding school, The Diary had become an institution. It'd morphed into a huge lever-arch file into which I wrote religiously every day. I added photos, letters and news clippings. It wasn't private. I let all my friends read it. I also encouraged them to add their own news and comments. In fact, it was – in those pre-internet days – a rudimentary blog. And I loved it. We would all gather round it, reading back over our entries from the previous year. 'Weren't we all so *immature and pathetic!*' we'd shriek about our antics in the lower sixth.

I didn't just write The Diary. I wrote most of the end-of-year comedy skits, taking the mickey out of all the staff. I published an (unauthorised and rather incendiary) school magazine and wrote 'odes' for all my friends – long, comic poetry – on birthdays and for other significant events. I wrote (terrible) stories that I'd submit in loopy, flowery handwriting to *Just Seventeen* and *Mizz* magazines.

Over the years, all the words dried up. Or perhaps, more accurately, got washed away, like letters in the sand obliterated by an incoming tide. I barely wrote a thing except emails, thank-you letters (I do a *good* thank-you letter) and work stuff for twenty years.

But now I have the strangest sense of having come full circle. I've travelled miles over the last eleven months, and yet I seem to have ended up back at the beginning, back with the girl I once was, back to writing The Diary every day, sharing it with my friends and encouraging them to add their comments.

Then I think about all the messages and emails I've had from readers who've said *You should write a book about your last year.* And I think maybe, just maybe, they're right. Maybe that's how I can give something back, to help all those women (and men) who are where I was last March, and perhaps that's the way I can make it up to that ten-year-old girl with the HEAD GIRL badge pinned proudly on her chest and hope in her eyes.

THE MONTH WHEN I THROW A PARTY

HOUSE PARTY

Last night was Caroline's birthday party.

I've known Caroline since my Cambridge days. The minute I met her, in the Spread Eagle pub near Downing College, I knew she was a kindred spirit. We were both slim brunettes with a lust for life and a sense of the mischievous. Yet, for the last few years, seeing Caroline has been a bit like looking through a break in the space-time continuum. For she remained a size eight, looked great for her age and carried on just drinking at parties, whereas I began drinking every day, looked ten years older than I was and ballooned to a size fourteen.

Caroline had invited twelve of the old university gang to her house in the country for dinner, and to stay the night. We'd all managed to offload the children, so it was a rare 'grown-ups only' weekend. I took a six-pack of the trusty Beck's Blues down with me, and stashed them in the fridge.

And you know what? I've pretty much cracked the whole partying sober thing. For a start, it really helps when you feel physically good, which after eleven months off the booze you do. I didn't feel totally 'hot', but did feel, at the very least, 'warm'. I wore a red lace dress and, according to John, everybody said I looked great (admittedly, they hadn't seen me since the whole cancer thing, so their expectations were probably pretty low).

I happily drank my alcohol-free beers before dinner. (I did worry slightly that I'm now a hostess's worst seating-plan dilemma. *Who on earth do I sit next to the teetotal cancer victim?*) Then, once we'd sat down, I let the guy on my left pour me a glass of red wine, but just drank the water. (I've discovered that people feel edgy if their dinner companion has an empty glass. So long as it's full, they don't care, or notice, if you drink it or not.)

I had great fun at dinner catching up with old friends, then I won a table football tournament hands down (easy when the opposition are all drunk), and did lots of silly dancing. Plus, I discovered that I have a new role at parties. People want to *talk to me.* They offload. They ask advice. This hasn't happened to me for years! No one wants an in-depth conversation with the out-of-control lush.

I talked to one friend about his insomnia, another about her new business ideas and yearning to escape London and a third about being a stepmum. Proper, life-enhancing conversations *that I still remember*! Then, at about 1.30 a.m. I sloped off to bed, knowing that no one would notice, and that the only bit of the party I was missing was the bit that nobody would recall clearly.

And this morning! A house full of hangovers. What a treat. I'm trying really hard not to feel smug, because that would be mean and unsympathetic of me. I'm failing.

As we're leaving, Caroline gives me a hug and says 'I feel awful. I think I may join you on the whole no-booze thing.'

We pick the children up from my parents' house, and take them out for lunch. I'm eulogising about the fact that Pizza Express have started stocking alcohol-free beer. (Vive la révolution!) Kit pipes up 'Mummy, how long has it been since you had any wine?'

'Nearly a year, sweetheart,' I reply. 'Why? Do you prefer it when I don't drink wine? Am I different?'

'Yes,' he says, 'you're more . . .'

We all wait in anticipation while he searches for an appropriate adjective. (Kit, as detailed in his school report, is not big on adjectives.) Beautiful? Patient? Kind?

'. . . *Mummyish*,' he concludes, with a flourish.

So, there you have it. Quit drinking. You'll still have a ball at parties, and you'll be more . . . *Mummyish*.

DAY	3	4	2

CATCHING UP WITH MR BIG

Back in October and November, when I was a newbie at the breast cancer clinic, and still going through the *Am I going to die?* phase, I used to watch the 'graduates' breeze into the waiting room with a huge degree of envy. These were the ladies coming back for their check-ups. Often they sported short, gamine, post-chemo hairstyles. They looked confident, happy and *healthy*. The breast nurses would greet them by name, give them a big hug and make a fuss of them.

Meanwhile, I'd be sitting, pale-faced and traumatised, waiting for the results of my MRI scan, or lymph biopsy, or whatever, thinking *One day, maybe, that'll be me: through the worst and out the other side*. Well, today it's my turn. I have an appointment with Mr Big, who I haven't seen for two months.

The way the whole cancer thing works is like a conveyor belt. Your consultant surgeon does the initial diagnostic work and the operation. They then hand you over to the oncologist. They, in turn, pass you over to the radiotherapist, and when they've done with you, you get sent back to the consultant surgeon again for 'check-up and sign-off'.

I've been looking forward to it. Because once this one's out of the way, I don't have another hospital appointment for *six whole months*. I'd been planning to take chocolates for the nurses, and make a mini party out of the event. But now I'm scared.

What if I don't graduate? What if I discover that I've failed, that I'm not 'all clear' and I have to start again at the beginning? I've just started to move on from the whole *cancer* thing. It's been feeling a bit like that episode of *Dallas* where Bobby steps out of the shower and realises that the whole of the previous series has been a dream. My lefty is all healed, and looking pretty good (everything is relative). At the moment, I seem to have virtually no tamoxifen side effects. I'm pretty much back to 'normal'. *I can't do it all over again.*

I have that familiar knot of anxiety in my stomach (the one that feels very much like an alcohol craving). In fact, if it wasn't ten thirty in the morning I'd crack open a Beck's Blue. I'd reassured John, breezily, that he didn't need to take time off work to come with me, as it was all 'routine'. Now I'm regretting that.

If you're going through hell, keep going. One foot in front of the other, one day at a time.

Luckily, I've discovered a great new way of dealing with the stress: swearing.

Generally, I think swearing is just a bit *lazy and unimaginative.* I try to encourage the children to find much more interesting invectives if they're stressed. (Apart from anything else, it's great for the vocabulary.) So, Maddie might drop something on her foot and say 'Aarrrggghh! Dastardly, pox-ridden camel's buttocks!' You see? Much more fun.

I think this aversion to swearing comes from my childhood. I remember vividly the *one occasion* when my dad told my mum to 'f**k off'. She left the house, and didn't come back for TWO

DAYS. As my dad couldn't even make toast without setting off the smoke alarms, it was a disaster. None of us ever swore again.

Anyhow, back to the point: yesterday, when I posted on my blog about going back to the cancer clinic, two of my lovely readers said 'Fuck cancer!' And I thought, *Well yes, why the hell not?* So, I went up to my bathroom, locked the door (the children were downstairs) and shouted **FUCK FUCK FUCKEDY FUCK FUCK! FUCK RIGHT OFF AND DON'T FUCKING COME BACK, FUCKER.** And, you know what? I felt *much, much better.*

I make my way to the clinic, where I'm greeted like a long-lost friend by all the nurses – bless them. After a short stint in the waiting room, which feels like for ever, I'm called in for an ultrasound. I've only had one breast ultrasound, last October, and it was *terrible.* There's that awful moment when you catch sight of a black mass on the screen, and the friendly, chatty sonographer goes quiet. Then they start measuring it, just like they measured your foetus's head and spine when you were pregnant, but less jolly. Because it's not going to grow into a gorgeous, squirming baby – it's going to kill you.

This time I'm hoping it's going to be very different. A charming, fatherly Australian squirts (thoughtfully warmed) gel all over my boobs and starts running his large wand-like thing (probe? stick? sorry, I can't think of a way of describing it that doesn't sound inappropriately *sexual*) over them. Within just a few minutes he says 'That's all absolutely fine.' No black mass. No taking measurements. All done.

'Thank you, thank you,' I whisper, 'I've been really worried.'

'I know,' he replies. 'I realise that just one word can change your life.' And that moment of empathy nearly has me sobbing all over his paper sheets.

Ten minutes later it's my turn with Mr Big, the genius-surgeon-with-terrible-bedside-manner. He does a recap of all my stats: 22mm, grade 2 invasive lobular carcinoma, negative lymphs, ninety-two per cent chance of non-recurrence, blah blah blah, after which he invites me to remove (again) all my clothes above the waist. He cops a feel, which he seems happy about (in a medical sense, you understand), checks my ultrasound printout and dismisses me with a firm handshake.

On the way out I meet a lady ten years or so older than me. She has one of those wonderful faces that looks like it has a host of stories to tell. Like me, she's skipping, and hugging her reprieve close to her heart.

We do the 'Survivor' thing of exchanging case histories, like most people chat about the weather. You tell me your story, I'll tell you mine. She was first diagnosed fourteen years ago, with a recurrence (of primary breast cancer, not the terminal secondary variety) four years ago. She says, 'I've stopped talking about it now, because no one really knows what it's like unless they've been there.' And we smile at each other as I realise that, yet again, I'm a member of a club no one wants to join; and I feel I've known her for ever.

I go straight from the clinic to the school gate to collect Kit and Maddie. I have an overnight bag with me for Kit, as he's been invited to spend the night with his bestie. His teacher pulls me aside.

The children's teachers are all really young, bouncy, gorgeous and 'with it'. It's totally different from my schooldays, when teachers were *ancient,* wizened and completely out of touch. Then, it strikes me, yet again, that the world around me hasn't actually changed that much, it's my perspective on it that's different.

'The boys told me that they're having a *hangover* tonight!' says Kit's form teacher. 'It's a cross between "hanging out" and a "sleepover", apparently. I asked them if they knew what a hangover was. They said no, so I told them that Mummy and Daddy would probably know.'

(Ain't that the truth!)

'The boys both blushed, and said "Is it what Mummy and Daddy did to make us?" It was a rather awkward classroom moment!'

How hysterical is that? My son has no idea what a hangover is. And you know what? I can't remember feeling so proud! (He obviously needs to work on his biology, however.)

MENOPAUSE

Menopause. It's one of those words that makes me want to stick my head firmly in the sand. You know it's coming, but there's not a lot you can do about it, so best to not think about it, right? Well, I've been forced to think about it recently, as the side effects of tamoxifen mimic the menopause. Plus, there's been a fair bit of chat on my blog about menopause. So, I do some research. And it's fascinating.

Many women start drinking *more* during menopause because it's hard. It comes with symptoms that range from annoying to debilitating, it's a reminder of the ageing process and our own mortality, it can cause or worsen anxiety and depression and it coincides with a time when, often, our children are leaving home and our parents are in need of serious help. Even writing that list makes me want a large drink.

The problem is, drinking during menopause is *the last thing you should do*! Here are the many reasons why quitting alcohol is a very good idea for any women approaching *the change* (don't you just love that euphemism?):

As you get older, your tolerance for alcohol drops off, because the proportion of water in your body decreases and you become less efficient at metabolising ethanol. This means that a few glasses of wine get you more drunk, more quickly, than they used to. Which means worse behaviour, worse hangovers, more self-hatred. You get the picture.

Then there's the issue of *fat*. One of the most pissy-offy menopausal (and tamoxifen) side effects is weight gain. Not all over, in a Jessica Rabbit kind of way, but around the middle – like a child wearing a blow-up rubber ring in the swimming pool. That's exactly what drinking wine does for you too. So, if you're menopausal *and* drinking, you're getting a double whammy. Before you know it, you're looking down and there's *no sign of your feet*!

Osteoporosis is another biggie, one of the more dangerous side effects of menopause. It's a thinning of the bones that can lead to fractures and complications. And it's irreversible. Guess what one of the other main causes of osteoporosis is? Yup, you got it: *heavy drinking.*

Also, many women find that menopause causes, or exacerbates, depression. All those fluctuating hormones, on top of everything else. But using alcohol as a prop does not help. Because alcohol (and I realise I run the risk of repeating myself here) makes depression *worse*. It gives you an immediate dopamine high, followed by an inevitable crash.

Which leads neatly on to *mood swings*. Why do we women have to live with these accursed hormones? I feel hugely sorry for John, as in our household my menopause is going to coincide with two girls going through puberty – a veritable bubbling volcano of hormones. John, who has no sisters and went to a boys' boarding school from the age of seven, is already finding the whole puberty thing somewhat unnerving.

This morning he asked 'What are we all going to do today?' Evie was angling for a family trip to her favourite French restaurant, so she said, 'Why don't we look for a little brasserie?' John looked horrified.

'Darling,' he said, 'you know I am a modern man' (he so is not), 'but I do have to draw the line somewhere, and shopping for *undergarments* is very much a Mummy thing.'

I left Evie to explain to her father the (very many) differences between a **brassiere** and a **brasserie**.

Hormones. How can something so tiny wreak so much merry hell? And one thing guaranteed to make hormonally induced mood swings worse is alcohol.

Menopause also messes around with our sleep. As does (are you seeing the theme here?) *alcohol.* Enough said.

One of the more weird and debilitating effects of the meno-pause is hot flushes. Sudden rises in body temperature that make you want to crawl into the fridge and nestle there among the cheese and pots of yoghurt for a while. But, you know what's the first suggestion most doctors give for dealing with hot flushes? QUIT DRINKING! (Cutting down on caffeine also helps.)

So, there you have it. Seven good reasons why going sober makes *the change* less of a change.

Now I've been banned from even *thinking* about HRT because of the whole breast cancer thing, so I do some research on how to manage menopausal symptoms without resorting to hormone replacement. One of the most effective remedies is acupuncture. Don't ask me how it works, but it does, apparently.

And, sure enough, with a combination of not drinking and

monthly acupuncture sessions at the Haven, I've managed to avoid any of the hot flushes, night sweats, major mood swings and weight gain that often go hand in hand with tamoxifen. Long may it continue.

DAY |3|5|2|

SOBER BIRTHDAYS

It's my birthday next week. I've never had a sober birthday before, apart from when I was pregnant. Birthdays were an excuse to indulge myself as much as possible. In recent years, it would take me three or four days of self-loathing to recover from them.

Now I realise that birthdays are not actually all about me. The smalls are super-excited. When you are seven, a birthday is the most amazing thing in the universe. Since my birthday falls on a work day, they have insisted on throwing a pre-celebration today so daddy can join in.

I have pretended not to notice the whisperings, the secret shopping trips, the wrapping and hiding of presents. I am practising my 'that's the thing I most wanted in the entire world' face – like Meryl Streep before the Oscars. I'm planning that gesture that she makes where she clasps her hands together, as if she's praying, presses them against her lips and goes all misty-eyed.

This time last year, I decided to throw a party. I invited about twenty-five adults and twenty-five children. I prepared Sunday lunch for them all, and booked a man to turn up with *live animals* – snakes, spiders, a chinchilla, an owl and the obligatory meerkats – to entertain the kids. I bought cases and cases of wine to entertain the adults. It cost a fortune. And I didn't enjoy it.

Well, I enjoyed the beginning. The first few glasses of wine. And the end – when I could get really stuck in, and congratulate myself on having *made it.* But the middle was pretty awful. Catering for fifty people when half drunk is *super-hard.* And being a good hostess is impossible after too many vinos. I tried introducing people initially, but I'd keep forgetting names, and quite quickly gave up. I couldn't relax and enjoy myself. I charged around the house, glass in hand, constantly convinced that I ought to be *somewhere other than where I was.*

The next day I felt like death. Plus, I was paranoid that no one had enjoyed themselves because I'd been such a terrible hostess. I knew I'd not be able to shift the black mood for days. And that's the day I found myself clutching that World's Best Mum mug of red wine and quit. For ever.

So, this year I'm throwing a different kind of party. On Friday. My first ever sober party. After my recent dice with death, I want to be able to say thank you to all my friends for being there, and to celebrate life in general. I've even invited the friends who weren't there, the ones who disappeared, as, if I'm completely honest with myself, I know that I used to be a fair-weather friend myself – there if you fancied a few drinks, but not if you really needed help.

Then, in a wave of magnanimity, and determination to be a grown-up and let bygones be bygones, I even invite Thing One and Thing Two.

I'm not hosting at home (too much hard work). Instead, I've booked a private room in a swanky restaurant. I'm spending all the money I saved by not drinking alcohol on alcoholic drinks and canapés for seventy-five people. How ironic. I'm a bit nervous about it, but the nervousness is swamped by building excitement.

Seventy-five of my best friends, all in the same room, and I'll be sober enough to talk to them all! I'll be able to introduce people, make witty conversation. Perhaps I'll even do a speech. Without slurring, forgetting what I was saying mid-sentence and falling off the chair. And I'll remember every single minute of it, and wake up the next day feeling . . . great (if broke).

Whoop whoop!

GENETICS

It's half-term, and the children have got me thinking about genetics. There is a fair amount of evidence that some people have a genetic predisposition towards addiction. Not just addiction to alcohol – any addiction.

Look at me and John. We both started smoking at boarding school, because it was what the 'cool kids' did. He carried on for another decade as a 'social smoker'. (I mean, what is that *about*? How does one *do that*?) Whereas I ended up having cigarettes for breakfast. Same with my mum and dad – Mum was an occasional smoker for years, Dad a rampant addict. (Both Dad and I quit fifteen years ago.)

I'm sure that, eventually, if John and my mum smoked enough fags they, too, would have become addicted, but they would just never want to. One or two were always enough.

It's exactly the same story with alcohol. John and my mum – happy to have a glass and stop. Dad and I would compete to finish the bottle. I have, quite simply, an addictive person-ality. I just don't get *moderation.* And that's not entirely bad. I do think that addicts are people who throw themselves into life with huge gusto. They are – we are – *fabulous people* who grab hold of life by the scruff of the neck. We are the all-or-nothing tribe.

But I worry about my kids, and I'm always alert to the signs of constantly looking for *more.* I've been wrestling with their latest addiction all half-term: *Minecraft* (and, to a lesser extent, other computer games like *Clash of Clans* and *Jurassic World*). When they're not playing these games themselves, they like to watch other people playing them on YouTube. The multi-millionaire YouTuber, Stampy, spends so much time in my house that it's like having a fourth child.

I so wish it was like my childhood, where the only screen was the television, and kids TV (provided by the good old nanny BBC) was always semi-educational: *Jackanory. Blue Peter. Take Hart.*

I try really hard to limit the time they spend doing these things, but it's *exhausting.* I have to keep finding activities out of the house, which gets expensive, and eventually you just run out of ideas. How ironic that I should spend my whole life being the voice of moderation!

What worries me about kids and *Minecraft* is that I see all the same addictive behaviours: the obsession, the tantrums when it's restricted and the increasing lack of interest in anything else.

What makes it even more tricky is the 'code of silence' around the whole issue. None of the mums want to admit that their child spends too much time on screens (or is it really just me?), because it makes them look like a *bad parent.*

One of my favourite mum friends told me that her son is

only allowed a screen on Saturday mornings *before breakfast.* He doesn't even watch TV (unless it's David Attenborough). I nearly died of shame. This mum is a proper professional. She has a postgraduate degree in *Actions Have Consequences* (the module I keep failing at). When her kids were playing up before Christmas she, after one firm warning, returned their presents to John Lewis. That's proper hardcore.

Today, Kit and Maddie have playdates, so I take Evie and her friend Brooke to Go Ape. Go Ape is a three-hour adventure trail, way up in the trees, of zip wires and aerial walkways. I was booking tickets for the two girls online last week when an alert came up saying that as they were under thirteen they had to be accompanied by an adult.

I thought, for a while, about fibbing. They definitely look – and act – like teenagers. But then I remembered a post I'd written on my blog that morning, and the phrase I'd highlighted: *Outside the comfort zone is where the magic happens.* Time, I thought, to practise what I preach, and I booked myself in.

I'm regretting this *big time* now, as I sway in my harness thirty feet off the ground. Evie and Brooke are swinging through the trees merrily, like the pre-teen offspring of Tarzan, yelling back encouragements to me – the adult, supposedly in charge. Then we get to a point where we have a choice of two directions. One is labelled DIFFICULT and the other EXTREME. What kind of a choice is that?!?

The right way to go is obvious, but the girls think otherwise. 'We can't do EXTREME unless you come with us!' they tell me. 'PLEEEASE!'

I stand there, up in the canopy, wishing with every fibre of my being that I had both feet on terra firma. I am definitely out of the comfort zone and right now there's no sign of the sodding magic.

'Okay,' I sigh.

I think I might be about to die. In fact, if I weren't strapped into a harness attached to a safety line, I would have done, as at one point I slip off the wobbling pole I'm expected to tightrope-walk along, and end up dangling from the wire like a pair of rather old and baggy pants on the washing line. But I make it.

When we (finally) reach the ground Evie takes my hand and says 'Mummy, I am *so proud* of you.' I'm already feeling some-what shaky, so this makes me all tearful.

'There were no other mummies doing the EXTREME route. And, you know the people in the group behind us, who did the easy route?' *Eye roll.* 'Well, they came up to me and said *"Your mum is **the bomb**!"'*

'The bum?' I ask, confused.

'No, **the bomb**.'

I have no idea what on earth that means, but apparently it's a really good thing, rather like the time a group of teenagers described my perfectly healthy dog as 'sick'.

THE PARTY

It's Friday night. The night of The Party. And I'm having serious wobbles. What on earth am I doing throwing a party when I can't even have one glass of champagne to take the edge off? It's too soon! I'm crazy. Plus, my dress is all wrong, but I can't afford to buy a new one. In fact, I can't afford the party at all. And no one's going to have any fun. CANCEL THE WHOLE THING!

I have that squirming knot of anxiety in my stomach – the one that I would have drowned out with booze, back in the *drinking days*. Which is why I'd pretty much stopped having parties. I would have had a glass or two of vino at lunchtime (to quieten down the squirming snakes), then another two 'sharpeners' while getting ready. Then at least two while waiting for people to arrive. I'd have hit my 'perfect drunkenness' by about 7.30 p.m., so by 9 p.m. it'd be seriously messy.

But today I'm having to live with the restless serpents. I remind myself that *absolutely everything* that is worth doing, everything that is game-changing in life, is accompanied by that feeling. *If you're avoiding anxiety you're not properly living*, I remind myself. I felt the same before every job interview, every first date, before getting married, before giving birth, before going off backpacking. Where would I be now if I'd avoided doing all those things (or got totally drunk beforehand)? Anxiety is a sign that you're pushing boundaries, moving forward, grabbing the bull by the horns. IT IS GOOD.

John and I turn up ten minutes early, and sit on our own in a big, echoing room for twenty minutes while I sip my virgin mojito and mutter, through gritted teeth, 'Nobody's coming!'

An hour later and the place is heaving. People exclaiming over old friends, making new ones. I work the room, chatting to everybody. Introducing people. Feeling the thrill of a party where *I know everyone*! Then, I stand up on a chair (couldn't have done that drunk).

I look out over the crowd. At Sam, who got me the appointment with Mr Big; at Harriet who cheered me up with posh stationery; at Jane, mother of Spike, Buster and Keith; Katie, the ex-flatmate with the pyrotechnic boyfriend (now her ex-husband); Laura, hostess of my first sober dinner party; Selina, my best friend from school, and the man she eloped with nearly thirty years ago; and many, many more. I make a speech, thanking them all for their support and help through the cancer thing.

Everyone says I 'look amazing'. I know they kind of have to say that to the lady who's paying the bar bill and has just recovered from cancer, but I honestly think at least some of them mean it. Because – apart from anything else – I'm two stone lighter than this time last year.

Then, at midnight, the bar closes. Iver and Wendy, friends from Scotland, are staying with us, so the four of us walk out on to the street where my car is parked, bang smack outside. Five minutes into the journey, Iver suddenly sits up from his semi-drunken slump and yells 'Good God, Clare, why are you driving the minicab?!' I tell him it's actually my car, and I am totally, and legally, able to drive it.

We get home and pay the babysitter, then the other three have a nightcap while I brew up a green tea. We exchange notes about the evening, and I go to bed so buzzed that I can't sleep until 2 a.m.

I honestly can't remember the last time I enjoyed a party more. Yet I'd been totally sober for the whole five hours. Who knew?

OUTED

I'm shopping on the King's Road, thinking how far I've come since my mini breakdown outside R. Soles. An email pings up on my iPhone. It's from my friend Diana. I assume it's a thank-you for the party, but it's not. I scroll down, feeling increasingly queasy. I'm rooted to the spot on the pavement like a traffic bollard, shoppers swarming past me on both sides.

> Dear Clare,
> I wonder if you remember that at your wonderful party I mentioned that I am no longer drinking, and it turned out that you have also given up?
> Now, it so happens that I found a blog or two about women drinking – because I think the world, and women in particular, have gone a bit overboard on booze and it's just all crazy – and there's one blog I love.
> And, you know what? I think it's you!
> **Are you SoberMummy?**

Suddenly, my two worlds collide. I'm horrified. Sharing all this *stuff* with 'strangers' is one thing, but people you *actually know* knowing all about you is, paradoxically, terrifying.

We spend our lives carefully curating our social media to make everything look *just perfect*. I know women who would find it difficult to confess to an ingrowing toenail, let alone an addiction issue.

Part of the reason there is so much shame around alcohol addiction in particular is that while other addictions are seen to be the fault of the drug, alcohol addiction is assumed to be a problem with the *user*, the 'alcoholic'. There's an assumption that most people are capable of drinking responsibly, and that only the weak and the selfish, *the diseased*, can't manage to.

This view is so endemic that we even believe it ourselves. We refuse to acknowledge that we have a problem for as long as possible and then, when we eventually face up to it, we feel terribly ashamed. At least I do.

Also, I'm aware that people make huge assumptions about alcohol addicts. If I confess to having a problem, they will picture me pouring vodka on my cornflakes and leaving my children to run feral while I sell their favourite toys for whisky.

So, I'm worried that I'll become a pariah at the school gates or, even worse, the children will get bullied and told they have a dreadful mother.

But, on the other hand, and despite all these fears, it's strangely liberating being outed. I've been feeling slightly schiz-ophrenic – like I'm two completely different people simultaneously. Maybe it's time. Maybe SoberMummy's had her day and I should tell everyone who I am. Shouldn't I be proud of what I've achieved, not ashamed? Aren't I too old, too grown-up, to care about what other people think?

Dear Diana, I type. *Yes, it's me. How amazing that you found me.*

THE MONTH WHEN I LOOK
BACKWARDS AND FORWARDS

DAY |3|6|5|

ONE YEAR

Three hundred and sixty-five days. Twelve months. One whole year. And what a difference a year makes.

I think back to Day Zero. The day I hid behind the kitchen counter, clutching a mug of red wine at 11 a.m.

Back then I'd thought that all mums drank copiously. After all, the school gate at pick-up time and social media are littered with jokes about Mummy's little helper. Wine is our reward for getting to the end of a gruelling day, our way of winding down and feeling adult again.

Now I realise how easy it is for drinking to evolve from social lubrication to self-medication. You start off drinking at times of celebration. Then you begin drinking for relaxation. Then commiseration, apprehension and agitation. Before long, you're using alcohol to deal with any emotion at all.

Life for modern mothers isn't easy. And social media, with all the pressure it provides to be perfect, to do everything brilliantly, from baking the best cupcakes to creating the best home-made costumes, makes it even more difficult. So, we turn to booze as a coping mechanism, a prop.

But when you get used to using wine to numb your way out of tricky situations, you get to the stage where you're unable to cope with them in the raw. In fact, you're unable to cope with almost *any* situation in the raw. You become more anxious, more fearful, more depressed. You stop growing and start retreating. Your world gradually becomes smaller and smaller.

I also see now what alcohol does to us physically.

It makes us gain weight, especially around the middle, it interferes with our sleep, it does terrible things to our skin, making us look older than we are. It gives us awful hangovers as our bodies fight to deal with the toxins. And, eventually, it does real harm to our livers and causes our bodies to self-destruct by growing cancers.

You would think that, given all that, the decision to stop would be easy.

Far from it.

We worry that life without booze will be boring, that *we'll* be boring and lose all our friends. We worry that it'll be too hard. We worry that, rather than supporting us, people will *judge us*. That they will assume we are weak, irresponsible, physically and mentally flawed, just because we got addicted to an addictive substance. Because alcohol is the drug that no one wants to see as a drug, despite the fact that, according to the Nutt Report, it does more harm, to the individual and society combined, than any other (legal or illegal). People would rather blame *you* for your addiction than blame their favourite tipple.

So, 365 days ago, I was terrified. I knew I had to do something because somewhere along the line, my life seemed to have shrunk. I'd gone from being someone who was always out and about, pushing boundaries, taking risks and grabbing life by the short and curlies, to being a stay-at-home mum, who did little other than stay at home (and drink).

Ironically, while my life had got smaller, I'd expanded. The lithe, gorgeous girl I'd once been had been blown up with a bicycle pump. I'd gained two stone, a huge wine belly and jowls.

I wasn't even a good mum. I spent most of my time trying to avoid my children – in favour of sinking a glass of vino. In fact, I spent most of time drinking in order to avoid life. I also seemed to have left my balls somewhere. I was constantly anxious and fearful. Even the smallest tasks seemed like mountains to climb, and necessitated a drink 'to take the edge off' as soon as it hit 'wine o'clock' (which was creeping inexorably earlier).

I thought that, vast alcohol intake aside, I was generally healthy. I still exercised a fair bit, and ate well. But all those toxins were silently wreaking havoc, and I was secretly harbouring a malignant tumour in my left boob, which I didn't find for another eight months.

I had a suspicion that the booze had something to do with the fact that my life had veered so far off track. I realised that I'd stopped controlling it some years previously, and it was now controlling me. I'd had enough. So, I decided to quit.

I thought that going sober would change me physically. I hoped I'd lose some weight and sleep better. I also hoped that, after a while, the infernal internal monologue in my head (the wine witch) would disappear. BUT I feared that life without booze would be flat and featureless. I tried to reconcile myself to being dull and sensible, not the wild, hedonist of my youth.

I had no idea that quitting alcohol would change, not just a few things, but everything. I had no idea that life without booze would be more thrilling, more exciting (yet also more peaceful) and more colourful than ever before. I had no idea that, along the way, I'd find a person I thought I'd lost.

I feel like, over the last twelve months, I've come full circle. Slowly, slowly all the layers of stuff I've hidden behind have been stripped back. The process is painful – like being rubbed raw with a cheese grater – but underneath it all is the girl I was in my late twenties.

She's still there! That kind, brave, adventurous, optimistic and funny person I vaguely remember. And, like I did back then, I now greet every day (well, maybe not *every day*, most days) with enthusiasm, and small things – like the changing of the seasons – with wonder.

I've got my body back. I've lost two stone and look, apparently, at least five years younger. I've rediscovered my self-respect, my courage and my mojo. I *like myself* again.

Best of all, I'm a better wife, mother and friend. I've started looking outwards again instead of inwards. I'm more patient, more kind, more forgiving. Instead of constantly trying to escape, both physically and mentally, I'm properly present. I'm still a work in progress, obviously, but I'm getting there.

I couldn't have done it without my blog. When I started writing it I didn't expect many (if any) readers. I was writing for myself. But I remember the thrill when I saw that one person had read my stuff, and, gradually, more people started to visit and to leave comments and send me emails. I realised that I was not alone.

My readers stopped being just anonymous numbers, and started being virtual friends. Then I *had* to keep going. If ever I felt like a drink I thought about all those people willing me on, and those relying on me to show them the way. I couldn't let them down.

When, in October, I found *the lump*, I couldn't tell anyone – not even John. I was too scared. All I wanted to do was to drink until I passed out and didn't have to think about it any more. But I didn't. What I did instead was to blog about it, and I will never forget the waves of love and support from people all over the world that got me through that time, those who mailed me with their own cancer stories, those who prayed for me.

320

What dealing with cancer has taught me is that, when life throws you lemons, the last thing you need is alcohol. You need to be strong, clear-headed and sober. Empathetic Breast Nurse told me that in an emergency you need to fit your own oxygen mask before you can fit them on your children, and that's what I've done. I'm breathing clean air, and I'm ready to help them with whatever cards life deals them.

Facing my own mortality made me realise that life is too precious, too miraculous, to view it all through a half-drunk haze, and it's made me brave. Right now, I feel like I could deal with anything. I am a superhero.

In the last year, I've beaten the wine witch, and I've kicked cancer's butt too. So, bring on year two, because I'm on a roll. I've been given a second chance, a clean sheet of paper, and I'm not going to waste it.

EPILOGUE

JAMAICA

I'm sitting on our terrace, sipping green tea, watching the sun set over a turquoise Caribbean sea, and listening to the faint *thwock* of croquet mallets connecting with wooden balls on the immaculately manicured lawn below. I'm wearing a bikini – a garment I never thought I'd see again. I can see the beach from here. A perfect, croissant-shaped stretch of white sand that the beach boys are raking, removing any pesky, unsightly strands of seaweed that have had the temerity to wash up and blot the view.

Jamaica Inn is a beautiful old colonial-style hotel. John was sold when he discovered that it was a favourite of his hero, Winston Churchill. The typical guests are American and British couples in their forties, fifties and sixties, not rowdy young singles on the pull. I've not seen a single drunk guest, it's just not that kind of place. BUT, everyone is drinking pretty much *all the time.*

At 11 a.m., on the dot, they serve a complimentary drink to anyone who's on the beach. There's a choice of a yummy fruit punch or – the much more popular – Planter's cocktail. Made with plenty of rum. *At eleven in the morning!* In the old days, I'd have been in heaven! Then, at lunchtime, the terrace is littered with large glasses of rosé and cold Red Stripe beers. (They also serve Beck's Blue! Oh joy.) By four in the afternoon the bar staff are busy serving wine and cocktails on the beach. Then there are the obligatory sundowners, and wine with dinner. Most people seem to be drinking more than the government-recommended weekly limits every single day.

And it's just not *necessary*. I honestly couldn't be more relaxed than I am right now. (It helps that, for once, someone else is picking John's soggy towels off the floor.) I can't see how I could be enjoying myself more. And, as I'm not drinking, I wake up early – feeling amazing – and can make the most of every beautiful day.

Now, this seems like a perfect moment to broach the subject I've been mulling over for the last few weeks, so I turn to John and say 'Do you think I should turn the story of my last year into a book? I thought it might help other women like me. You know, addicts, cancer sufferers, or just people who want to change their lives.'

I wait for him to splutter with indignation, to choke on his gin and tonic (serve him right) and declare me totally mad.

'I think that's a totally brilliant idea,' he says. Blimey.

I'm so blindsided that I find myself arguing against my own proposal.

'But I'm not sure I have the nerve to come out of the closet. What if everyone hates me? I'll definitely get trolled. It'd be a disaster. In a world where everyone curates their public persona to perfection, how can I expose every flaw? I've spent a lifetime trying to present my best self to the world – applying foundation, tinting the grey roots, choosing the best outfits. Do I really have the courage to show what lurks underneath? And I'm not sure if I can cope with all the inevitable rejection letters from agents and publishers. It'd drive me to drink.'

'You know what? There'll undoubtedly be some tricky patches, but it will be *an adventure*! And don't we all need a bit of adventure in our lives?'

(Have I mentioned that he's a good man?)

I remember a quote by William Blake: *The road of excess leads to the palace of wisdom.* I'm not sure that my wisdom would fill a palace, but I have gained some insight over the last year, which I'm sure could help other people like me. While I like to think that I'm unique, an individual, and that my story is special, one thing I've learned is that in so many ways we are very similar; in the reasons we drink, the reasons we decide to quit and the experience we go through once we're sober.

My friend Philippa, a huge advocate of AA and the twelve steps, pointed out to me recently (not at all smugly, she's far too nice for that), that despite my fear of AA, and my insistence on going it 'alone', I have, over the last twelve months, managed to complete pretty much all the steps.

I admitted that my life had become unmanageable. I came to believe that a power greater than myself could restore me to sanity (the internet in my case, rather than God). I did a 'searching and fearless inventory' of myself and admitted (to the world!) 'the exact nature of my wrongs'. I considered who I'd harmed and made amends and I tried my hardest to spread the word and reach out to others.

I also learned the truth and the value of some of the AA mantras, like *One day at a time* and *You're only as sick as your secrets.* But the greatest lesson from AA is that sharing your story is the most powerful way of helping other people. It's time, I think, to share mine.

I am, frankly, still terrified by the idea of 'coming out', but the great thing about getting cancer and facing your own mortality is that you realise you have absolutely nothing to lose.

So, striking while the iron is hot, I pull out the laptop, create a new document and start to type.

DAY o. SOMETHING HAS TO CHANGE.

THE END

To donate money to SoberMummy's appeal for the Haven
please visit www.justgiving.com/sober-mummy

ACKNOWLEDGEMENTS

This book would never have been published without a huge number of people believing in me more than I believed in myself, and understanding that there are many women (and men) out there who might find this story helpful.

Thanks to my wonderful agent, Annette Green, for picking me off her slush pile with such enthusiasm and for all her guidance along the way. Thanks to Charlotte Hardman, my fabulous editor, for helping me, with such wisdom and grace, turn my ramblings into something readable. Thanks also to the rest of the team at Hodder and Stoughton, particularly Emma Knight, Alice Morley and Fiona Rose without whom you would never have stumbled across this book.

I'd also like to give a huge, virtual hug to all the readers of my blog, Mummy was a Secret Drinker, who followed this story as it was happening, giving me such great support along the way, and then persuaded me to write this book. There are far too many of you to mention by name, but here are just a few: Lushnomore, 007Mum, Elizabeth, Eeyore, Graham, Ulla, Laura from Belgium, Annie, Northwoman, SWMum, manconcerned-forhiswife, Ang75, Soberat53, Nana Treen, Edinburgh Housewife, SFM, '69, Finding a Sober Miracle, mythreesons, claireperth, w3stie, Dr C, Rose, justonemore, Putting Down the Glass, Silver Birch, DJ, Jacs60 and Lia.

Many thanks to my fellow sober bloggers, for all their support and for believing, like me, that stories can change the world. Again, too many to mention here, but including the wonderful Mrs D, Ainsobriety, The Wine Bitch, Kary May, Hurrah for Coffee, Groundhog Girl, Tipsynomore, Hapless Homesteader, Mrs S, Irish Mammy, HabitDone, RedRecovers, thewinothatiknow, Rachel Black and Suburban Betty.

A huge thanks to my early readers – for ploughing through my first draft and convincing me to keep going: Diana Gardner-Brown, Philippa Myers, Caroline Skinner and Jane Blackburne, and to my early confidantes, for propping me up whenever I felt like throwing my manuscript in the bin: Annabel Abbs, Sam Corsellis and my favourite barista at the Craven Cottage Café.

A huge number of my friends and family allowed me to plunder their lives for this book, and even to use their real names. Thank you, thank you, all of you.

But the biggest thanks of all goes to my family. My hugely longsuffering husband, known by my blog readers as 'Mr SM', and outed in this book as 'John,' for his unwavering love, support and humour throughout the drinking days, the sober days and the cancer days, and (I hope) all the days to come. And, finally, to my three incredible children, for showing me something new every day, for teaching me what's important in life and for making me want to be a better person.

WHERE TO FIND HELP

For more information on cutting down or quitting alcohol completely, look up Drink Aware (drinkaware.co.uk)

For group based recovery programmes try Alcoholics Anonymous (aa.org) or Smart Recovery (smartrecovery.org.uk)

For supportive online communities, try Club Soda (joinclubsoda.co.uk), Soberistas (soberistas.com), Living Sober (livingsober.org.nz), Hello Sunday Morning (hellosundaymorning.org) and Sober, Sassy Life (sobersassylife.com)

There are also many fabulous blogs out there, and more being created every day, all over the world. For a list of my favourites, visit my blog, Mummy was a Secret Drinker at mummywasasecretdrinker.blogspot.com

For regular inspiration and information check out the SoberMummy Facebook page at Facebook.com/SoberMummy